ONE WEEK
LOAN

This book is due for return on or before the last date shown below.

RESTORATIVE JUSTICE AND CIVIL SOCIETY

EDITED BY

HEATHER STRANG
Australian National University

and

JOHN BRAITHWAITE
Australian National University

CAMBRIDGE UNIVERSITY PRESS
Cambridge, New York, Melbourne, Madrid, Cape Town, Singapore, São Paulo

Cambridge University Press
The Edinburgh Building, Cambridge CB2 8RU, UK

Published in the United States of America by Cambridge University Press, New York

www.cambridge.org
Information on this title: www.cambridge.org/9780521805995

First published 2001

A catalogue record for this publication is available from the British Library

National Library of Australia Cataloguing in Publication data
Restorative justice and civil society.
Bibliography.
Includes index.
ISBN 0 521 80599 6 (hbk.).
ISBN 0 521 00053 X (PBK.).
1. Restorative justice. 2. Civil society.
I. Braithwaite, John. II. Strang, Heather.
340.115

ISBN 978-0-521-80599-5 hardback
ISBN 978-0-521-00053-6 paperback

Transferred to digital printing 2008

Contents

Contributors

DAVID BAYLEY is Distinguished Professor in the School of Criminal Justice, State University of New York at Albany. He is a specialist in international criminal justice, with particular interest in strategies of policing, police reform and accountability.

JOHN BRAITHWAITE is Chair of the Regulatory Institutions Network and a Professor in the Law Program of the Research School of Social Sciences, Australian National University. He is working on integrating the theory of restorative justice and the theory of responsive regulation.

LISA CAMERON works with Education Queensland in behaviour management and has a background in teaching and school counselling.

CHRIS CUNNEEN is the Director of the Institute of Criminology at the University of Sydney Law School. He has published widely in the areas of juvenile justice, policing, Indigenous issues and hate crime.

SINCLAIR DINNEN is a Research Fellow in the Department of Political and Social Change, Research School of Pacific and Asian Studies, Australian National University. His current research focuses on conflict and conflict management in Melanesia.

PAUL MCCOLD is the Research Director for the International Institute for Restorative Practices in Bethlehem, Pennsylvania USA. He has taught criminal justice and is engaged in a number of restorative justice research activities. He has also published widely on restorative justice.

JOHN MCDONALD is a Director of Transformative Justice Australia. He has worked as a teacher, policy officer and an adviser to the New South Wales Police Commissioner and the Australian National University.

DAVID MOORE is a Director of Transformative Justice Australia. He has worked as an academic, researcher and government adviser and has published on politics, justice and related fields.

BRENDA MORRISON is a postdoctoral fellow in the Centre for Restorative Justice, Research School of Social Sciences, Australian National University. Her theoretical work on the social psychological processes underlying restorative processes is currently being applied to the analysis of bullying and victimisation in schools.

TERRY O'CONNELL is a former member of the New South Wales Police Service, where he had a significant role in the development of the Wagga Wagga model of restorative justice conferencing. He has worked closely with police and other agencies in Britain and North America in promoting this model.

GEORGE PAVLICH is a Professor of Sociology at the University of Alberta. He has written extensively on community justice, governance, critique and criminology.

SIR CHARLES POLLARD is Chief Constable of Thames Valley Police. He has been at the forefront of discussions on reforms to the criminal justice system in England and Wales and has been instrumental in introducing restorative justice interventions for young offenders in Thames Valley.

JAMES RITCHIE is a former consultant to the New South Wales Police Service, where he designed and implemented a comprehensive program of reform to improve crime reduction initiatives and boost officer morale. He has worked with police services in Britain, the United States, Japan and Scandinavia.

CLIFFORD SHEARING is a Professor of Criminology and Sociology at the University of Toronto and at the School of Government at the University of the Western Cape. He writes and researches on developments in regulation where he has explored shifts in the governance of security.

LAWRENCE SHERMAN is the Greenfield Professor of Human Relations in the Department of Sociology and Director of the Jerry Lee Center of Criminology at the University of Pennsylvania. Both his empirical and theoretical work focus on the consequences of social control systems, and especially sanctions, for levels of compliance and defiance.

HEATHER STRANG is Director of the Centre for Restorative Justice, Research School of Social Sciences, Australian National University. She has directed the Reintegrative Shaming Experiments, examining the effectiveness of a restorative justice alternative to court.

MARGARET THORSBORNE is the Managing Director of Transformative Justice Australia (Queensland), a consultancy committed to increasing job satisfaction and productivity by improving workplace and community. She has a background in education and counselling.

TED WACHTEL is Executive Director of the International Institute for Restorative Practices in Bethlehem, Pennsylvania USA. He and his wife founded the Community Service Foundation, which operates schools and group homes for delinquent and troubled youth.

Preface

This volume arises from a conference conducted in 1999 by the Restorative Justice Group in the Research School of Social Sciences, Australian National University. The conference was sponsored by the Reshaping Australian Institutions project and opened by the former Chief Justice of Australia, Sir Anthony Mason.

The objective of the conference was to shift restorative justice discussion away from the debate over which fraction of the state (police, courts, juvenile justice and so on) should 'control' restorative justice. Instead the discussion focused on the contest between control by institutions of civil society and state institutions. Does state justice inevitably capture community justice? Are there better and worse ways of thinking about how the justice of law can influence the justice of the people and vice versa? What are the implications of restorative justice for democratic theory? Do citizens view restorative justice as procedurally fair? How can restorative justice be advanced so as to make it both more democratic and more effective? What does the empirical evidence say about such questions?

The contributors to this volume address all these issues, as they grapple with the place and meaning of restorative values in institutions of civil society. The collection reflects the extraordinary diversity of restorative practices and the vigour and intensity of the debate.

Heather Strang and John Braithwaite

CHAPTER 1

Introduction: Restorative Justice and Civil Society

John Braithwaite and Heather Strang

This is a collection of essays that is diverse by intention. Our intellectual agenda is to begin to forge coherence from bringing together two of the 'hottest' but most inchoate topics in the social sciences – civil society and restorative justice.

We adopt as broad a working conception of civil society as possible – all those institutions that are intermediate between the individual and the state. This lets in families (as in family group conferences, a restorative practice discussed in most chapters), schools (the chapters of Wachtel and McCold, Ritchie and O'Connell, Morrison, Cameron and Thorsborne), churches (Sherman, Dinnen), private policing organisations (Bayley, Shearing), private workplaces (McDonald and Moore), Indigenous organisations (Cunneen), social movements such as the victims of crime movement and the women's movement (Strang), and most inchoate of all, communities (Shearing, Pollard, Pavlich).

Restorative justice is conceived in the literature in two different ways. One is a process conception, the other a values conception. The process conception has been the more dominant one to this point. On this view, restorative justice is a process that brings together all stakeholders affected by some harm that has been done (e.g., offenders, their families, victims and their families, affected communities, state agencies such as the police). These stakeholders meet in a circle to discuss how they have been affected by the harm and come to some agreement as to what should be done to right any wrongs suffered.

On the second view, it is values that distinguish restorative justice from traditional punitive state justice. Restorative justice is about healing (restoration) rather than hurting. Responding to the hurt of crime with the hurt of punishment is rejected, along with its corresponding value of proportionality – punishment that is proportionate to the wrong that has been done. The idea is that the value of healing is the key because the

1

crucial dynamic to foster is healing that begets healing. The dynamic to avert is hurt that begets hurt. We return later to what we have learnt from this volume about the other values that may be defining of restorative justice. For the moment, let us simply mark the significance of this contest by two illustrations. Someone strongly committed to a process definition might say that while a family group conference is a restorative justice process, a mediation between a single victim and a single offender is not – because in the latter there is no circle that includes or even invites all stakeholders, most of whom are excluded. Someone strongly committed to a values conception of restorative justice might say that a community conference that sits in a circle and then decides to cane or incarcerate a child, or even that conducts its deliberation around the framework of discovering the just punishment, is not restorative justice. In contrast, a victim–offender mediation that heals, rejecting the punitive paradigm, satisfies the values definition of restorative justice.

In our view it is best to see restorative justice as involving a commitment to both restorative processes and restorative values. Both define continua. Most values are of course defined in a continuous way – there can be more restoration or less. And the processes at issue here can be conceived in a rather continuous way as well – from formal courtroom processing that involves no attempt to empower the voices of stakeholders, to mediation that involves only two stakeholders, to whole-of-community healing circles such as we have seen in some North American First Nations communities where all local citizens are welcome to speak. Most restorative justice advocates are not going to want the extreme end of the restorative justice continuum – maximally restorative process involving maximally restorative values – in a range of contexts. For certain kinds of highly dangerous violent offenders, they may want punitive values to substantially displace restorative values; they may want to see the offender locked away in a place that limits opportunities for healing encounters with his family. For matters that involve delicacy and intimacy – such as sexual abuse of one child by another – the value of privacy may be of more profound significance than openness of a restorative process to all community stakeholders. Even within such open community forums, there may be times when it makes sense to break out into one-on-one encounters in which things can be said that would not be said before the whole group. Courts will be better than conferences for resolving certain kinds of disputes over facts. In sum, even the most radical restorativists will not want to be at the extreme end of the restorative justice continuum all of the time.

Why Restorative Justice is a Hot Topic

We live in an era of disillusionment about justice and the state. Restorative justice advocates contend that while collections of essays on state institutions like police or prisons might have coherence of focus, that focus is tired and sometimes trivial in terms of its prospects of illuminating how to deal with problems of crime and violence. But belief in the centralised state as capable of crime prevention planning has been more tenacious than trust in the capabilities of the state for industry planning. The ghost of Hayek is ubiquitous in discussions of industry policy, especially on the right. But until recently it has only been idiosyncratic criminological figures of the left, such as Clifford Shearing (Chapter 2), who would invoke a Hayekian view of local community knowledge being superior to state intelligence of crime and how to solve it.

Shearing tells an inspiring story of peace forums in South Africa that mobilise local knowledge to deal with crime problems of daunting dimensions. These peace forums are at the expansive end of the continuum of stakeholder participation, moving from the 'community of care' of much restorative justice writing to a 'community of life'. They seek to govern the future rather than simply restore a balance that has been upset in the past.

While few domains of state failure are as profound as failure to prevent crime, with any major fall in the crime rate that does occur because of changes in demographics, employment, or tastes for illicit drugs, there will be a politician or police chief with an interest in claiming that his or her enforcement policies deserve credit for the fall. Conversely, when crime goes up, it will be decaying community values or unemployment that will be blamed. But the more fundamental reasons for the resilience of statist analyses of crime are traversed by David Bayley (Chapter 14). Law and order politics has a simplicity of political appeal. For people who are insecure about their jobs and their children's futures, the politics of exclusion is appealing, especially when the exclusionary impulse averts explicit racism, alighting upon the exclusion of criminals (who are only coincidentally black or of minority ethnic background in disproportionate numbers). With criminals, the politics of inclusion has always been regarded as risky; no politician wants to be accused of being soft on crime. On the other hand, just as Morrison (Chapter 13) shows that parents are more supportive of restorative principles than teachers assume they are, voters are more supportive of restorative justice and less supportive of prison than politicians assume they are (Doob, 1999).

Restorative justice is inserting another new political dynamic into this equation. First it is a social movement that taps into late-modern cynicism about the capacity of state institutions to solve problems like crime. It invites a disillusioned public to demand that law and order politicians produce evidence that the vast expenditures of their tax dollars on building more prisons actually prevent crime. While the truth at this time is that there is only limited evidence that restorative justice prevents crime, the rhetorical appeal was well illustrated by Chief Justice Bayda of

Saskatchewan in introducing a recent lecture by Norwegian restorative justice figure Nils Christie. Bayda invited his audience to imagine they were alone late at night in the dark streets of a metropolis. There are two routes home. On one street live 1000 criminals who have been through the Canadian prisons system. On the other street are 1000 criminals who have been through a restorative justice process. Which street do you choose?

The second way restorative justice is challenging the law and order political dynamic is on a front where the empirical evidence has recently become surprisingly clear. The more people actually experience restorative programs, the more support for them rises. They go away from them more satisfied that justice has been done, that the process has been fair, more optimistic that the outcome will do something to prevent future crime (Braithwaite, 1999a). This is not universally true, especially for victims, who in a significant minority of cases are less satisfied as a result of restorative justice processes, but it is clear that the majority of citizens with first-hand knowledge prefer them to court.

Some of the momentum for restorative justice has come from research suggesting that restorative justice programs do actually reduce crime. Reoffending in conferenced cases in the famous Wagga Wagga program of the early 1990s was 20 percent, compared to 48 percent in cases that went to court (Forsythe, 1995). Even more dramatic success was reported for the Singaporean family group conferencing program with only 2 percent reoffending, compared to 30 percent over the same period for offenders who went to court (Chan, 1996). Chief Constable Charles Pollard (Chapter 11) reports similarly encouraging results for his path-breaking Thames Valley conferencing program.

But none of these evaluations is convincing because we must assume that adequate controls would reduce or reverse these effects owing to the tendency for more serious cases to be sent to court rather than conference. There are a few studies with more persuasive efforts to introduce controls or match conferencing and court groups that show positive effects of restorative justice on reoffending (Braithwaite, 1999a; 27–35), such as Burford and Pennell's (1998) research on family violence conferences. However, sample sizes in these studies are small.

The most rigorous test to date of the crime reduction potential of restorative justice has been the Reintegrative Shaming Experiments (Sherman et al, 1998, Strang et al, 1999). Here a randomised research design was used to compare the effectiveness of conferences with normal court processing. While no significant difference between the two dispositions was found for young property offenders, the experiment found a 38 percent reduction in repeat crimes by violent youth who had attended a conference compared with their counterparts dealt with in court (Sherman et al, 2000).

While the jury is not in on whether restorative justice 'works' in terms of crime prevention, reducing the cost of the criminal justice system, and the like, it is fair to say that the early research results are encouraging rather than discouraging. And this establishes restorative justice as an emerging topic for the social sciences in the next decade.

Why Civil Society is a Hot Topic

Few books have so quickly become a social science classic as Robert Putnam's (1993) *Making Democracy Work: Civic Traditions in Modern Italy.* Putnam shows that the regions of Italy that have both flourished economically and suffered less corruption are those that have fostered social capital formation (see Morrison, Ritchie and O'Connell, Chapters 13 and 10). They are regions where civil society flourishes, in the sense of membership of voluntary associations intermediate between families and states. And they are regions where citizens are more trusting of one another in civil society. Putnam has been able to show that the direction of historical causality operating here is not that economic success generates a trust-based culture but that a strong fabric of trust, woven in institutions of civil society, has economic benefits.

This social capital research tradition has been used by Non-Government Organisations (NGOs) to advocate why there should be investment in the NGO sector as a path to economic development, corruption control and control of other crime problems such as family violence. But it has also been picked up by influential global institutions such as the International Monetary Fund and the World Bank. The social capital paradigm shift has seen those institutions abandon their previously myopic focus on nurturing the development of free markets as the path to development. On the eve of the millennium, 'good governance' is seen as vital and causally prior to market development in IMF/World Bank circles, partly born of their disastrous experiences in Russia and some other post-communist societies. For example, to get market makers into a stock exchange, you need trust to work in civil society so that a deal based on a handshake on the floor of an exchange will be honoured; you need self-regulatory norms in professions like law, accountancy and stockbroking; you need banks that self-regulate each other's risk management systems and do something if (as in the Russian case) organised crime seeks to take over the banking system.

Dinnen's chapter on Papua New Guinea (Chapter 7) is included in this volume because no case better illustrates this changing paradigm in its interface with the crime problem. Perhaps this is because in no society is crime as big an economic and social problem as in Papua New Guinea – though South Africa (Shearing, Chapter 2), Russia and Colombia would be credible competitors for this honour. Tourist numbers to Papua New Guinea are among the lowest for any nation, partly because of tourists' fears for their safety; violence has shut down the Bougainville copper mine, which had been the country's biggest foreign exchange earner and funded more than a third of the Papua New Guinea budget.

Development aid to Papua New Guinea in the 1970s was dominated by the market development paradigm. In the 1980s crime was identified as a major obstacle to economic growth. Massive resources were poured into aid projects to develop policing, the prisons system, juvenile justice. These were diagnosed as failures in the 1990s; the problem was seen as getting worse. At the millennium, the development agencies in Papua New Guinea are becoming more oriented to 'good governance' nurtured in civil society as a crime prevention paradigm – community development, working with NGOs and yes, a major new commitment to restorative justice.

Civil society is of importance to the restorative justice debate because of the pessimism criminologists have that any single state intervention in a delinquent life can turn it around. It does seem romantic to expect that a single two-hour conference could reverse the thousands of hours of peer and family influences in the months before and after a conference. On the other hand, if the social movement for restorative justice is about more than just changing the practices of states, if it can have an impact on an entire culture, if it actually succeeds in changing families and schools towards more restorative practices, the effects on crime might be much more considerable.

Hope v. Pouring Cold Water on Hot Topics

When David Bayley made his presentation at the conference that gave birth to this collection, he read from our email inviting him to participate. It said David was invited in his capacity as a 'crusty old copper-loving criminologist' whose job was to pour cold water on our upbeat analyses of restorative justice and civil society. Apart from resiling from being old, he accepted this challenge with relish. In Chapter 14 he has met it admirably. Even if the restorative justice and social capital in civil society paradigms realise all their promise, which he doubts, Bayley rightly points out that sound state policy will continue to have a central role in any strategy for confronting crime. The justice of state crime control may be inequitable. But Bayley enquires: whither equity in a world where we know volunteerism in civil society is more likely to flourish in rich communities than in poor ones? Equity is a domain where Bayley's warning is especially apposite: it might be desirable to responsibilise communities, but it cannot be desirable to deresponsibilise the state. Sherman (Chapter 3) gives the equity and civil society question a different twist again in his contrast of high crime as the upshot of the Quaker egalitarianism of Philadelphia, lower crime the legacy of Puritan hierarchical Boston. Egalitarian justice may undermine civil society which is strongest under a culture of Calvinist hierarchical communalism. But if the new culture finds a way to encourage egalitarian leadership (for example, the kind of restorative policing espoused in Charles Pollard's chapter) then we may evolve a new basis for a strong civil society. Both Pollard and Sherman in their chapters propose an International Institute or Society for Restorative Justice. Ted Wachtel, a man of action, upon returning from the ANU conference, promptly proceeded with establishing an International Institute for Restorative Practices.

The paradigm shift to good governance for social capital formation in civil society is not only about the cultivation of the virtue of trust. It is also about cultivation of the virtue of hope. A game tourists play when visiting the cradles of European civilisation, preeminently in Italy, is to see if they can guess which virtue is represented in the carved stone of a magnificent cathedral or chateau. The virtue of piety and the vice of gluttony are always easy to pick. The virtue we moderns seem to have most trouble identifying is hope. Hope is the least modern of virtues. Indeed to most moderns it seems less a virtue than cynicism. In this collection, Morrison in her conclusion is our guardian of the ancient virtue of hope, Bayley of the modern virtue of cynicism. For this volume and in our work on restorative justice generally, we do seek to cultivate hope, the possibility for a richer vision of how to transform cruel and ineffective punitive practices. As Morrison contends, without hope nothing changes. For us, Shearing's Zwelethemba does indeed mean 'place of hope or renewal' (as it does in the South African Xhosa language). Yet hope must be tempered by doses of reality and Bayley helps us to that. On the paradox of equity and leadership, he is joined by the analyses of Sherman and Pollard. Strang joins the paradox at another level with her observation that both the victims' movement and individual victims (whom we know to be poorer and more dominated than non-victims of crime) support the leadership of police in restorative justice processes. In some cases, this is a plea for restoration of their lost security through the presence of a police uniform in the room where restorative justice is transacted.

Pavlich pours a more postmodern kind of cold water on community as the core value of both the restorative justice and civil society paradigms. Unified community is an essential ingredient of totalitarianism. Even partial communities in civil society can be Ku Klux Klans. Responsibility to the 'common good' leaves out those excluded from presently dominant conceptions of community – the other, the unfamiliar, the strange, the outlaw. Derridian deconstruction is advocated for disrupting privileged unities of community. Since any community must have a boundary, it must exclude those outside the boundary; this means an inevitability about hostility to and from the excluded. So Pavlich poses the question of how to make the move from hostility to hospitality. The 'deconstructive opening' Pavlich suggests is replacing community with solidarity – hospitality without boundary, a virtue of care hospitable to the non-member. For those of us of republican–feminist bent, replacing fraternity with solidarity (liberty, equality, solidarity) seems an appealing move from the deconstruction site to a normative construction site. Still, no idea in political theory big enough to inspire hope for transformation is beyond corruption: many a tyranny has been enacted at the hands of cadres chanting solidarity forever. The method of deconstructive openness is Pavlich's remedy, just as checks and balances in a separation of powers are the remedy to tyrannies of solidarity for the republican.

Ironies of State and Civil Society

Ritchie and O'Connell see large state bureaucracies like police departments as inherently afflicted with imperatives to processing rather than relationships, rules rather than people, control rather than participation, enforced compliance rather than deliberative decision-making. In these senses large bureaucracies are ill equipped to deliver restorative justice and well equipped to crush it. While relational approaches, restorative practices to use Wachtel and McCold's expression (Chapter 8), work better than coerced compliance in helping large bureaucracies deliver valued outcomes like crime prevention, the power-brokers who rise to the top within them see relational approaches as a threat to their control (which they are). The paradox of bureaucracy is that those who value performance over control are less likely to make it to the top in state bureaucracies. This does make the state an unreliable ally of the social movement for restorative justice.

A theme of much restorative justice writing is that state leadership, particularly a threat of state coercion lurking in the background, is a risk to the integrity of restorative justice processes. There are echoes of this perspective in this volume in the contribution of Shearing (Chapter 2), for example. However, we have also seen that a feature of the contributions of Bayley, Sherman, Pollard and Strang is an irony that a certain kind of state, indeed police, leadership may be necessary to activate a restorative civil society.

Ironies of state and civil society are most profound in Dinnen's chapter (7). He traces the history of Papua New Guinea civil society from pre-colonial violence through colonial peacemaking, and then from the rule of law project which accompanied Independence to the hybrids of state–local regulation now emerging. Irony indeed that the purely local

(Indigenous) and the more purely central (statist) controls on violence seemed to fail utterly, while the highly discretionary paternalism of the *kiaps* (white police of sorts) which harnessed tribal cultures of self-regulation were more effective. Dinnen sees the developing hybrids of state–local regulation, much of it of a restorative character, which draws on local knowledge in securing compliance, as potentially the most successful strategy for the future.

Alan Rumsey (1999) has documented the famous hybridised intervention of the Kulka Women's Club to end a New Guinea Highlands tribal war. What the Kulka Women's Club (civil society actor) did on 13 September 1982 was to march between two opposing armies under the national flag (symbol of national community), exhorting both sides with gifts (restorative gesture) to put down their arms, which they did. Note that as in so many of the important non-Western forms of restorative justice, the victims moved the offenders by giving them gifts rather than asking for compensation. The distinctive peacemaking intervention of the Kulka Women's Club seems to have been one-off, rather than a recurrent Melanesian cultural pattern, but its importance is that it had a long-lasting effect, the peace having held until the present, during two decades when hostilities among surrounding tribes escalated. Though the intervention seems unique, Maev O'Collins (1999) links it to peace and reconciliation meetings organised by women in war-torn Bougainville and women marching in Port Moresby to protest against male violence. Rumsey's (1999: 9) work is important because it shows the need for highly contextualised analysis of the macro-transformative moments of restorative justice: 'the very factors that make one area relatively conducive to peacemaking are the same ones that make it more difficult in the neighbouring region'.

From a republican normative perspective, it may be that what one wants is for both state and civil society to be strong so that each can act as a check and balance on the other (Braithwaite, 1998b). A vigilant state can be a check on the abuses of power of a Ku Klux Klan or a family group conference that decides to make a child wear a T-shirt saying 'I am a thief'. A conference, as Pollard's chapter illustrates for Thames Valley, can be a forum where citizens criticise police for racist bias in a way judges would never give them the latitude to do. The crime prevention effectiveness that Ritchie and O'Connell (Chapter 10) see as only achievable by creative, relational organisations (as opposed to routine processing coercive ones) might be achieved by external democratic demands for performance and internal ones for voice. Again the paradox may be that the path to relational organisational governance may be state imposition on bureaucracies of participatory decision-making and accountability to local communities. Restorative justice needs state authority to prevent powerful fractions of the state from destroying restorative justice

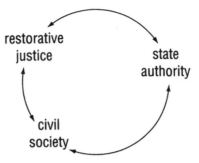

Figure 1.1 A Virtuous Circle Where Restorative Justice Supports Civil Society and State Authority

so that a virtuous circle of restorative justice, civil society and state authority is created (see Figure 1.1).

A thread running through our chapters is that the power of restorative justice may be connected to the fact that it does not subordinate emotion to dispassionate justice, as in the blindfolded icon of justice balancing the scales. Nor does restorative justice subordinate emotion to rational bureaucratic routines. Space is created in civil society for the free expression of emotions, however irrational they may seem. If emotions are deeply felt then the relational perspective requires that others attend to their existence and ponder what might be done to heal them. Of course, civil society will not produce a civil society unless there is civility – mutual respect and non-violence – in how emotions are conveyed. Frankness and civility are not found to be objectives sharply at odds in restorative justice practice. Most critically, hurt never demands violence and abuse for its effective communication; on the contrary, it is more effectively communicated with grace.

McDonald and Moore (Chapter 9) contribute an extremely important reformulation of the role of the emotions in restorative justice theory. They suggest replacing *Crime, Shame and Reintegration* as a template of restorative process with *Conflict, Acknowledgement and Transformation*. The *Conflict, Acknowledgement, Transformation* model has nuts and bolts implications for good conference design – for example, it is generally better for victim supporters to tell their stories before offender supporters. The reformulation from crime to conflict enables a wider ambit for restorative process, where schools, churches, businesses and all sorts of other non-justice sites can be included, a move Wachtel and McCold (Chapter 8) also make. When there is moral ambiguity over right and wrong in a conflict, Wachtel and McCold, like McDonald and Moore, prefer allowing the ambiguity to stand rather than coerced allocation of responsibility. Speaking to participants in advance of a conference and inviting them to own as much responsibility as they feel able to volunteer can be enough to trigger a virtuous circle of owning responsibility instead of a vicious circle of denial and blaming the other.

Hence, if deliberative, respectful confronting of conflict works well, acknowledgement of harm and shame concerning it is likely. At the individual level Morrison (Chapter 13) reports on Eliza Ahmed's (1999) research on school bullying which shows that bullies fail to acknowledge shame and instead transform shame into anger and their victims are caught in a cycle of persistent shame, while non-bully/non-victims acknowledge and discharge shame. But for McDonald and Moore, the more profound acknowledgement of shame is collective rather than individual (as in Ahmed's research). A conference is a means whereby a group of people harmed by a conflict begin to see themselves as sharing a concern. According to McDonald and Moore collective experience of shame marks the transition from negative to positive emotion, from conflict to cooperation. A recognition of collective vulnerability to the shared problem motivates a transformation of human relationships and thereby discovery of a way of dealing with the problem. A key move, as revealed by the wisdom of North American native peoples' healing circles, is putting the problem rather than a person in the centre of the circle as the focus for emotions that transform relationships around the circle.

Cunneen's analysis of Australian response to the Stolen Generation of Aboriginal children is an example of how not to implement the *Conflict, Acknowledgement and Transformation* model. Instead of acknowledgement and transformation following from a deep national conflict, what followed was denial, rationalisation and trivialisation. For such profound collective wrongs as genocide and apartheid, the world is slowly learning that undominated and state-assisted storytelling is needed, so that truth can lay a foundation for reconciliation, and so that collective shame which is acknowledged collectively can motivate just societal transformation. Cunneen's approach also throws down the important challenge of whether restorative justice gives rights a sufficiently central place.

Wachtel and McCold (Chapter 8) have their own reformulation. *Restorative* justice is authoritative/reintegrative dispute resolution which combines high social support (encouragement, nurture) with regulation which sets serious limits. *Neglectful* conflict resolution is neither supportive nor limit-setting; *permissive* approaches are supportive but not limit-setting; and *punitive* approaches are characterised by high levels of control but low levels of support.

Principles of Restorative Justice

The process and values conceptions of restorative justice discussed earlier are revealed by our essays to be interrelated. If one of the values of restorative justice is to enrich democracy, to implement participatory deliberation in an important domain of people's lives, then it follows that a process is needed in which all stakeholders have an opportunity to speak. If it is an important process requirement that all stakeholders have an opportunity to speak, it is important that speech is not dominated (that restorative justice instantiates the value of non-domination). Ultimately, we therefore think that to be fully restorative justice, both restorative process and restorative values tests should be passed. Equally, it is clear that these joint requirements can define a continuum of how restorative any given practice is. As Wachtel and McCold's chapter (8) so nicely shows, many problems of daily life are not big enough to justify assembling all affected stakeholders in a circle. One-on-one is fine – but restorative one-on-one oriented to values of healing and social support is likely to be better than punitive or neglectful encounters.

Moreover, the ferment in the chapters over values suggests that many more books will be written before there is consensus on any list of restorative values. Democracy, healing, social support (caring/love) and non-dominated speech seem the most recurrently supported restorative values, followed by community, though Pavlich has put that interesting challenge as to whether solidarity would serve us better than community. Apology, making amends and forgiveness are frequently cited in our chapters as desirable restorative values, though many in the victims' movement caution against seeking to persuade victims that they will feel less bad about themselves if only they can forgive. Cameron and Thorsborne make the interesting suggestion that a restorative value might be 'never giving up' on the wrongdoer, a more specified version of the philosophy of hope we see in Morrison and Ritchie and O'Connell's chapters. Acknowledgement – the crucial stage in McDonald and Moore's reformulated transformative *process* – can be conceived as a value, and indeed is conceived as one of Morrison's six principles of restorative justice.

Connected to these values around which there are stirrings of agreement across our chapters, Wachtel and McCold suggest six principles of restorative practice, which we suspect enjoy considerable agreement: 1. Foster awareness; 2. Avoid scolding or lecturing; 3. Involve offenders actively; 4. Accept ambiguity; 5. Separate deed from the doer; 6. See every instance of wrong-doing and conflict as an opportunity for learning. And we might add, as an opportunity for grace. More broadly, a serious conflict, say over an act of violence, can be seen as a transformative opportunity; as McDonald and Moore, following Ruth Morris (1995), point out, it is an impoverished way to view the opportunity a crime affords as no more than an opportunity to repair harm and prevent recurrence. It is an opportunity to confront an underlying drug or alcohol problem, to transform hurtful relationships in a family, to build peace in the Highlands of New Guinea, to forge more loving families and communities. The bigger the wrong, the deeper the conflict, the better the prospect for McDonald and Moore's collective emotional transformation to motivate real justice, including social justice.

Reframing the Research Agenda

Our case studies of restorative justice in civil society reveal some virtue in combining process and value conceptions of restorative justice as a normative ideal. They reveal a need for hope tempered by the wisdom of the cynics and cynicism tempered by the vision of optimists. We come to see the restorative justice agenda not as a choice between civil society and state justice, but as requiring us to seek the most productive synergies between the two. Restorative justice programs in civil society can become a testing ground for some big ideas in democratic theory. The research agenda of refining the principles and values of restorative justice has wider relevance to developing the values of a richer democracy. Finally, our case studies show that democratic practice requires an understanding of the emotions as well as reason. The volume includes insightful contributions to the literature on emotion, reason and social theory. Empirical assessment of these ideas will be a fruitful endeavour for decades to come.

CHAPTER 2

Transforming Security:
A South African Experiment

Clifford Shearing[1]

We have still to begin the task of anatomizing the new relations
of power brought into play on this new multiple and fragmented
territory of government. In doing so, we should not assume
that all is for the worst in this 'post-social' age. We need not
simply to condemn the injustices and disadvantages entailed
in the de-socialisation of government, but also to engage
inventively with the possibilities opened up by the imperatives
of activity and the images of plural affinities. The role of such
analyses should not be to praise or to blame, but to diagnose,
to identify the points of weakness that might be exploited if
we are to maximize the capacity of individuals and collectivities
to shape the knowledges, contest the authorities and configure
the practices that will govern them in the name of their
freedom and commitments.

(Rose, 1996: 353)

Introduction

In what follows I want to reflect upon work that has been taking place
since late 1997 in Zwelethemba[2] (a Xhosa name that means place of hope
or renewal), a black suburb on the outskirts of Worcester, a country town
about 120 kilometres north of Cape Town. This research is exploring ways
in which poor people, in this case poor black South Africans, can and
should respond to the global transformations that David Bayley and I
(Bayley & Shearing, 1996) have termed the 'multilateralisation' of governance. By this we mean changes that have led to the emergence of a variety of auspices for, and providers of, governance other than states – the
changes that Rose in the opening quotation terms 'post-social'.

What relevance one might ask does this have to restorative justice?
The answer is that while the processes I will describe have been informed
by work within a restorative justice tradition they arise in response to a

14

theoretical framework and normative agenda that differ in significant ways from the thinking that has given rise to restorative justice. Juxtaposing these differences places restorative justice within a wider context of a 'post-social age' that I, at least, find helpful in understanding restorative justice and in thinking about its development.

The Zwelethemba Agenda

The contemporary normative literature on governance challenges the previously taken for granted assumption that the business of government is, and should be, monopolised by states. The argument advanced in a variety of programmatic texts is that activities of government should be undertaken outside, as well as within, states.

This idea has achieved widespread acceptance and is shaping the agendas of governments around the world. It is also having a major effect on the way in which international development agencies such as the World Bank and the United Nations Development Program are going about their business. A good example of this is a February 1999 draft of a 'Tool Kit on Good Urban Governance' developed by Leo Fonseka. Fonseka argues that governance can no longer be left to the state alone but requires the active partnership of the state with what he calls 'civil society' and the 'private sector'. For Fonseka civil society refers to a variety of institutions that include non-governmental organisations, community-based organisations, academic and research institutes, religious groups and the media. The private sector includes small, medium and large enterprises, trade and investment associations and chambers of commerce. Fonseka argues that:

> All three [the state, civil society and the private sector] are critical for sustaining human development. Since each has got its weaknesses and strengths, a major objective of good governance is to promote the highest possible constructive integration among them in order to minimise individual weaknesses and utilise the strengths optimally. The intricate intercourse between and among these three domains will indicate the direction of the society's economic and social flight path. The more integral, balanced and inter-dependent the three are the better it is for that society. (1999: 3)

For Fonseka the appropriate balance between these governmental partners is one in which:

- states provide 'the foundation for Equity, Justice and Peace' (thereby 'creating a conducive political and legal environment');
- civil society provides 'the foundation of Liberty, Equality, Responsibility and Self-expression';
- while the 'private corporate sector provides the foundation through economic growth and development'. (1999: 4)

This conception of balance between partners reflects what has come to be called neo-liberalism. There is nothing new about this and indeed it has as Rose and Miller (1992) argue always been central to liberalism in ideas such as Adam Smith's 'invisible hand'. What differentiates the neo-liberal position from classic liberalism is that where the older liberal position simply assumed the existence of non-state institutions capable of engaging in such partnerships, neo-liberals argue for a constitutive regulatory environment that 'makes up' the civil society and the private sector (Shearing, 1993). Within neo-liberalism this job of creating and sustaining non-state nodes is seen as a defining feature of the state's role.

In addition to this, many neo-liberals conceive of the state role as one of coordinating and providing direction to the network of governance that multilateralisation has produced. This conception of the neo-liberal agenda has been advocated in a variety of normative texts such as Osborne and Gaebler's *Reinventing Government* (1993) and Eggers' and O'Leary's *Revolution at the Roots* (1995). The argument advanced is that the correct balance between state and non-state partnerships is reached when state governments provide the overall direction and control of governance and provide a regulatory environment that will encourage non-state participants to engage in the 'rowing' of governance. E.S. Savas spells out the reason for this balance nicely when he writes:

> The word government is from a Greek word, which means 'to steer'. The job of government is to steer, not to row the boat. Delivering services is rowing and government is not very good at rowing (cited in Osborne & Gaebler, 1993: 25).[3]

Underlying this liberal conception of governance is an argument that the mobilisation of local knowledge and capacity is essential for effective governance. This is a direct challenge to the position associated with welfarism that state governments should monopolise governance and should do so by hiring agents with the knowledge and capacity required to realise their governing agenda. An example is the 'criminal justice system'.

Rose summarises these developments as follows:

> A new ethical politics has taken shape – of the environment, of animal rights, of reproduction, of health, of everyday life itself – which refuses the idea that politics is a matter of state, parliament, election and party programme. Anti-political themes are on the rise in right-wing, left-wing and 'no-wing' varieties, stressing the inefficacy, the limits, the inevitable failings of state provision of welfare, crime control, education and much more, and demanding that individuals, families, communities, employers take back to themselves the powers and responsibilities that, since the nineteenth century, have been acquired by states, politicians and legislators. (1999: 2–3)

While these 'anti-political' arguments have only recently begun to take centre stage in political debates, the developments that have shifted the balance of governance away from states have been taking place for much of this century. In the domain of the governance of security one can trace these shifts to the 1940s and 1950s (Johnston, 1992). Much of this early development took place as corporations took the initiative in governing new spaces of collective life that were emerging, in particular the spaces that Shearing and Stenning (1992: 228–229) have termed 'mass private property'.

This desire to play a more active role in governance was facilitated by a regulatory structure, particularly contract and property law, that accorded corporations the right to govern these spaces of governance. Central among these new spaces were commercial malls, industrial 'parks', recreation areas and residential 'gated communities'. Corporations who used these spaces as places of business took advantage of the 'rights' set out in property and contract law and developed mentalities, institutional arrangements, technologies and practices for governing them. Within the arena of security these developments have operated to shift auspices and provision of governance away from the state into new governing assemblages. This shift in the location of knowledge and capacity was accompanied by a shift to future- or risk-based objectives and technologies for realising them that are not as reliant on force as those of state governments (Shearing, 1992; Shearing, 1997). Developments in private security provide an obvious example.

One of the consequences of the emergence of corporate entities as auspices and providers of governance has been that communities associated with them have challenged 'the idea that politics is a matter of state, parliament, elections and party programme' (Rose, 1999). One of the ways in which they have done so is through the creation of 'contractual communities' (Shearing, 1992) in which arrangements for governance are agreed upon through contract. This happens, for instance, when one buys a home in a gated community and agrees as part of the terms of the contract to particular governing arrangements. These contractual communities create new 'spacio-ethical zones' (Rose, 1999) within which members assume responsibility for some of their own governance.

These developments, while having much in common with neo-liberalism, do not fit easily with its more state-directed forms. With the emergence of these corporate governmental nodes both the rowing and the steering of governance are accepted as a responsibility of non-state nodes. To the extent that this has happened contractual communities have been able to realise the value of self-direction so central to democracy in ways that do not depend on conventional claims that 'politics is a matter of state, parliament, election and party programme[s]' (Rose, 1999).

During the early period in the development of this 'new ethical politics' (Rose, 1999), while state laws did provide the legal opportunity for the emergence of corporate governance, states did not actively promote it. Nor were they interested in limiting or directing the emergence of corporate governments. This was so even though many state agents, especially the police, became concerned about the implications of these developments and sought to resist them. In sum they took place without the active state involvement that has marked more recent neo-liberal developments (Shearing and Wood, forthcoming).

These mid-century developments are quite different, as I have just suggested, to the situation that exists today. States, and their agents, at present are more actively involved in promoting and shaping nodal governance. A key feature of much of this shaping has been an active attempt to bring these new governments under state direction. Today, the reigning political rationality is very deliberately promoting forms of nodal governance in which the state is conceived of as a broker or manager of programs of governance for which others must be persuaded to accept responsibility (Garland, 1996). This is nicely illustrated in 'community policing' programs that seek to 'responsibilise' (Burchell, 1993; O'Malley & Palmer, 1996) so that others will be willing and able to assist the police by taking on parts of the rowing of policing.

This desire to shape what non-state nodes do is made clear in a recent proposal by Ian Blair (1998), a serving Chief Constable in Britain, who has argued that nodes participating in governance should be 'police compliant'. With these late-century developments, states have sought to deliberately both encourage and regulate the involvement of local 'partners' in ways that are 'state compliant'.

While this concern with state steering and direction has been evident with respect to 'civil society' 'partnerships', states have, despite proposals such as Ian Blair's, tended to adopt a 'hands off' stance with respect to the 'private sector'. This difference in focus has had significant consequences for the relations that have developed between states and these two sectors. Again this is particularly evident with respect to the governance of security where the more well established corporate nodes have far greater autonomy from state direction than do 'civil society' nodes that have developed under the impact of programs designed to responsibilise local citizens and organisations. This has served to bifurcate developments in the multilateralisation of governance. As a result governmental arrangements developed under the auspices of corporations tend to be more independent of state direction than the civil society arrangements deliberately promoted by states working within a neo-liberal mentality.

As the collectivities involved in the self-directed forms of governance that have developed within private sector initiatives are more likely to involve the well-to-do, these collectivities have tended to fare better, with respect to enhanced autonomy, than their poorer neighbours (see for example Cruikshank's (1999) discussion of the 'empowerment' of people within neo-liberal programs). It is this inequality (see Bayley & Shearing, 1996), and how it might be addressed and rectified, that is the principal normative focus of the Zwelethemba project.

In the project we have asked how to create a regulatory environment and institutions, technologies and practices within it that will enhance poor people's ability to take greater control over the steering of their lives. South Africa is a particularly appropriate site in which to be doing this as the 'governance gap' just noted is especially stark. Over the past several decades the well-to-do (particularly well-to-do white South Africans) have done much to shift the control over the governance of their lives away from the state into the hands of a variety of corporate governments. This is particularly evident with respect to the governance of security. Here, not only is the ratio of private security personnel to state police agents among the highest in the world, but corporate governments now routinely undertake many of the functions that states have regarded as central to their role – for example, emergency response (Carrier, forthcoming). This situation has not changed since South Africa's first democratic election.

This contrasts sharply with the situation of poor people. They too had developed considerable governmental autonomy prior to the election through a range of civic structures within local areas. Since independence, however, the new government has sought to dismantle these processes and replace them with more state-directed programs. Again what has happened in policing provides an excellent example. The various 'popular policing' initiatives developed in response to apartheid (which were often very violent) have been dismantled and replaced with community policing initiatives that seek to ensure that the steering of policing remains in state hands, and more specifically in police hands. While this is never made explicit, the clear implication is that while corporate governments can be trusted to develop nodal governments that are independent of state steering that comply with the constitution and other state laws, this is not true of poor communities.

It is this context that has established the project's normative agenda. Namely, to develop a model for the nodal governance of security that enhances the autonomy of local 'community' nodes in ways that bear a family resemblance to what is already happening within the private sector. Specifically the project has sought to develop a 'model' for the local governance of security – what we call 'local capacity policing' – that promotes a mode of self-governance that enhances self-direction and is compliant with state law but which is not necessarily police compliant. Central to this agenda of legal compliance is the insistence that there should be no challenge to the state's claim to monopolise the distribution of physical force.

Although I am using the term 'model', we do not mean this in the sense of a blueprint that sets out and directs a course of action in a closed manner. The procedures the model endorses are open-ended and encourage discovery and inventiveness, albeit within bounds and according to principles that the model endorses.

The Model

There are two aspects to the model. The first has to do with problem-solving. There are, in turn, two aspects to problem-solving, namely, peacemaking and peacebuilding. Peacemaking refers in our terminology to problem-solving with respect to ongoing disputes that will establish peace with respect to that particular matter. Peacebuilding refers to problem-solving with respect to more generic issues.

The second aspect of the model is concerned with sustaining the processes of peacemaking and peacebuilding over time.

Problem-Solving: Peacemaking

Self-Direction, Knowledge and Capacity

At the heart of the model is a technology, similar to that used in family group conferencing, for mobilising local knowledge and local capacity to engage in both the rowing and the steering of governance. In adopting this technology the model adopts a stance that is consistent with the general trend in governance noted above that gives priority to local knowledge and capacity (in Nils Christie's phrase 'let us have as few experts as we dare' (1977: 12)). The aim is to create a problem-solving Forum that will bring together local knowledge and capacity that can be mobilised to provide a solution to a dispute. It is this bringing together of knowledge and capacity to seek a solution, rather than any particular desired form of outcome (for example, 'restoration as a healing component' for victims, restoration as 'accepting responsibility' for offenders and restoration as 'denouncing wrongful behavior' for communities (Law Commission of Canada, 1999: 27)), that is at the heart of the model. The only restriction it imposes is its insistence that what is done should be legal and conform to the model's Code of Good Practice.

In providing for legality the model takes a conservative stance. It requires, first, that force should never be used as a consequence of a Peacemaking Forum to solve a problem. If the conclusion is reached at a Forum that a coercive solution is required this is defined as grounds for

> **CODE OF GOOD PRACTICE**
>
> Members of Peace Committees use these guidelines in the course
> of their work as Peacemakers:
> - We help create a safe and secure environment in our community
> - We respect human rights
> - We do not use force or violence
> - We work in the community as a cooperative team, not as individuals
> - We are impartial
> - We report back to our peacemaking colleagues
> - We do not gossip about our work or about other people
> - We are consistent in what we do
> - Our aim is to heal, not to hurt.

referring the matter to the police, or some other state agent. Second, it
requires that the members of the Peace Committees (that is, local groups
of Peacemakers) should never engage in adjudication. This stance is
encouraged by a practice, that again resonates with family group conferencing, of not blaming persons. The focus is on discovering what can be
done to reduce or eliminate the problem (see below for a discussion of
the instrumental, future-focused nature of the model and the practices it
facilitates).

The non-directive feature of the model just outlined encourages a
variety of ways of problem-solving and leaves to the Forum participants
the decision as to just what this will be. What gives these 'cases' a family
resemblance is not so much what is done but rather the mobilisation of
local knowledge and capacity in and through the temporary collectivities
created through the process. Each Forum is different and transitory,
although its members are drawn from a broader territorial collectivity.
During a regular review process (see below) Peacemakers (the community members who facilitate the Forums) are encouraged both to reflect
on what has occurred in particular cases as well as to make comparisons
across cases.

The model also includes typical steps that Peacemakers are encouraged to follow.

Again, these steps operate as guidelines rather than as rules. Both the
Code of Good Practice and the problem-solving steps were developed
through an iterative process. During this process we reflected on how
they worked and the extent to which their elements were contributing to
our objectives.

STEPS IN PEACEMAKING

1 Meet separately with the people directly involved in order to find out what happened.
2 Encourage them to come together in a peace circle and to bring with them any other people who they think will help re-establish peace.
3 Meet with all these people together in a peace circle:
   - make sure that everyone has the opportunity to speak without being interrupted
   - let all the people affected by what happened tell how they feel about what happened and what it did to their lives.
4 Let the people start thinking and talking about how to make peace.
5 Work out a plan of action:
   - make clear what everybody's role will be
   - appoint some suitable person from the circle to monitor the agreement
   - get everyone to agree to the plan.
6 Let people end the circle in some way that will show that they have made peace: e.g., by shaking hands, embracing, or saying a prayer.

In both the Peacemaking and Peacebuilding Forums the emphasis is not on problems but on the knowledge and capacity available within circles for solving them. The model's technology seeks to 'make people up', to 'hail them out', not as people who have problems – and certainly not as people who give their problems away (Christie, 1977) to other experts (state or non-state) – but as people who are capable of developing solutions.

To return briefly to our introductory analysis, the argument implicit in the model is that the difficulty with state-directed versions of the neo-liberal political rationality is not its insistence that local capacities and knowledges be deployed in governance but the mechanisms promoted for accomplishing this. What the model distances itself from is forms of 'empowerment' that seek to mobilise local knowledge and capacity in order to enhance the capacity of state agencies to realise their own aims (cf. Drucker, 1994; see also Osborne & Gaebler, 1993).

The model views disputes as occasions around which to demonstrate to people that they have the capacity and knowledge required to self-govern.

These resources are assembled by inviting neighbours, friends and relatives to join the problem-solving Forums. This procedure brings together what may be thought about not simply as what John Braithwaite calls a 'community of care' but a 'community of life' – that is, a community drawn from the collectivity within which one lives one's daily life. Once the group is assembled, the Peacemakers use the steps described above as guidelines for setting in place a process that mobilises local resources.

These procedures work to encourage members of the Forum to engage in problem-solving. However, in this 'responsibilisation', the consequences are different from those advocated by the likes of Drucker and Osborne and Gaebler. This difference is a direct result of the difference in agenda. The processes encouraged by the model are not designed to engage the participants as role players in programs constructed by others. In contrast, the model works to promote innovation and self-direction. In doing so it promotes practices that are similar to developments in corporate governance that enable corporate collectivities to promote agendas that, while legal, are not simply expressions of state agendas. The effect is thus quite different from programs – for example, much that takes place under the sign of community policing – that seek to make up people as implementers of state agency programs. None of this, of course, should be taken as implying that the practices that are promoted are unregulated. In part this regulation arises from state law but the Peacemakers, as I have noted, also work within a self-imposed regulatory framework that interprets and goes beyond this.

Nature of the Problem

One of the consequences of the fact that many restorative justice programs are set up as diversion schemes is that a considerable amount of definitional work is done before the issue arrives at the dispute resolution Forum. This means that by the time the issue reaches the Forum it has already been defined as a legal infraction and parties to the infraction have been identified as offenders and victims. It is this 'problem' that is returned to the 'community' to be resolved. The definitional work that has been done provides the framework within which a resolution is to be found. This directs the whole resolution process. There is nothing new about this observation. It is nonetheless an important one. A recent restatement of it is provided by the Canadian Law Commission's discussion of how 'many of our most important issues are only imperfectly forced into [an adjudicative] model' (1999: iii, 49).

Where problematic events are identified before a state-driven definitional process takes place, two things happen. First, events that would pass through the state net may be and often are identified as deserving attention. This feature of pre-state engagement has been discredited by Stan Cohen (1985), among others, as net-widening. However, this critique is premised on state involvement and state action. It assumes that issues that would not have been dealt with through state processes and would not have been settled through the imposition of state sanctions would now get caught in a state net. This is not what the Zwelethemba model promotes. Yes, what occurs is net-widening in the sense that problems that would not otherwise be addressed, and would very likely escalate into 'state-attention-problems', are identified and attended to through a peacemaking process. But this is not the net-widening Cohen had in mind. Indeed the process avoids precisely the problems that Cohen was concerned about, by reducing the state 'catch'.

Secondly, what our cases indicate – over 100 in the first seven months – is that whatever the nature of the issue, it gets 'problematised' or 'made up' in ways that typically do not parallel the definitional practices of state agents. Two features are particularly noteworthy. One is that events are firmly embedded in a wider and deeper terrain. Thus, for instance, a stabbing is not 'pulled out' of the context of daily life as an 'assault' that has an offender and a victim. Rather it is located within a wider context of often ongoing and long-established patterns of action that include groupings such as families, neighbours and so on. Within this broader context, who is the 'offender' and who the 'victim' very often oscillates depending on just when a snapshot of events is taken – a 'victim' today may well have been an 'offender' yesterday. This is particularly important in light of the model's concern with 'hailing out' Forum participants as people who resolve problems rather than as disputants who create them.

The central issues that have emerged as providing the context for many of the specific events that have been dealt with through Peacemaking Forums are 'sex', 'money' and 'nuisance'. It is precisely these broader issues that states, as state agents constantly remind us (Wood & Shearing, 1998), typically do not have the capacity or the right to resolve.

Governing the Future

While the model is neutral on just what constitutes a resolution of a problem, a pervasive practice has emerged whereby Forums shift attention away from the past to the future. What tends to happen is that the event 'arrives' at a Forum as a problem defined by the disputants in a way that focuses attention on the past – the focus is on what has happened and the harms claimed to have been caused by the event. This takes place in most cases because the person who initially claims the status of 'victim' has set up or established the initial problematisation. If the 'victim' had taken the problem to the police this construction would be supported and formalised. It is this construction that is typically brought to non-state dispute resolution Forums as a result of diversion.

This tends not to happen within the Zwelethemba process, for four principal reasons. The first, as I have noted, is that the discussion typically places the event that precipitated the Forum within a wider context. Within this context the objective of repairing the past through either restorative or more conventional means becomes less self-evident. As this happens, the conception of what is a solution tends to become bringing-an-end-to-the-cycle-that-has-produced-the-dispute, rather than with sorting out the complex details of conflict and allocating responsibility and blame. What the discussion reveals to participants is that the focus on remedying the past is not as 'natural' as it appeared to be initially. This process mirrors what tends to happen in corporate governance and contributes to the 're-hailing' of disputants (see above).

A second and related reason for the move to a future-focus has to do with the existence of a wider group of people than the disputants at the circle, in particular, a group of people that extends beyond the participants directly associated with the principal disputants. While the persons initially identified as victims and offenders frequently initiate a discussion that is past-focused and backward-looking, as others enter into it there is very often a shift in focus to the future. While this can be, and sometimes is, initiated through persons identified with the particular disputants, it is most likely to be initiated and pursued by participants who are affected but not directly associated with the disputants, for example, neighbours who are concerned about the trading of insults and fighting between disputants. What these others tend to do is argue that the matter is not simply a dispute between a limited number of people that requires resolution but one that has had an effect on a wider 'community of life'. The dispute has, it is argued, disrupted the peace of the wider community. The objective this wider community brings to the circle is one that promotes a different future. Again this echoes what happens within the corporate governance of security.

A third related reason is the choice made during the early development of the model to think of the process as one designed to bring peace to Zwelethemba. This was partially a matter of the way in which we, as facilitators of the processes, thought about matters. More importantly, however, was the way in which our construction resonated with people who had been living with high levels of disorder for decades. One expression of this was the choice made by members of Peace Committees to describe themselves as Peacemakers and to call the association that was formed the Zwelethemba Peacemakers Association. This is similar to the explanation provided by those who argue that the risk focus – that is so prevalent today – can be explained, at least in part, in terms of people's responses to relatively high levels of disorder (Garland, 1996; see also Beck's (1992) more general discussion of what he refers to as the 'risk society'; Ericson & Haggerty, 1997).

Finally, a fourth feature that discourages a focus on the past is the model's insistence that solutions not involve the use of punishment or force. While, as is clear from restorative Forums that this alone need not shift the focus to the future, in conjunction with the other features just noted it tends to do so.

This focus on the governance of the future does not, of course, eliminate a discussion of, or a concern for, the past. What happens is that the past tends to be addressed to ensure that the future is different. That is, to the extent that dealing with the past becomes a focus, this tends to happen because it is believed that the past must be addressed in order to enable the participants to move forward in ways that will lead to peace in the future. This focus on dealing with the past as a way of enabling participants to move on into a new and different future is of course a feature of many restorative processes that view restoration as a basis for settling the past in ways that release persons from its grip. While this certainly has been a feature of the processes the model has facilitated – as is evident, for example, in the relatively large proportion of circles that conclude with some gesture of reconciliation (see below) – the emphasis has tended to be more instrumental and utilitarian. This emphasis parallels the focus within 'corporate policing' (Shearing & Stenning, 1981). This tendency is one that Braithwaite (1999a) has noted in corporate dispute resolution and something that he believes that analysts have tended to neglect as they have examined the practices within restorative Forums. An example of this is the emphasis in many restorative Forums on contractual agreements that are intended to bind disputants in the future.

This greater focus on the future is used by participants to assess the success of Peacemaking Forums. While they regard restoration and reconciliation as important, and perhaps even necessary, they are believed to be insufficient in themselves. Peace Forums are assessed on the basis of the extent to which they govern the future rather than on the extent to which they restore a balance that has been upset in the past. Thus, while symbolic expressions of restoration, like the holding of hands, are encouraged and valued, they are not regarded as essential. Much more important are those features of the process, such as contracts, that seek to bind participants to a future course of action. It is in this context that gestures such as handholding tend to be given meaning. For this reason these tend to involve not simply the disputants but all those present. What is symbolised through them is a joint commitment to contribute to a different future. While none of this means that the past is not given any weight, it does mean that a concern with the past tends not to trump efforts to 'colonise the future' (Giddens, 1991).

Authority and Participation

A feature of this process that is closely akin to restorative justice processes is the reliance it places on sources of authority that are brought together in the course of the peacemaking. The model insists that Peacemakers should define themselves as having no authority to resolve the dispute or to insist that agreements made in the course of the resolution process are kept. Initially we were concerned that this might mean that the Peacemakers, and their Forums, would not be taken as seriously as they would be if the facilitator had been a state agent, such as a police officer or a someone with status within the community (what people in Zwelethemba sometimes refer to as a 'grey hair'). This concern proved groundless, as sources of authority were almost always located within the Forum itself.

This definition of Peacemakers as simply facilitators has meant that there are few, if any, bars to participation based on status. Peacemakers vary enormously in background, and include both men and women and several young people in their late teens and early 20s. Although they do not bring any special authority to the Forums, they do participate actively in the discussion. They do this by drawing people in and summarising what has been said and acting as members of the community of life who can make suggestions.

The number of Peacemakers who decide to attend a Forum varies from two people to about ten. The principle that has emerged is that as many Peacemakers as possible will attend. This ensures considerable opportunity for them to learn and observe variations in the way in which facilitation is accomplished.

In setting up Forums disputants are encouraged to bring along anyone they wish. However, other persons not specifically invited by the principal disputants may and do attend. As we have suggested, this extends participation in the Forums beyond the disputants' 'community of care'.

The emphasis on inclusion not only draws on ties within collectivities, it also strengthens and creates them. Typically a Forum will operate to build new ties between members as well as strengthen existing ones. Links that perhaps had not previously been recognised will be identified and new sources of cohesion will be established. Similarly new links often develop as a consequence of post-Forum agreements that require people to coordinate their activities in some way.

In response to our concerns that there may be problems that require adjudication by an 'outside' authority, such as 'grey hairs', the project has worked with the South African Law Commission (which has recently published a discussion paper setting out the model I am describing) to develop the idea of a Community Forum. This would be different from the Peace Committees in that it would involve adjudication by either a single person or a panel. We have envisaged this as following an arbitration logic where disputants whose dispute has not been settled within a Peace Committee could opt to take their case to the Community Forum for settlement. To date, with well over a hundred disputes considered at the Peace Committee level, we have not had an instance where this option has seemed attractive.

Problem-Solving: Peacebuilding

To this point our focus has been on the resolution of current disputes. While Peacemaking Forums typically tend to shift attention to the future, they seldom take this discussion beyond the immediate issue. That is, the participants typically consider how the repetition of a particular set of events is to be avoided but do not take the next step and consider more generic issues. For example, they might consider how it is that future thefts by a particular person, or from a particular home, can be avoided but they are unlikely to consider how burglary can be reduced more generally. Shifting to peacebuilding in a generic sense, we have found, requires Forums dedicated to this. Like the Peacemaking Forums, they are designed to mobilise local capacity and knowledge and to hail people and collectivities as having the knowledge and capacity to accomplish this. Unlike Peacemaking Forums, these Forums require many meetings as people work through the issues and experiment with different solutions. This long-term commitment is more difficult to establish and sustain. In our experience to date, these Forums are most likely to succeed if they bring together established corporate entities that have an interest in developing longer-term solutions to problems.

In identifying generic issues as candidates for successful resolution, Peacemakers look back over the sorts of problems that face the community and identify matters that come up regularly. This is done in two ways. First, by considering the problems that have been brought to Peacemaking Forums. This is done both through memory by Peace Committees and on a formal basis as part of an audit process (see below). Second, the model promotes the use of two forms of surveys. One is a victim survey that we have undertaken on a regular basis, both to ascertain residents' perceptions of the sorts of security issues they face and to keep track of the levels of awareness regarding the work of Peacemakers. The other is an exit interview that we have recently initiated that asks questions of the principal participants at Peacemaking Forums. We have been assisted in the development of both these survey instruments by Tony Doob.

On the basis of the list of peacebuilding possibilities, which shifts as experience changes, the next step the model proposes is to discover a match between an issue on the list and a group of participants who are likely to be willing to tackle the issue in the longer term. One example of an issue that has been addressed is the disorder that results from the existence of illegal drinking establishments called 'shebeens', that exist throughout South Africa. Although these businesses are not legally sanctioned, state agents typically take a tolerant attitude towards them. They constitute the principal settings in Zwelethemba for adult recreation. In the case of the 'shebeen problem', the Peace Committees have worked to create a self-regulatory schema whereby shebeen owners agree to a Code of Conduct and seek collectively to promote it.

The guiding steps that have been developed for peacebuilding are as follows:

STEPS IN PEACEBUILDING

1 Identify the issue
2 Build ideas about why it happened
3 Choose one or two ideas to try out
4 Build a program, based on the ideas, to resolve the issue
5 See what happens after the program has been tried
6 Improve the program
7 Share what you have learned

These steps, incidentally, were initiated at a discussion in Zwelethemba attended by David Bayley, John Braithwaite and Enrique Font, a colleague who is working with us in Argentina.

We have found that peacebuilding, outside of the Peacemaking Forums, is the most difficult part of the process to develop and sustain. While the peacebuilding steps work well, we need to think more about how to set up and sustain Peacebuilding Forums. Our most successful Forums at present, as I have indicated, are ones that involve local entities that have some existence apart from our Forums. An example would be the Peacebuilding Forum made up primarily of shebeen owners.

Another difficult issue has been finding satisfactory ways of enabling peacebuilding resources to relate to state agencies. Relevant to our thinking has been a recent development in South Africa, taken from developments in Europe and North America, namely the establishment of Partnership Forums that operate to bring state agencies together to engage in precisely the sort of peacebuilding I have just outlined. These

Forums, called Community Safety Forums, are just being established. We intend to use these Forums as institutions whose resources our Peace-building Forums can seek to mobilise. Given the agenda set out at the start of the chapter, it is critical to the model that this engagement take place only once a strategic plan for mobilising resources has been established at a Peacebuilding Forum level.

This discussion brings me to the second part of the model I mentioned at the outset, namely, the mechanisms we have set in place for sustaining peacemaking and peacebuilding.

Sustainability

A question often raised by Peacemakers during the course of the model's development was: 'What do we get out of all of this work?' In raising this they were broaching the classic 'free rider problem'. They were saying, 'We are doing this work to provide a communal good from which everyone in the collectivity benefits but we are getting no special compensation for this'. They raised this issue most often in the context of family pressures that they were facing to contribute to the collective income of the household. Other household members, they noted, were critical of the way they were spending their time and wanted them to 'get out there' and make some money. This concern led to much discussion. Much of this was around experience with past responses to this issue in other settings within the South African context. Of particular concern was the experience with the practice by governments and non-governmental organisations of formalising roles such as these as either full-time or part-time occupations for which people were paid. This response, it was felt by many people, both within and outside the project, has been profoundly problem-ridden. Among these problems, one that was frequently raised was the way in which this response served to set people who were paid apart from their fellow residents as people with jobs and as new relatively affluent members of the collectivity. A related concern was that the monies paid to contributors were not 'spread around' within the collectivity and served to create undesirable status distinctions. Perhaps most importantly, from the point of view of our agenda, was that this response simply created another level of experts who deprecated local knowledge and capacity.

The procedure we developed, and the one our model endorses, is one in which monies are paid to the Peace Committee for the work they do. Payment is made in terms of outcomes, not time spent working as Peacemakers. While this principle applies to both peacemaking and peacebuilding, as peacemaking efforts are more discrete we are clearer about how to reward outcomes associated with peacemaking than we are with those associated with peacebuilding.

So payments are now made to Peace Committees for both peacemaking and peacebuilding work according to a schedule. Payments are made after a review of cases by the fieldworkers of the Community Peace Programme. The review considers whether or not the procedures followed conformed with the principles of the model, particularly as these are set out in the Code of Good Practice. Payments are made irrespective of whether the process was successful in promoting peace – the outcome is a peacemaking or peacebuilding activity that takes place in accord with the Code. In making these payments the Community Peace Programme, during the model-building phase, took the role of local governments which, in terms of the model, should be responsible for providing the funds for these payments. These payments are paid into two funds. First, an Administrative Fund that is used to support the work of the Peace Committee by providing for refreshments, stationery and so on. The second, and larger share of the payment, goes to a Chumani Fund (or Growth Fund) that is to be used for two purposes: first, to create income-generating opportunities within the collectivity served by the Peace Committee, and second, to support that collectivity through 'poverty relief' (interpreted to date as supporting services to disadvantaged members of the collectivity, for example supporting an old age home).

In dispensing the monies in the Chumani Fund, the Peace Committee acts as an investment cooperative. To promote income generation, the Chumani Fund is being used to develop micro-enterprises within the collectivity. While participation within these small businesses is not limited to Committee members, the model, in its present form, gives priority to them. The Chumani Fund provides support for developing micro-enterprise in the form of assistance in business planning and the management of the businesses once they are established. The model also provides for a Revolving Fund that provides loans to business ventures. It also includes templates for record-keeping that the payments for peacemaking and peacebuilding require and the records that poverty relief payments and micro-enterprise entail.

These procedures have worked to sustain the willingness of Peacemakers to volunteer their time to peacemaking and peacebuilding activities. They have done so by providing answers to the question 'Why should we be doing this?' that are persuasive within the context within which we are working. There are several reasons for this. One is the widespread assumption that contributing to the wider collective through contributing to peace and the economic well-being of communities is self-evidently worthwhile. In addition, the opportunities to directly participate in micro-enterprise are seen as providing an acceptable response to the free rider problem noted above. We interpret the willingness to continue to engage in peacemaking and peacebuilding under these arrangements as evidence that the contribution Peacemakers feel they make to communal interests, along with the opportunity to directly benefit, provide a workable recipe for sustainability.

In addition to the arguments just presented as grounds for this arrangement, an additional argument that influenced our choice of this approach has to do with the issue of 'empowerment' and the problems attached to conventional programs raised by Cruikshank (1999) and others. One of the features of programs of empowerment that have developed under the neo-liberal approach to re-inventing government has been a tendency to pass on the work of governance without a corresponding shift of resources. Carol LaPrairie (1999) has discussed the problem of 'responsibilisation without resources', while Pat O'Malley has defined the issue in these terms:

> ... there is nothing necessarily wrong with making people responsible, but in order to do so you have to provide the real conditions for responsibility. Most neo-liberal governance thinks it can do this by provision of attitudinal resources and knowledge – empowerment – but most often there is a need to provide infrastructure and material support (cried down of course because of its associations with welfare). (Personal communication)

Bayley and I (1996) responded to this need to provide resources with an argument for block grants to communities that would create a policing budget as opposed to a police budget (see also the recommendations of the Independent Commission on Northern Ireland (Independent Commission, 1999) on the creation of policing budgets). In the Zwelethemba model this idea of a block grant is given concrete expression through the processes I have just outlined.

Accountability and Transparency

There are obvious dangers that the practices that take place will not remain within legal or ethical bounds as the process develops over time and the number of Peacemakers expands. This is particularly worrying in South Africa, where there has been a history of such problems. Indeed it was not long before these problems emerged in Zwelethemba. The most difficult occurred when a well established 'problem-solver', who many people in the community turned to for assistance, joined the Peacemakers and started to practise his brand of problem-solving (which violated the Code of Good Practice) under their sign. In response to this, and the general concern just raised, a set of procedures have been established as part of the model to guard against abuse.

The procedures the model endorses include some safeguarding features. The overriding principle is that people in collectivities have a right to undertake peacemaking and peacebuilding so long as what they do is within the law and is undertaken in a transparent manner so that the legality of their actions can be assessed. A similar principle is applied at a political level: the position the model takes is that no political approvals are necessary or required so long as the process is legal. This is true for governments, political parties and for the 'community'. Political support is, however, regarded as desirable. We have taken a similar position with respect to criminal justice agencies. Again, support is regarded as very desirable. While these arguments are based on principle, there are also practical grounds for endorsing them. In particular, that one should be careful of unnecessarily setting up gatekeepers by asking for approvals that are not required.

Peace Committees are typically formed after general community meetings in which the peacemaking and peacebuilding are introduced to a group of residents (as we have moved the model into areas outside of Zwelethemba, this is done by both Peacemakers and members of the Community Peace Programme). To ensure transparency we attempt to make known, to as many people as possible within the collectivity, what procedures will be used, for example, by publicising widely the Code of Good Practice and the peacemaking and peacebuilding steps. This is also done at the outset of Forums.

As there is no adjudication by the Peacemakers, responsibility for decisions rests with the participants at the Forum. The Peacemakers' role is to facilitate this and to ensure that the agreements arrived at conform to the Code of Good Practice and the ethical and legal framework it embodies. The procedures and the agreements reached at all Forums are reviewed by members of the Community Peace Programme as part of the assessment process for allocating resources to the administrative and the growth funds. As the project expands and as monies for these funds are made available by governments, this process will be formally authorised by them. We keep audited accounts of payments and expenditures.

Regular meetings are held with 'stakeholders'. In particular, in the sites in which we are working at present Peacemakers and members of the Community Peace Programme meet regularly with the local police and the local Community Police Forum. Community Police Forums are statutory bodies established to provide liaison between the community and the police. Regular meetings are also held with local magistrates.

Membership in Peace Committees requires that persons be familiar with the procedures and formally agree to abide by them. Membership in a Peace Committee is for four-month renewable terms. Renewal decisions are made on the basis of the member's history and, in particular, the standards set by the Code of Good Practice.

Conclusion

In developing the Zwelethemba model we have sought to take up Nikolas Rose's (1996) challenge to do more than engage in a simple dismissal of governmental developments taking place under the sign of 'neo-liberalism'. Instead we have explored how they might be responded to, and shaped, so as 'to maximise the capacity of individuals and collectivities to shape the knowledges, contest the authorities and configure the practices that will govern them in the name of their freedom and commitments'. The model argues that for this to happen it is necessary not only to develop mentalities and procedures that make up problem-solving Forums and 'disputants' differently, but that this must be done in ways that, in Pat O'Malley's words, will 'provide the real conditions for responsibility'. We are continuing to explore how the procedures advocated by the Zwelethemba model might be extended, and further developed, elsewhere in South Africa and further afield. As part of this we intend to promote a variety of exchanges (both 'real' and 'virtual'), at a variety of levels, to explore how both the objectives set out in this chapter, and the technologies developed for their accomplishment, might be advanced.

Notes

1   On behalf of the members of the Community Peace Programme and participants in the development of the Zwelethemba model.
2   This model-building project was supported by the Raoul Wallenberg Institute, Lund University, through a grant from the Government of Sweden.
3   Fonseka (1999: 3) spells out this definition as follows: 'The term "Governance" is derived from the Greek words "kybernan" and "kybernetes". It means "to steer and to pilot or be at the helm of things".'

CHAPTER 3

Two Protestant Ethics
and the Spirit of Restoration

Lawrence W. Sherman

Meddle not with government ...
I have said little to you about distributing justice ...
for I should desire you should never be concerned therein.
William Penn

Government is equally as necessary to mankind
as bread and water, light and air, and far more excellent.
John Calvin

Restorative community justice is an idea whose inspiration is the same Protestant ethic that sparked the 1995 bombing of the Oklahoma City Federal Building. Ironically, that ethic is primarily known for its commitment to non-violence and its opposition to war. But its fundamental values can lead to violent civil disobedience, a hatred of all government, and a social incapacity for building strong civil society institutions outside of government. The social structure of the restorative justice movement itself provides further evidence for at least part of this claim, given the movement's fragmented leadership and dearth of strong institutions. The possibility that restorative justice may amplify modern cultural trends weakening civil society and democracy is a major issue for the future of that movement.

The Protestant ethic that sparks both pacifism and bombings is the radical egalitarianism and individualism of the antinomian (literally 'against laws') sects founded in the first century after Luther, including Quakers, Mennonites, Amish and Anabaptists (Fisher, 1972b: 73). These religions are at once democratic and anarchistic, literate and anti-professional. Their theology stands in sharp contrast to the Calvinist Puritan ideals of hierarchical communalism, the high 'calling' of judges, and deference to the authority of highly educated people. As E. Digby Baltzell's

(1979: 94) analysis of these two Protestant ethics puts it, the Calvinist Puritan ethic is 'optimistic about institutions, pessimistic about man', while the antinomian Quaker ethic is 'optimistic about man, pessimistic about institutions'. It is the pessimism about institutions that may lead the antinomianism of restorative community justice to undermine government and civil society – just as communities founded by these religions have been left, centuries later, far weaker in state and civil institutions than communities founded by Puritans. The history of these two ethics suggests the growth of restorative justice would foster an egalitarian individualism that breeds disrespect for all institutions, including law itself.

Yet it is equally plausible that restorative justice would have exactly the opposite effects, arriving just in time to save democratic legal institutions from a crisis of legitimacy bred of an outdated hierarchical relationship to citizens. As modern democracies place an increasingly 'consumerist' emphasis on the quality of the state's treatment of individual citizens, the values and procedures of restorative justice may offer a far better fit to modern culture than the legal forms of the past millennium. Just as Digby Baltzell predicts a weaker civil society from the Quaker ethic that restorative justice promotes, Francis Fukuyama (1992) predicts that the state would become stronger by greater attention to its symbolic recognition of the importance of each and every citizen. While both Baltzell and Fukuyama suggest similar diagnoses of how we arrived at our present state of culture, they imply divergent visions of the effect of egalitarian justice on the institutional fabric of democracy, one pessimistic, one optimistic. But in order for the optimistic vision to gain credence, the civil institutional support for restorative justice may have to strengthen itself substantially.

The question of what macrosociological effects restorative justice would produce emerges from an analysis of the history and social effects of the two major Protestant ethics in Western culture since the Lutheran Reformation. That history offers ample reasons to deduce that diverting criminal offences from formal law courts to egalitarian community restoration processes poses a threat to the strength of the state, and also threatens institutions of civil society. But history is most useful when it goes beyond mere correlation to a fuller understanding of changing context, which Neustadt and May (1986: 253–254) call thinking in timestreams: 'imagining the future as it may be when it becomes the past – with some intelligible continuity but richly complex and able to surprise'. Thus a prediction about the effects of the Quaker ethic dominating the criminal law may well be wrong in the context of the current age.

The counterpoint to Baltzell's historical analysis is the new cultural conditions of what is arguably a 'post-materialist age', one in which Francis

Fukuyama (1992) argues that government has become more important for its symbolic functions (such as a statement of ideals) than for its instrumental functions (such as provision of armed forces). If Fukuyama is right, the central purpose of government is to provide identity and recognition to each individual as an important member of society. In such a world, the legitimacy of government declines as citizens perceive disrespect by the agents of the state. Thus it may be that the antinomian ideals of restorative justice are just what government needs to maintain its legitimacy in the face of declining trust in hierarchical government. If economic and historical forces are driving our age towards an era of egalitarian individualism, then democratic government may need to reinvent its relationship to citizens, especially in the enforcement of law. Law itself may require new principles of legitimation, principles linked more closely to emotions than to logic, to inclusiveness more than to erudition. This theory predicts that the growth of restorative justice would lead to stronger institutions of both government and civil society.

This essay explores both Baltzell's history of the two Protestant ethics and Fukuyama's predictions about the future of state and society. It applies these analyses to the vision of a world in which most criminal offences are processed by egalitarian citizen groups with emotional ties to the principals in each case, under the general oversight of courts. It concludes by suggesting several models under which restorative justice can help build support for civil institutions – including those advocating restorative justice – as well as the rule of law itself.

Two Protestant Ethics

Max Weber's (1958) 'Protestant ethic' was actually a Puritan ethic, quite distinct from other branches of the Protestant Reformation. As Baltzell (1979) argues, the Puritan ethic was only one of the two great influences of the Protestant Reformation on modern democracy. These two ethics have clashed for over three centuries, with the Puritan ethic dominating Western political culture for most of that time. But since the 1960s, Baltzell suggests, the other Protestant ethic has been gaining ground, and has arguably won the battle for dominance in political culture. That ethic is Quaker, not Puritan.

While both the Calvinist Puritans and the antinomian Quakers placed governmental authority in the vote of the people, their interpretations of that authority were very different. John Calvin's Geneva was a radical new system of order and communalism led by learned magistrates, whose calling was judged to be the highest of any vocation, outside the pulpit itself (Barr, 1961). George Fox's Quakers practised individualistic defiance of authority, refusing to grant anyone else the right to lead them either to

God or to battle. Calvin's Geneva was a school for leadership, not in commerce as Weber suggests, but in government and politics. Its English refugee 'graduates' (who escaped to Geneva from Protestant-murdering Queen Mary) returned home to create sects that built a theocracy in Massachusetts and imposed Cromwell's strict government. Fox's English followers were schooled in resistance to government in ways large and small, including William Penn's landmark London trial and appeal establishing the right of jurors to refuse a judge's directed verdict (Turow, 1999). Penn and his faithful went on to found the state of Pennsylvania as a business venture, a community where each citizen could pursue their private lives with minimal interference from the state.

The Quaker and Puritan ethics were manifestly different in the relationship of the individual to the group. Puritans were intensely involved in groups, including not only church congregations, but also lecture groups and town meetings. When they colonised Massachusetts, they built their homes around a village green, commuting to their farmlands outside the village. Quakers, in contrast, had much less intense ties to their groups, with much greater tolerance for both solitude and diversity of opinion. When they colonised Pennsylvania, they settled on family farms far apart from their neighbours. Over the next two centuries, graduates of New England colleges were generally far more successful in the group-dominated profession of law than in the individually inspired field of science; graduates of Quaker colleges were far more successful in science than in law (Baltzell, 1979: 515). The Puritans were classically 'other-directed', valuing the respect of their fellow citizens (Riesman, 1950), while the Quakers were 'inner-directed' and less concerned about peer group pressures.

Baltzell (1979: 94) links the differences in cultural consequences of the Puritan and Quaker ethics to differences in their theologies. The most fundamental difference is in the ultimate source of sacred authority, and the Quaker doctrine of the 'inner light'. The Bible is the sacred authority for Puritans; the 'inner light' of divine inspiration of each individual is the sacred authority for Quakers. Puritans hold true to the faith of their fathers, for whom God is one transcendent for all men the same. Quakers say 'to thine ownself be true' in honouring a God who is immanent in all persons in unique ways. Puritans stress the Old Testament and its Ten Commandments, but Quakers stress the New Testament and its Sermon on the Mount. Puritans value the head, Quakers the heart. Puritans stress God's laws – understood through systematic study and reasoning, while Quakers stress the Gospel understood through love and feeling. Puritans feel anxious and compelled to duty and honour; Quakers seek peace of mind through honesty and good conscience. Some Puritans (and not others) are predestined to be part of God's 'elect',

Table 1   Cultural Consequences of Puritan and Quaker Ethics

Puritans: Hierarchical	Quakers: Egalitarian
Communitarianism	*Individualism*
Build institutions through compromise	Reject institutions as imperfect
Ideal calling: public service	Ideal calling: private life
Ideal place: city	Ideal place: rural or suburb
Ideal government: representative republic	Ideal government: direct democracy
Speaking aristocracy and silent democracy	Speaking democracy and silent plutocracy
Level up (opportunarian)	Level down (egalitarian)
Patriarchy	Sexual equality or matriarchy
Ethnocentrism, provincialism	Xenophilia, cosmopolitanism
Respect for erudition	Anti-intellectual
Respect professional experts	Reject professionalism
Human nature: sinful, must be controlled	Human nature: perfectible, must find inner guidance
Emotions tightly controlled	Emotions openly expressed
Attitude towards government: pride and trust	Attitude towards government: shame and distrust

(*Source*: adapted from Baltzell, 1979, p 94)

while all Quakers manifest God in every person equally. Most important, Puritans see the source of evil in a good world caused by the sinfulness of individuals, Quakers see the source of evil in a sinful world that corrupts good individuals. Puritans seek to transform the world; Quakers prefer to withdraw from it.

Baltzell summarises the cultural consequences of these differing theologies as 'hierarchical communalism' and 'egalitarian individualism', as selectively detailed in Table 1. The selection of cultural consequences is based on the dimensions most relevant to restorative justice as it has been practised in Canberra, Australia, based on the 'Wagga model' of community justice conferences (Braithwaite, 1999a; Sherman et al, 1998). Perhaps the most important dimension is the issue of who talks in the two traditions: Puritan democracy is silent except for speech by learned leaders, while Quaker democracy is spoken by all save the wealthy. Yet

Puritans talked more than Quakers, with more frequent assemblies, lecture groups, and even libraries: six of nine public libraries in England prior to 1640 were founded in Puritan towns (Phillips, 1999: 27), while Quakers relied upon (and talked about) few books other than the Bible. Thus while Puritans reserved public speaking for more learned voices, there was more widespread participation in government by Puritans than by Quakers. Quaker culture follows de Tocqueville's classic definition of individualism:

> ... a ... feeling which disposes each citizen to isolate himself from the mass of his fellows and withdraw into the circle of family and friends; with this little society formed to his taste, he leaves the greater society to look after itself. (1848; 1969: 506)

This withdrawal is even seen in such acts of community intervention as charity, which a Puritan culture pursues through institutional philanthropy (such as the endowment of university professorships) and a Quaker culture pursues through spontaneous acts of charity (such as giving food and shelter to victims of flood or fire).

Like all ideal types, these two Protestant ethics greatly simplify a highly complex and dynamic picture of Protestant sectarianism over four centuries. For example, on the eve of the American Civil War, one historian divided the sects by party as follows: 'devotionalist' Protestants generally joined the Whig Party, including Unitarians (who descended from Puritans), Quakers, 'new School' Calvinists, 'Free Will' Baptists, 'perfectionists' and Finneyites, while the Democratic Party attracted most of the 'confessionalists', including German Lutherans, Dutch 'true' Calvinists, Old School Presbyterians, and antimission (later 'Southern') Baptists (Phillips, 1999: 392). When the Democrats ultimately became the party of the southern cause, such Yankee Calvinists as President Theodore Roosevelt's father (who was married to a southern belle) refused to fight in the Civil War (Morris, 1978). Yet he went on to found a leading New York museum and helped build other major institutions of civil society. The point is not that these types imply perfect prediction of political behaviour on the basis of religious background. The value of Baltzell's two Protestant ethics is the high probability of accuracy with such predictions.

Baltzell's own experiment is the comparison of Puritan Boston to Quaker Philadelphia. The Quaker city was the largest in the US in 1800, twice the size of New York and three times that of Boston; even today it is twice the size of Boston. Yet the Puritan culture of Boston has produced three Presidents to Philadelphia's none; it is Massachusetts that produced 112 years of Supreme Court service compared to only 83 from Pennsylvania (Baltzell, 1979: 495); it is Philadelphia where the top lawyer in the US – a millionaire – twice refused a Supreme Court appointment on the grounds that the salary was too low (Baltzell, 1979: 11). More important, it is the far wealthier Philadelphia that failed to build its civil society institutions, endowing only one chair at its leading university by 1877; Harvard's first chair was endowed in 1721, with a total of thirteen endowed by 1872 while the University of Pennsylvania still had none. Most of Philadelphia's elite families sent their children elsewhere for education, while Boston's elites committed themselves to local educational institutions. Massachusetts led the nation in requiring public education for every child as a function of local government from the 1600s, while Pennsylvania left secondary education up to poorly supported charity and religious schools well into the nineteenth century (Baltzell, 1979: 269). By the dawn of the twentieth century, muckraker Lincoln Steffens found that while Boston had corruption, its voting was relatively honest and its civil society groups were fighting hard against public payoffs. But Philadelphia, 'corrupt and contented', was a city where the machine had literally stolen the franchise from the people, a city where a sample of registered voters found 63 percent of them to be non-existent (Baltzell, 1979: 378).

Today, Boston has created (across the river) the nation's richest university, a wealth of other civil institutions, and one of the lowest urban homicide rates (6 per 100,000). Philadelphia has a moderately strong civil society, especially a rich array of churches, but far less substantial civil institutions than its (far smaller) Puritan comparison city. The homicide rate in Philadelphia was three times higher (22 per 100,000) than Boston's in 1998 (Federal Bureau of Investigation, 1999). When faced with a rising homicide rate in the early 1990s, Boston mounted multiple collaborative efforts among religious, civic and governmental institutions to combat the problem; Philadelphia launched no such effort until 1998, after discovering that its police had been intentionally and substantially understating the level of all serious crimes except homicide. While Boston enjoys an expanding economy and a growing population, Philadelphia's declining economy has lost 10 percent of its resident population in a decade. At every turn, where Boston appears capable of building coalitions across racial, ethnic and political boundaries, Philadelphia continues to struggle to achieve consensus on a clear course of action. As Eli Kirk Price said of the construction of the Philadelphia Museum of Art – perhaps the city's greatest building – 'Every stone in that Museum was placed there against someone's opposition' (Baltzell, 1979: 44).

Baltzell's comparison of two cities may be more persuasive than his more sweeping claim (1979: 455) that since 1963 the US has moved from dominance by the Puritan ethic to dominance by the Quaker. Yet many social indicators and analyses by other scholars point to that conclusion.

Most striking is the declining trust in national government measured in the United States since 1963 – the year of President Kennedy's assassination (which Baltzell compares in cultural consequences to the execution of Charles I) and in many other nations since 1980. Public opinion polls show that the percentage of sampled white Americans who answer 'most of the time' or 'just about always' to the question 'How much of the time can you trust the government to do what is right?' dropped from 75 percent in 1964 to 20 percent in 1994 (LaFree, 1998: 102). Unpacking this trend reveals some growth in the belief that people in government are crooked (30 percent to 50 percent), large growth in the belief that government serves a few big interests (30 percent to 75 percent), but almost equally large growth (35 percent to 70 percent) in the belief that 'public officials don't care what people like me think' (Orren, 1997: 82). This last measure may explain why the loss of legitimacy is greatest for the federal government and lowest for local government (Orren, 1997: 83), where legitimacy has actually increased over time: people may trust government more where they feel that officials are more likely to recognise and act on their views.

Yet these trends are not simply an American phenomenon. Inglehart (1997: 223) reports declining respect for authority from 1981 to 1990 in 18 of 21 countries surveyed (the exceptions being three countries that democratised during that period: South Korea, Argentina, and South Africa). In countries as diverse as the US, Finland, Mexico and Great Britain, respect for the police and armed forces declined markedly, as did 'pride' in their nation. At the same time, 14 out of the 21 reported increasing trust in other people. All of these measures indicate a shift from Puritan to Quaker ethics, as Baltzell has defined them, far beyond America's shores. While some might attribute this change to the ripple effects of American culture in global entertainment media, there are far more compelling explanations in the material changes simultaneously affecting all of these nations.

The massive three-decade decline of public trust in liberal democratic governments suggests a paradox of success: as democracies become more materially successful and better educated, their perceived need for governance declines and their expectations for government 'consumerism' increase (Fukuyama, 1992; Orren, 1997; Inglehart, 1997). The crisis of government legitimacy has been prompted less by declining quality of government conduct than by increasing public dissatisfaction with institutions in general. Nye and Zelikow (1997: 270) examine 17 hypotheses about public loss of trust in government, including theories of government integrity and effectiveness. But only one hypothesis 'fits all institutions and all countries': the social changes normatively challenging the legitimacy of virtually all forms of social hierarchy authority (although not wealth). Thus even at a time when advanced societies have become increasingly *less* egalitarian in their distributions of material wealth (LaFree & Drass, 1996), the post-materialist lack of struggle for daily survival may have made them *more* egalitarian in their cultural expectations of government and the rule of law. As Baltzell (1979: 103) observes, 'from the beginning, the Quakers were levelers of authority rather than levelers of wealth'. Across the world, this great awakening (and its material preconditions) may have constructed a widespread preference for the antinomian recognition of individual dignity over the Calvinist recognition of communal authority.

Fukuyama (1992), after Hegel, hypothesises that the quest for recognition is the central engine of 'history', which he defines as the evolution of ideology and government. The quest for recognition through fame by princes and generals fuelled millennia of warfare, while the quest for recognition by writers and philosophers fuelled creative ideas for how government should be constituted. The 'end of history' Fukuyama hypothesises is liberal democracy, the final form of ideological evolution. In this form of government, nation-states do not go to war (at least with other modern democracies). But they face strong internal demands by their citizens, whose human rights include the dignity of recognition, or what Plato called *thymos*, a source of the powerful emotions of anger, pride and shame:

> *Thymos* emerges in the *Republic* as being somehow related to the value one sets on oneself, what we today might call 'self-esteem.'... Socrates suggests a relationship between anger and 'self-esteem' by explaining that the nobler a man is – that is, the more highly he evaluates his own worth – the more angry he will become when he has been dealt with unjustly. ... *Thymos* is something like an innate human sense of justice: people believe that they have a certain worth, and when other people act as though they are worth less – when they do not recognize their worth at its correct value – then they become angry. The intimate relationship between self-evaluation and anger can be seen in the English word synonymous with anger, 'indignation.' 'Dignity' refers to a person's sense of self-worth; 'in-dignation' arises when someone happens to offend that sense of worth. Conversely, when other people see that we are not living up to our own sense of self-esteem, we feel *shame*; and when we are evaluated justly (i.e., in proportion to our own true worth), we feel *pride*. (Fukuyama, 1992: 164–165)

The emotions of shame, pride and anger figure heavily in the 1989 book that provides a theoretical foundation for a major branch of the restorative justice movement. John Braithwaite's (1989) *Crime, Shame and Reintegration* hypothesises that fear of shame and pride in being law-abiding are the major social forces for preventing crime, but that modern criminal justice has become disconnected from those emotions. Instead, he argues, the criminal justice system often creates anger (and indignation) at the state by offending citizens' dignity, undermining their respect for law and their willingness to obey it. He recommends a process of shaming offences but not offenders, affirming each crime-committing (and admitting) citizen's dignity as a human being and inviting them to take pride in being law-abiding. He also invokes the New Testament theology of hating the sin but loving (and reintegrating) the sinner, thus bridging Fukuyama's Hegelian analysis with the Quaker Protestant ethic.

This analysis may also bridge explanation and prediction: understanding the decline in public trust and predicting the effect of restorative justice. To the extent that the declining threat to material well-being (food, water, shelter, and peace) has raised human consciousness on Maslow's hierarchy of needs, that may explain the declining ability of democratic government to satisfy voters that it is doing the right things, as James MacGregor Burns (1978: 72) observes '... the gratification of needs places an even greater burden on leadership – above all to raise its own goals as the needs of followers are transmuted into higher and higher searches for individual and social fulfillment'. Those goals are likely to include the state's treating all citizens with the respect they feel they deserve, even (or especially) when the government is personified by representatives (like judges and police) who feel they deserve respect from the citizenry. Thus rising prosperity may feed a battle for respect between state and citizen, one in which equality is unlikely to result from the persisting use of hierarchical institutions such as courts. Braithwaite's analysis opens a door to bypassing this battle, using restorative justice as a means for the state to re-affirm rather than deny the dignity of all its citizens. But whether this bypass will lead to a collapse of mainstream respect for law remains an empirical question.

Theoretically and theologically, the Puritan ethic provides a firmer foundation than the Quaker ethic for compliance with law. Puritan culture mobilises the emotions of shame, anger and pride far more intensely than Quaker culture. It also offers less freedom for personal disagreement with the strictures of group rules, including criminal law. The 'shamelessness' of post-materialist civilisation is not simply a function of changes in community structure, but also of the rising individualism fed by Quaker ethics. Not all shame, to be sure, is alike. Puritan culture favours stigmatic shaming (such as punishing adulterers by making them display the scarlet letter 'A', as described in Hawthorne's novel). In contrast, Braithwaite favours reintegrative shaming, shame for criminal acts that allows criminal actors to repair the harm they have caused and to proudly return to the company of law-abiding people without permanent stigmata from their criminal past. Yet even reintegrative shaming assumes a minimum of other-directedness to make pride attractive and shame unattractive. The inner-directedness of the Quaker ethic works in the opposite direction: by supporting private conceptions of justice, it can render the law irrelevant and legitimate even the most horrendous acts of violence.

Antinomian inner-directedness is the connection between Quaker ethics and the Oklahoma City bombing. While reintegrative shaming seeks an inner-directed desire to obey the law, the historical pattern of inner-directed culture is one of defiance and self-help. Defiance can include individual acts of conscience, such as Martin Luther's reported statement at the Diet of Worms when he refused to recant his heresy: 'Here I stand. I can do no other. So help me God. Amen' (Burns, 1978: 204). It can include idiosyncratic acts of social protest, such as disrupting dominant groups' church services like the two Quaker girls who in 1666 entered the Puritan church in Duxbury, Massachusetts stark naked (Phillips, 1999: 213). It can include organised acts of resistance to group pressure, such as Pennsylvania's Quakers and Baptists helping British prisoners of war in the 1780s to escape from the stockades near Lancaster, and the Anabaptist Ephrata Brethren declaring neutral status in the American Revolution because they were under a higher Magistrate and were 'consequently emancipated from the civil government' (Phillips, 1999: 213, 218). Most famously, it includes the Protestant sects' underground railroad that helped thousands of runaway slaves escape from their southern owners across the Mason–Dixon Line and north to Canada out of reach of the American law courts that would return them to their 'rightful owners'.

It is a short step from ignoring the law to creating the law with self-help. As Donald Black (1983) has suggested, much of what the law calls 'crime' is legitimated in the minds of criminals as 'righteous' punishment of people who deserve to be punished. This is the premise of any culture of honour (Nisbett & Cohen, 1996), in which insults must be punished severely in order to deter a feeding frenzy of subsequent incursions upon honour. This 'code of the street' (Anderson, 1999) is more a rational necessity than a moral imperative. But as Katz (1988) shows, crimes ranging in seriousness from shoplifting to baby-killing can be justified in the mind of the offender by self-righteous indignation at the moment the crime is committed. The moral outrage and vocabulary of motive in support of this tradition come not only from the Code Duello – which Puritans strongly opposed – but from the theology of the 'inner light'.

The theology of inner light has witnessed justification of both pacifist defiance of violence and anarchistic mayhem. The extreme violence it can produce was demonstrated shortly after the Lutheran Reformation began, when German antinomians looted castles, burned cities and killed tens of thousands of people. Inspired by the writings of Johann Agricola, they believed that the Ten Commandments were merely a Jewish Code that they need not obey (Fisher, 1972a: 334). The Munster Anabaptists followed these views in creating a violent theocratic kingdom on principles of communism and polygamy (Williams, 1972). Condemned by Luther himself and recanted by Agricola, this strain of Protestantism created thousands of martyrs who were burned, beheaded or drowned for refusing to recant their beliefs. But rather than reforming the institutional church with Luther, the antinomians saw themselves abandoning institutions altogether and returning to the primitive structure of the early church – as preparation for the end of the world. That, in turn, justified violence by a small subgroup within what was otherwise a strongly pacifist movement, the direct forerunners of today's Amish, Mennonites and Hutterites.

To Oklahoma City bomber Timothy McVeigh, blowing up a federal building was not a crime but a punishment: just revenge for the federal government's illegitimate 1993 attack on the Waco, Texas compound of another antinomian sect, the Branch Davidians, in which over 70 men, women and children died. To the government of laws of the United States, McVeigh's act of destruction was indeed a crime, the largest simultaneous mass murder on US soil in this century, for which the trial court imposed the death penalty. As an activist in the modern militia movement, McVeigh was exposed to ideas derived from centuries of distrust and even paranoia about government (Phillips, 1999: 14). His conduct was legitimated by the same sources that legitimated the American Revolution, in its attack on tyranny and injustice. These sources include not only the Enlightenment philosophers, but the Bible itself: 'the most influential indictment of pharisees, courtiers and tyrants ever printed' (Phillips, 1999: 48). It is of course not the literal text of the Bible, but the wide range of its interpretation allowed by the antinomian ethic, that lets murder be justified by God. The same is arguably true of Calvinist justification of war. The difference is that the latter reflects collective decisions arrived at by democratic lawmaking, while McVeigh's decision was inspired by his own antinomian 'inner light' entirely outside the law.

The Spirit of Restoration

The violence of radical antinomians notwithstanding, the Quaker ethic is radically peaceful. It stands in no sharper contrast to Calvinism than when the two ethics are compared on the issue of capital punishment. Puritans long employed the death penalty, and hanged at least several Quakers for their speech (not their deeds). It appears that there is no case, however, in which the Quakers executed anyone for anything, let alone executing Puritans for their intolerance. The modern American scourge of criminal justice – its soaring prison population – is actually the product of a Quaker invention for reducing capital punishment (Rothman, 1971). The 'penitentiary' was designed to allow prisoners to become penitent through reflection on their sins in the isolation of solitary confinement. No matter how inhumane the institution of prison has become, it was clearly inspired by the spirit of restoration: the hope that prisoners could be restored to the fellowship of good citizens.

The modern movement for restorative justice rejects both capital punishment and widespread use of prison as failing to restore victims, communities, and offenders to the state they were in before each crime was committed (Marshall, 1985, as cited in Braithwaite, 1999a). The movement seeks means by which each offender can seek atonement with each victim and each community – literally at-one-ment, rebuilding human bonds torn asunder by the criminal act of harm. The means to achieve this vary widely across the many varieties of restorative justice. But it generally uses forms and processes that are consistent with the values and culture of the antinomian sects, loosely and collectively described here as the 'Quaker ethic'. While the Mennonite churches and educational institutions which have fostered restorative justice can properly take issue with that name, the greater fame of the Quakers as pacifist justifies the convenience of that label.

One of the most widely taught, and most thoroughly studied, varieties of restorative justice is the 'Wagga model' developed by New South Wales Police Sergeant Terry O'Connell in the small Australian city of Wagga Wagga. This model has many of the features of a Quaker meeting, and provides a sharp contrast to the Calvinist features of law courts.

Perhaps the most important contrast is that this model of restorative justice avoids court altogether whenever possible. Weber (1922–23 [1948]: 318) reports it was considered taboo among antinomian sects to call on the law courts for any purpose (on pain of expulsion from the church). The Wagga model employs police to invite victims, offenders and their supporters to a meeting in which the offenders – who must not (for these purposes) dispute their guilt – can sit in a circle and discuss the harm the crime has caused, express the pain and emotional impact of that harm, and democratically deliberate as to how that harm should be repaired. Rather than a representative form of governance in which the judges act on behalf of the state, this system is more akin to the 'assembly democracy' of ancient Greece, town meetings and other direct democratic systems (Dahl, 1998: 100–112). The major exception to that characterisation is that the community as a whole is not invited to be present – although it may be just as well represented as it is in a typical court case; both courtrooms and the restorative community justice conferences tend to have only direct participants and their relatives and friends in the room.

Another dimension of Quaker ethic in the Wagga model is the egalitarianism of the proceedings. This equality begins with the architecture of the room. Unlike the elevated bench of the judge looking down on the courtroom of lawyers in an inner sanctum and lay citizens restrained behind a railing further back, the Wagga conference room seats everyone at positions of equal status in a circle. Like knights of the round table, all citizens in the room can look each other in the eye. The police officer moderating the proceedings offers only questions, not answers: What did the offender do? How did it hurt the victim? How does the victim feel about that hurt? How do the victims' friends and family feel? How do the offenders' family and friends feel about what has been said? What would be the right way for the offender to repay the debt to the victim and to society? Does everyone agree? Is there anything the offender wants to say to the victim ('I'm sorry'). Is there anything the victim wants to say to the offender ('I forgive you'). This is not what is said in every case, like a script. But the main points are generally covered, and the apology and forgiveness are far more frequent in the conference than in a courtroom (Sherman et al, 1998; Strang et al, 1999). Most important, everyone present is allowed to talk, just as in a Quaker meeting, and no one person dominates speech, as in a Puritan church or in an Anglo-American courtroom.

One corollary of the radical egalitarianism of the community justice conference is an anti-intellectual devaluing of learned professions (Hofstadter, 1963). In the Wagga model, no lawyers need apply. They are always on call, ready to be invoked to protect anyone whose rights may seem abused. But as long as the consensus remains to proceed in a conference, everyone in the circle has equal authority, regardless of how much education they may (or may not) have. Just as most Quaker meetings have no preachers (although Mennonites and other antinomians do), the Wagga circles have no one claiming to know any more than anyone else. This feature reinforces the view that justice is a simple matter of innate human decency, rather than a complex matter for wise and learned people. It stands in stark contrast to the view of the early Massachusetts Governors who rebutted attacks from some citizens for being too lenient in court with claims to special expertise:

> A magistrate was supposed to enforce the laws, but this did not mean an unbending application of the same punishment in every case. This much any fool could do. The calling of the magistrate demanded special talents to fit the punishment to the crime, to bend the law to the particular circumstance. (Morgan, 1964, as quoted in Baltzell, 1979: 77)

Restorative justice, in Quaker-like contrast, takes the view that 'any fool' can fit the punishment to the crime based on common sense and civic experience – and perhaps an implicit premise of the inner light providing divine guidance to each person to help do the right thing.

A final dimension of the Quaker ethic in the Wagga model is the open expression of emotion. Unlike the emotional restraint valued by Puritan culture and Western law courts, antinomian sects place high value on intensely emotional displays. In this respect Quakers and restorative justice also follow Hasidic Jews, whose antinomianism includes pacifism, refusal to recognise civil authority, withdrawal from a sinful world, and highly emotional forms of worship: dancing, singing, shouting and praying aloud. While Quaker meetings are sometimes completely silent, there is an intensity of experience that allows anyone to speak as the spirit moves them to do so. There is no ban on tears or wailing in either an antinomian sect or a restorative community justice conference.

A final difference is not as prominent in theology, but enormously important in practice: time for justice. Restorative community justice is a process of taking testimonials from all present, whatever their level of emotion. In this respect they resemble a revival meeting more than a conventional church service. Religions using more intense emotions generally have longer services than the more cerebral sects, often by a difference of eight hours to one. Restorative community justice takes, on average, some seventy minutes to resolve a case that courts may hear in a total of ten minutes or so. Court time, moreover, is spread across several different appearances for legal technicalities, most of which have no emotional significance for victim or offender and leave citizens feeling like cogs in a wheel. A community justice conference is all about the people present (rather than legal formalities), people who come only once, prepared to stay until the case is resolved.

These procedural dimensions of restorative justice are all intended to produce better results for the end-values or substantive outcomes for all stakeholders: victims, offenders, their families and the community. They are also consistent with Tom Tyler's (1990) research on the kinds of procedures that increase compliance with the law, regardless of the substantive decisions they produce: procedures which offer respect, inclusiveness, and apparent equality of treatment to all. Tyler (1998) also suggests that procedures like the Wagga model can help educate citizens as to the functions of the law, changing their views of right and wrong, and building consensus in support of legal institutions. Consensus is a different basis for obeying the law than deference to authority, merely because it has the right to rule. The deference model is tied to the Puritan ethic of hierarchical communalism, while the consensus ethic appears to be a better fit for a postmaterialist political culture dominated by an egalitarian Quaker ethic. Tyler's focus on the key issue of identity suggests that people are more likely to identify with the political community creating a legal system (for example, Americans) if they feel that they are welcomed and valued as members of that political community – rather than being considered marginal, or worth less than others in that community.

Tyler's hypotheses are supported by preliminary results from several controlled experiments in Canberra, Australia's capital city, comparing the Wagga model to court (Sherman et al, 1998; Strang et al, 1999). These experiments directly observed the treatment of offenders and victims in comparable cases assigned at random to be processed in court or in restorative justice conferences. Within weeks after the cases were processed, both offenders and victims were interviewed. The substantive results of the processing were fairly similar in the two kinds of justice, despite the major differences in the decision-making procedures employed. But the restorative justice conferences produced far better results for both Fukuyama's concerns about citizen recognition, and Baltzell's concerns about respect for legal institutions. Offenders sent to conferences were far less likely than similar offenders sent to court to say that they were pushed around, disadvantaged by their age, income or education, treated as if they were untrustworthy, or not listened to. Offenders sent to conferences were more likely to say that their experience increased their respect for the justice system and for the police, as well as their feeling that the crime they had committed was morally wrong. Offenders sent to court were more likely to say that the experience made them angry – a sign of insufficient recognition by the state.

These findings suggest that the Quaker ethic manifested in the Wagga model's spirit of restorative justice appears to increase the consensual basis for law and legal institutions. Yet the findings are limited to the microsociological level. Whether they would generalise to the macrosocietal level is another question entirely. The Canberra experiments were conducted in a social context of widespread court-administered justice. If the balance of cases were to shift radically, so that most crimes were dealt with in a conference rather than in a court, the effect on legal institutions could be quite different. It is possible that the same restorative justice procedures building support for law at a micro level could undermine law at a macro level.

Consider the following fact: a 1995 survey found that Australian citizens ranked the police at 65 on a scale of 0 to 100 in level of confidence in the institution. The same survey, however, ranked the legal system at 46, or almost one-third lower than the police (Bean, 1995). This could reflect a retributive dissatisfaction with the courts for too much lenience in sentencing, an outcome that Australians do not blame on the police. But it could also reflect an egalitarian ethic in Australia, in which the police are seen as a more egalitarian institution than the judiciary. The fact that police make no claim to belong to a learned profession, and eschew symbols of superiority to the citizenry, may help explain their higher public confidence rating. The fact that Australian police stations have front desks on the same floor level with citizens is a case in point, while American police are actually rebuilding some police stations to eliminate the judge-like difference in height between desk officer and the public (*Law Enforcement News*, July–August 1999: 5).

Whatever the micro-level effects of increasingly egalitarian procedures in criminal justice, the macro-level effects of a Quaker ethic could be substantial. A perfect match between the Quaker ethic and the procedures of restorative justice could include two long-term attributes of that ethic (see Table 1 above): a rejection of institutions generally as inevitably imperfect (with a preference for solving all problems on a face-to-face basis), and rising distrust and disrespect for government. In theory, it could lead to ideological support for neighbourhood level Balkanisation, in which each neighbourhood works with its own police officer to do whatever it feels is right. Such devolution is not unknown in the history of the American police, who were only removed from local control and placed under a rule of law with a great deal of political conflict (Richardson, 1970). Restorative justice could breed increasing egalitarian discontent with the judiciary, and the legal profession's emphasis on erudition, as the source of true justice. Just as the English Civil War and the beheading of Charles I unleashed a wide range of theologies and proposed levelling of social structures, widespread restorative community justice could unleash a plethora of ideas for more minimal legal institutions.

Civil Society in a Thymotic State

Whether a revolution in legal ideas would be useful remains to be seen. Whether such a revolution is necessary is a more accessible question. It seems just as plausible that any discontent with judicial procedures unleashed by widespread restorative justice could be met by reforms of the courts themselves. If New York's police can lower the height of the station house desk, for example, perhaps judges can tear down their benches and sit at floor-level tables. If judicial robes (or wigs) are offensive to a modern egalitarian world, perhaps they can go the way of the powdered wigs once worn by all ladies and gentlemen. If court procedures take too little time with each case, or fail to invite victims to witness and help deliberate, these could also be changed (albeit with substantially greater taxpayer investment in the hiring of learned judges). The modern Quaker ethic that supports these ideas need not inexorably lead to undermining the institution of law courts. But it could well do so if the courts remain unresponsive to such demands.

Fukuyama suggests that the end of nations seeking recognition through war may herald the age of citizens seeking more recognition from their nations. We might call a nation that responds with more recognition of

citizens a 'thymotic' state. It is one thing to say that states are becoming
more symbolic than instrumental, providing a source of security and identity to citizens engaged in a global economy. It is quite another to say that
a state is trying hard to make each citizen feel like a valued customer, just
as a first-class hotel chain would do. Thus a thymotic state may employ
some of the same techniques as those hotels: train all staff to smile, look
customers in the eye and say 'hello' each time you meet. Train all staff to
listen patiently to customer complaints. Train staff not to interrupt when
customers go on at some length about the causes of their dissatisfaction.
Train staff to be sympathetic, as well as empathetic, about the concerns customers relate. Train staff to try to correct conditions complained about, so
that every customer will feel valued by the company and will continue to
remain a customer. 'Though he might have been a Russian, a Greek, a
Turk or Prussian, he remains an Englishman', as Gilbert and Sullivan put
it in *HMS Pinafore.*

Whether or not the thymotic state is actually in competition for citizens, it would be designed to act as if it is. For city governments in the
United States, there is no question that such competition is crucial to the
very survival of those governments. Philadelphia has lost 10 percent of its
resident population and a large portion of its jobs in just the past decade.
While it has yet to become anything like a thymotic state, that may be the
only way it can remain a major city. The same is true for Washington, DC,
St Louis, Baltimore, Kansas City, New Haven, and other older cities with
concentrated poverty and racial segregation (Suarez, 1999). 'Though he
might have moved to Swarthmore, he remains a Philadelphian.' Yet
there is no question that suburban police are more polite to their tax-
payers, more responsive to their requests – and have more free time available to recognise each citizen because there is less crime in a poverty-free
suburban environment. The paradox of the thymotic state in a free market is that some governments can recruit the kind of citizens they prefer
to serve, while other governments are left with the kinds of citizens whose
needs and demands overwhelm the available resources. This results in a
stratification of thymos. Recognition of citizens by governments, as in
recognition of customers by hotel chains, operates on what Robert Mer-
ton called the Matthew effect: to them that hath shall be given, to them
that hath not shall be taken away.

Similar dynamics may operate at the nation-state level as well, with
immigrants seeking out nations offering better human rights as well as
economic opportunities. If material needs become increasingly satisfied
(barring global warming and its weather disasters shattering that hope),
then government sensitivity to citizen demands for recognition may
become a major factor in attracting both capital investment and skilled
labour. A global market could provide substantial monetary incentives

for governments to treat citizens in a manner more consistent with the Quaker ethic.

First and foremost among such changes might be a conversion to restorative justice for resolving a majority of criminal offences when offenders can be identified. At that point, restorative justice could become either a reform of mainstream legal institutions (just as Puritanism reformed the Church of England) or an alternative, anti-institutional devolution of authority to small bands of citizens (just as Quakers abandoned the institutional church). Or it could become something in between. No matter which form it would take, it could lead down the path of individualism and decreasing respect for centralised lawmaking institutions. The same tendencies that support lynch mobs (another form of 'community justice') would have to be restrained through a variety of institutions. But the reinforcement of the Quaker ethic that restorative justice would provide may weaken the state's ability to restrain lynch mob justice.

An alternative scenario is completely different, but just as destabilising for legal institutions. In an egalitarian, Quaker ethic political culture, there may be increasing demands for a more thymotic state. Yet because law is a conservative institution, it remains unresponsive to those demands. Restorative justice does not flourish and grow, but remains an isolated idea with a few scattered experiments. Other aspects of governance offer citizens more recognition and respect, thus making the hierarchicalism of legal institutions all the more offensive. Anger at legal institutions increases, and compliance with the law declines. More severe penalties are imposed and perceived as illegitimate, prompting even more defiance of law. Police join with citizens in a general cultural attack on judges and lawyers, fuelling private justice (self-help) and even summary punishment by police (as in Brazilian death squads, or in a less extreme case, systematic beatings of known criminals).

Both these scenarios might be avoided by the development of civil society institutions in support of both restorative justice and the basic institutions of law. Large membership groups advocating gradual changes in criminal justice procedures could have a stabilising influence, in two ways. One way is to ensure that needed changes occur to make the courts more culturally appropriate to an increasingly egalitarian age. The other way is to ensure that restorative justice is tightly linked to and supervised by the central legal institutions of legislatures and courts. Both ways may help prevent the rise of any extreme forms of antinomian justice.

What sort of civil society institutions would be required to accomplish these goals? National or even international advocacy groups modelled on the 'green' environmental defence groups may serve the purpose well. The 'Restorative Justice Society' could have branches in each democracy and a world headquarters for information and strategic resources. Charles Pollard in his contribution to this volume develops in a slightly different, but thoroughly compatible way, the idea of an 'International Institute for Restorative Justice'. Such an institution would be little different from the civil groups that helped to create modern police and prosecution services financed by the government (Radzinowicz, 1948). With an annual meeting for presenting academic papers and research findings, it might appear little different in its early years from such existing groups as the World Victimology Society or the International Society of Criminology. It could even follow the path of a professional society, such as the American Public Health Association, consisting largely of people employed in that line of work. As the number of people working in restorative justice grows, the potential for professional associations increases directly. But a broader influence on the politics of adopting restorative justice, or making courts into more thymotic institutions, may require more than a professional association.

The best protection for the rule of law may result from a rich diversity of national and international associations, comprised of both interested advocates and professionals (or lay people employed) in the field. There is probably even virtue in competition and conflict among such groups, just as we find in the conflict among the several organisations advocating gun control in the United States. But the existence of any such civil institutions would be a radical departure from the current state, in which a handful of consulting and training organisations constitute the entire institutional fabric of restorative justice. Without a strong set of civil institutions to raise money, create publicity and lobby relevant legislatures and police, restorative justice may go either nowhere or too far.

Yet the absence of civil institutions supporting restorative justice is no surprise. The antinomian outlook of people attracted to the values of restorative justice naturally militates against investment in institution-building. A recent meeting of restorative justice activists convened by an international foundation provided a clear case in point. While the foundation invited the individuals to collaborate and cooperate, several days of meetings failed to develop an institutional agenda. Rather than cooperate in the construction of imperfect institutions, the participants mostly returned to fostering programs in civil society at the margins of the criminal justice system. This is consistent with the Quaker ethic. It takes a Puritan ethic to believe in such institutions, and to invest time and energy in building them for the sake of the larger – in this case world – community. But the Puritan ethic, and its respect for the leadership that builds institutions, is passé. The paradox of bottom-up restorative justice is that it may not happen, or may not be for the good, if there is no top-level leadership to make both things possible.

The purpose of social science, of course, is not just to understand the world, but to change it. Perhaps the antinomian supporters of restorative justice who read this chapter may be moved to break their orthodoxy, and to view the two Protestant ethics as two tools in a toolbox rather than as a profound choice of dogma. The diversity of most democracies makes any dogma increasingly rigid, and the virtue of mixed political ethics increasingly clear. The healthy civil society may have to draw on Puritan ethics to build institutions, Quaker ethics to run them, and Muslim or Roman Catholic or Confucianist ethics to provide all the thymos that the times demand.

CHAPTER 4

The Force of Community

George Pavlich

> If by community one implies, as is often the case, a harmonious group, consensus, and fundamental agreements beneath the phenomena of discord or war, then I don't believe in it very much and I sense in it as much threat as promise ...
> *(Derrida, 1995: 355)*

Introduction

A close cousin of civil society, the community has long been heralded a bastion of individual freedom. Recent attempts to increase 'non-coercive' controls over individuals in the name of community reflect its continued political appeal (Cohen, 1985). The popularity of free community structures is particularly evident in contexts where old images of 'society' are fragmenting under the weight of trenchant neo-liberal assaults on welfare state institutions (Pavlich, 1999, 1996). Where once only the radical critic championed (say) releasing the 'mentally ill' from society's asylums into the 'community', now treating such 'clients' in community-based programs is the norm. Community justice, community policing, community corrections, community psychiatry, community work, and safer community projects provide but a few examples of the wider control trends before us. In short, as welfare states roll themselves back to expose their recent neo-liberal inclinations, so community control emerges as a mode of regulation whose time has (again) come.

Such an ethos has spawned several new discourses articulated to amorphous images of 'community'. Perhaps the most influential of these is an academic-cum-popular discourse hailed as the 'new communitarianism' that aims to develop a 'responsive community' (Etzioni, 1998; Tam, 1998). Related to 'third way' political frameworks, the new communitarians claim to transcend a political environment that contrasts right with left positions, preferring not to favour communities over individuals, or vice versa (Giddens, 1998). Instead, they seek a balance between '... community and autonomy, between the common good and liberty, between individual rights and social responsibilities', focusing their efforts on developing 'responsive', meaningful and empowering community structures (Etzioni, 1998: X).

New communitarian concepts are said to derive from 'grassroots' activity, providing local community activists with conceptual horizons that reflect cumulative activist wisdom. For example, in the realm of community justice communitarian ideas delineate strategies to achieve strong, consensual and harmonious community relations, capable of housing alternative dispute resolution processes outside of law's courtrooms (e.g., Shonholtz, 1988/89; Wright & Galaway, 1989; Consedine, 1995). Reflecting communitarian allegiances, community justice advocates harbour a deep mistrust of the coercive controls used by the modern welfare state and its tentacular bureaucracies (see Merry & Milner, 1993; Pavlich, 1996). Similarly, advocates of 'restorative justice', or 'reintegrative shaming', or 'community conferences' (implicitly) assume an identifiable, common and unified community capable of being restored and/or reintegrated (Morris & Young, 1987; Braithwaite, 1989; New Zealand Ministry of Justice, 1995). In such frameworks, conflict is seen as threatening the integrity of communal relations; if disrupted, such relations are to be restored through healing processes like community mediation, family group conferences, and so on. (Zehr, 1990; Consedine, 1995).

These various invocations of community suggest specific rationales and calculations of collective solidarity. Yet most embrace an overriding theme: the community is conceived as a non-coercive space that regulates autonomous individuals through freely chosen, agreed-to and peaceful relations. Communal orders are not coercively imposed, but develop spontaneously from the 'bottom up'. The community, thus defined, stands opposed to coercively engineered state control by creating domains of free association that empower members to develop common, agreed-upon ways to regulate themselves.

Needless to say, such a sanguine portrayal of the growing spread of community control does not resonate in critical discussions. For example, some critics see recent quests for community control as little more than a state-orchestrated managerial reform of control institutions (Harrington, 1985). Other critics view it as an 'interpenetration' between state and community spheres that is more about 'control through community' than genuine 'community control' (Ratner, 1999; Cohen, 1985). Still others portray it as an attempt to redress profound crises now confronting capitalist societies (e.g., Abel, 1982; Hofrichter, 1987). Despite

their differences, all describe the rise of community control as an example of the welfare state trying to expand and strengthen its control network under the dubious pretexts of claiming to yield power to the
'community' (Santos, 1982). With the exception of Ratner's penetrating
account, however, critics tend to focus somewhat narrowly on whether
state control is intensifying or diminishing through community controls
(see Pavlich, 1996). There may be much to gain, I want to suggest, by
extending this discussion to examine how community control has
already taken on a life of its own, beyond shrinking social welfare state
controls (e.g., LaPrairie, 1995b; Crawford, 1998).

With these considerations in mind, the following discussion explores
a basic danger surrounding the now prominent quest for consensual,
restorative, informal, etc., community controls. I aim to show how calculating human solidarity through images of an assumed community wields
a double-edged sword, succinctly accosted by returning to the latter's ety-
mology. Specifically, the word community derives from the word 'common' with its Indo-European base (*moi, mei*) that came via the Latin
commununitatis to English (Ayto, 1990: 126). On the one hand, this ety-
mology suggests notions of 'shared by all', common, commune, etc. –
traces resound through the new communitarians' attempt to cultivate
consensual relations that yield a diverse but shared, responsive, rewarding, safe and harmonious community of communities (see Etzioni, 1998:
IV). On the other hand, community is also closely related to the word
'*communio*' connoting a military formation; the latter term reflects
notions of commonality (*com*), but it also defers to the Latin term *muni-
tio* (as in 'ammunition'), which derives from the verb *munire*, to defend,
or to fortify (Ayto, 1990: 23). Here we begin to glimpse a dark side to the
quest for community control, a potential danger that attends to the ways
a spontaneously shared community often involves images of exclusion,
fortification, military defence, and so on. That is, calls for a so-called free
and uncoerced community life may be laudable, but they are all too
often offset by the concomitant tendency to shore up limits, fortify a
given identity, and rely on exclusion to secure self-preservation.

Indeed, the quest for a clearly defined community always contains the
seeds of exclusionary parochialism that can lead, and has in the past led,
to atrocious totalitarian exclusions. Let us not forget that the 'community' featured prominently in the diverse hierarchies established under
the auspices of national socialist, apartheid and Stalinist calculations of
solidarity (Anderson, 1991). Indeed, images of community have featured
prominently among social calculations behind the most horrific cata-
strophes of the twentieth century; the mass slaughters of nationalistic
warfare, genocidal imperialisms, the gas chambers, ethnic cleansing,
apartheid torture, and so the list goes on. Under certain circumstances,

that is, the quest for community has proved more than capable of unleashing an obsession with member purity, xenophobia, and an extreme focus on excluding traces of the 'other', the 'strange', and so on. This reminder should put to rest the idea that imposing images of community over relations between people is an innocuous, or inherently positive, set of events. Of course, this is not to say that the calls for community are necessarily disastrous either; rather inscribing notions of community over given modes of association is always silhouetted against the threat of grave atrocities, some predictable and others unanticipated. And the task of critics is to outline the dangers of such perils wherever they may surface.

In this critical spirit, the following discussion is directed to an influential strategy within new communitarian discourses that establishes the 'community' as a discrete being capable of housing non-state controls (especially Etzioni, 1998; Tam, 1998). I call the dominant strategy a 'unifying' one, for it assumes the integrity of that which it describes, gathering definitions that impart images of the community as a unified reality. In turn, this strategy entices its advocates to demarcate 'strangers' from those viewed as insiders to given images of community. Whatever its benefits, this unifying strategy does not post a watch against totalitarian dangers that lurk beneath attempts to posit the community as an ontologically fixed entity, and to consider its participants as of primary concern – a point not missed by some advocates (e.g., Etzioni, 1998: XXVII). My discussion seeks to foreground another question: is there an alternative approach to collective solidarity that tries to guard against parochial community fortifications spilling over into dangerous exclusions? I shall argue that a deconstructive strategy focused on dissociation (rather than unity) holds promise, because it requires us to calculate solidarity dynamically by opening up (rather than closing off) defined limits. This requires all expressions of human solidarity to embrace the contingency of their limit formations, and to welcome the 'other' that forms the basis of any identity formation (i.e., this is the stranger that silently comprises familiar images of community). A dissociative strategy emphasises hospitality over exclusion by welcoming diversity, and pledging an ongoing responsibility to others. Whether it is possible to attach such a strategy to non-unified images of community remains an open question.

Unifying Discursive Strategies: Enunciating a Shared 'Community'

There are at least three key dimensions to the unifying strategies by which new communitarians and community control advocates evoke images of a shared community. First, they assume that the 'community' exists as a finite entity. However, this assumption masks a considerable discursive achievement by which the community is enunciated as an ontologically discrete being, and touted as the solution to previously identified problems. For instance, the famous neo-liberal critique of society as either non-existent, or too distant from individual being to be of value, affords unique opportunities for claiming 'community' as intermediary between the singular subject and wider collectivities (Pavlich, 1999). Similarly, the oft-propounded fiscal and legitimacy crises of the social welfare state's institutions of control provided an opportunity for the community to be (re-?)formulated as a viable solution. An erstwhile allegiance to 'society' could then be replaced with the idea of a 'community of communities', rendering the ontological importance of 'community' transparent. In this way, a certain space is cleared for purveying the community as an entity able to deal with contemporary political issues (e.g., Etzioni, 1998: X).

Secondly, having thus asserted the ontological priority of community, advocates then enunciate its core features. What is a community? How does the individual relate to the community? What can one expect from a strong (rather than weak, problematic, etc.) community? What are the needs of this community? What sorts of problems take social relations beyond the limits of communality? How might we strengthen and restore battered communities, or reintegrate wayward members? Even if diverse responses address such questions, most advocates gather definitions that isolate the common, essential and key precepts of community (see generally Etzioni, 1998; Goodin, 1998; Newman & de Zoysa, 1997; Vincent, 1997). So, Etzioni insists that 'communities are webs of social relations that encompass shared meanings and above all shared values' (1998: VIII), while Selznick (1995) offers ten guidelines for understanding what a community is (see also Rasmussen, 1990). Indicative of a widespread tendency, these authors try to identify what is common to all relations claiming the mantle of 'community', and so establish clear limits to 'proper' community structures.

The attempt to designate limits around 'the community' alerts us to a third unifying strategy: defining what a community *is* by deferring to what it *is not*. Here unifying strategies gather together notions of community by pointing to others who are not the same as, and who may threaten, 'normal' members of a shared, moral and peaceful community. The normal (the same) is thus demarcated from the other, the familiar from the strange. No doubt, as Bauman (1997: 35–45) usefully points out, all social orders (unities) create degrees of strangeness; but under postmodern conditions we face the difficult issue of many locally produced strangers being simultaneously identified by different quests for the community. Whatever else, this local proliferation of strangers may help to shore up specific claims to community, but it can also lead to dangerous patterns of exclusion that limit, if not preclude, the possibility of a wider solidarity (Crawford, 1998).

One could illustrate the point by example. As part of Etzioni's (1998) influential collection of essays, DiIulio argues that American society needs to rid itself of 'community-sapping disorders' related to serious crime; he identifies the following as threats to community: '... public drunkenness, aggressive panhandling, gangs loitering in parks, prostitutes soliciting on street corners, abandoned cars, rowdy taverns, unregulated sex and drug-oriented paraphernalia shops, gambling dens, unmaintained or abandoned buildings, and so on' (1998: 229). Against these and other 'threats', and as a way of protecting (fortifying) the community, he argues for a '... limited federal war on inner-city crime that we are not bound to lose' (1998: 235). Here one glimpses a strategy designed to buttress notions of community by setting up, in clear terms, what stands outside of (and in this case serves as a threat to) the 'community'. In the process, attempts to find what is common to the community are entrenched by designating certain people as discredited other. The latter are cast as enemies against which the community must be defended. The 'war' on the community's enemies is proclaimed in the name of protecting the fraternity within a predefined community. On its own, the incitement to war evokes traces of the most horrific tragedies born from the sheer virulence of exclusion. Compounded by the proliferation of communities and the excluded others, one begins to detect the outlines of an ominously divisive relational complex governed in large measure by processes of exclusion, or the threat of excommunication. (In fairness, not all communitarians would embrace DiIulio's formulation; Etzioni explicitly notes communities that glorify their own members by vilifying those who do not belong are at best imperfect (1998: XXVII). However, the tone of the latter part of the sentence does not entirely discredit forceful defences of community; it suggests rather that such defences render a given formation less than perfect).

Finally, proponents of unified communities usually locate the primary responsibility for their enunciations to 'members' as contextually defined and delimited. That is, the proffered images of community promise to benefit, and be directly responsible to, those who are identified and contained within that community. Equally, members within the community are deemed to have a wider responsibility to one another. So, as Etzioni puts it, 'A responsive community is one whose moral standards reflect the basic human needs of all its members' (1998: XXVII). This unifying strategy envisions its primary responsibility as the members of a predefined community. Again, to quote Etzioni, '... responsibilities are anchored in community. Reflecting the diverse moral voices of their citizens, responsive communities define what is expected of people; they educate the members to accept these values; and praise them when they do and frown upon them when they do not ...' (Etzioni, 1998: XXXVII). This betrays a conspicuous disregard for assessing the wider impact of given community identifications, especially on those placed at the margins of, or excluded from, such identities. That is, unifying strategies recognise a responsibility to fellow community members, but not to those who exist outside that community. Even where wider notions of responsibility are entertained, advocates tend to locate responsibility in the 'common good', in a wider community of communities. Those left out of presently dominant conceptions of community, the other, the unfamiliar, the strange, etc., do not feature as primary subjects of responsibility. As such, the otherness that makes possible the extraction of presented community identities becomes, at best, an ancillary responsibility.

The above strategies indicate how influential community advocates embrace practices of gathering together, unifying, a fixed image of community with specific features, limits and responsibilities. They enunciate new images of a far older promise – empowering community members to exercise freedoms that are absent from the coercive ambit of existing state structures. In so doing, they proffer their communitarian calculations of collective solidarity. However, there are significant dangers contained within unifying strategies. As noted, extreme dangers of totalitarianism attend to claims that enunciate realities as necessary (and so unmodifiable), especially when unity is emphasised at the expense of the excluded other. For instance, racism, xenophobia, ethnic cleansing, genocide, and so on, are always present within the discursive ambit of strategies that seek closure, limitation, exclusion and locate a primary responsibility to those included by their demarcations.

Deconstructive Openings

In another context, Derrida usefully theorises the problem thus: 'Once you grant some privilege to gathering and not to dissociating, you leave no room for the other, for the radical otherness of the other, for the radical singularity of the other' (Derrida, 1997: 14). This is not to suggest that such dangers are ineluctably attendant upon all unifying strategies; but discourses that focus on the ontological necessities of community – without a determined attempt to hold themselves responsible to excluded identities – do not guard against the peril of totalitarian neglect. There is, one might say, a short leap from the promises of contained community life to the claim that one pattern of community is superior, and therefore uniquely capable of deciding the fate of others. The latter hazard provides a fertile breeding ground for the most perilous and irresponsible of exclusions.

Does this mean that we should abandon any attempts at unity, such as formulating a notion of community? I shall return later to the question of community, but linguistic unities cannot be avoided entirely; to speak is in some measure to unify. After all, as Derrida notes, '... we need unity, some gathering, some configuration ...' (1997: 13). The issue is not about whether to vie for unity (rationality?) or multiplicity (relativism?). Rather unity is a condition of multiplicity and vice versa. Also, as Derrida wryly notes, '... pure unity or pure multiplicity – when there is only totality or unity and when there is only multiplicity or dissociation – is a synonym for death' (1997: 13). With this in mind, the aim is not to eliminate unifying discursive strategies; rather, at stake is the degree to which we privilege unifying strategies in our discourses. One could, for instance, elevate strategies of dissociation as a counterweight to, a vigilant watch over, the totalising tendencies within unifying strategies.

Continuing this line of thought, Derrida describes his deconstructive formulations as an attempt to '... prevent unity from closing upon itself, from being closed up' (1997: 13). That is, the 'privilege granted to unity, to totality, to organic ensembles, to community as a homogenised whole – this is the danger for responsibility, for decision, for ethics, for politics' (1997: 13). This interpretation of deconstruction does not entirely jettison unity, but emphasises the importance of disrupting any given unities, totalities, purportedly fixed identities, etc. Such disruptions are crucial elements for any attempts to open identities up to others, and to confront ethical responsibilities to others (see Critchley, 1992). Recognising such responsibilities we are able to confront the inherent dangers of unifying strategies, exploring alternatives that refuse to define the community within fixed, necessary limits.

Without rehearsing complex debates around deconstruction, one can entertain Derridian insights to approach collective human solidarity (see 1976, 1992, 1994, 1995). For instance, deconstruction can help to constantly open up the limits of a given present to its future. This is not a prescriptive venture which directs what ought to be done, nor is it simply a descriptive apology for existing institutions. Instead, as Derrida succinctly notes, deconstruction is located within, but critically directed to transforming, opening up, institutions:

> The paradox in the instituting moment of an institution is that, at the same time that it starts something new, it also continues something, is true to the memory of the past, to a heritage, to something we receive from the past, from our predecessors, from the culture. If an institution is to be an institution, it must to some extent break with the past, keep the memory of the past, while incorporating something absolutely new. (1997: 6)

Viewed thus, deconstruction does not completely abandon unity; instead it refuses to privilege unifying discursive strategies, and so close off institutions to what lies beyond their limits. Against totalitarian tendencies implied by the latter, deconstruction opens knowledge frameworks by forcing concealed hierarchies within language to the surface, exposing hidden oppositions and contradictions (Derrida, 1976). The point here is not to replace given with new hierarchies; rather it is to treat all totalities as provisional and contingent outcomes of specific socio-political-cultural struggles. The emphasis is on addressing the excluded as a way of reaching out towards, opening up to, otherness. Facing up to 'other' responsibilities is a basic characteristic of such thinking.

Derrida (1992) suggests an interesting way of understanding deconstruction's promise of justice. Inasmuch as deconstruction continuously opens limits to other possibilities, it keeps alive the pursuit of an elusive – yet consequential – promise of justice. For Derrida, deconstruction is bound to calculations of justice, even if promises claiming the name of the just forever beckon like mirages on the murky sands of the future (see also Pavlich, 1996: chapter 2). Confronting the promise of justice by deconstructively opening present notions of community to those yet to come could involve alternative discursive strategies by which to address spontaneous collective solidarity beyond the 'community'. For now though, I want only to make some orienting gestures towards a 'dissociating strategy' to explore the community beyond its current formulations. No doubt, such a strategy would involve practices that do not focus on what is common to all notions of community; rather in spaces generated when we refuse to grant given unities as necessary, one can open communitarian discourses up to a certain otherness, against which their claims to reality are silhouetted.

In this respect, Derrida rightly notes that, '... separation, dissociation is not an obstacle to society, to community, but the condition ... of community, the condition of any unity as such' (1997: 14–15). A dissociating strategy requires identities (e.g., community) to avoid heralding parochial self-definitions, and addresses the effects of exclusions created through processes of identification. Let us now turn to four strategies of dissociation before contemplating what this might mean for images of community.

Opening the Community: Dissociation and the Other Responsibility

First, dissociating strategies do not clear discursive spaces for enunciating an essential, immutable being of community. Seeking the spirit behind our ongoing quests for spontaneous collective solidarity overtakes concerns with ontology. Discursive spaces might then be sought, not to enunciate a fixed ontology of community, but to address the memory of a spirit that relentlessly calculates collective solidarity. In this respect, and only slightly tongue-in-cheek, one might defer to Derrida's (1994) concern with developing a 'hauntology' of the spirit, the trace. So, our initial strategy might be to clear spaces within which to enunciate equitable patterns of human association, viable and rewarding patterns of collective solidarity. Derrida (1994) senses this spirit, for instance, in Marx's attempt to calculate a communist alternative to capitalism's exploitative calculations of collective being. Perhaps, one could see in some contemporary quests for community justice a faltering attempt to reappropriate the spirit; however, there is a lesson to be learned from past attempts to align this spirit – necessarily – with any one calculation.

Secondly, the point of a dissociating strategy is not to capture the so-called essential, necessary, common and shared features of community. On the contrary, it seeks to prevent the community from being closed off in fixed entities, to confront the contingent processes that institute images, programs, or practices bearing the community mantle. The orientation eschews definitions that close in on themselves by claiming to be necessary and/or immutably fixed. Where such closure does occur, there lives totalitarianism. Dissociating strategies approach all calculations of collective solidarity as transient, open-ended, contingent and instituted again and again through the flows of human history.

Here, as elsewhere, dissociative strategies commit themselves to voices of the subjugated other (see also Foucault, 1980). Without an *a priori* commitment to unification, to what is common, there is no need to define the same through the exclusion of others. Dissociative strategies are more concerned with opening up given identities to their exclusions, and to doing this on an ongoing basis. One could then trace a spirit of solidarity that stands momentarily on the contingent grounds of present calculations, tracing past memories and yet gesturing towards the future. This stance implies welcoming otherness without escaping unity or exclusion entirely; it is more like being a host who welcomes without giving up a 'host' identity. No doubt, the host identity is modifiable, never fixed and negotiated in context; but the terms of that negotiation always take place from within a provisional and contingent identity. The orientating place is not fixed, and draws its breath from a continuous quest to open its limits up to future possibilities.

Finally, in all the above features of dissociative strategies, the calculation of solidarity is responsible to the identities excluded by its momentary, and transient formulations of identity (such as 'community' or indeed another calculation of solidarity). This approach hospitably opens up to the other whose future coming implies the possibility of new patterns of engagement; in this way deconstruction affirms its ethical responsibilities towards otherness. It extends an inclusive welcome to those excluded by its contingently erected identities. In so recognising a responsibility towards others, deconstruction remains open to promises of justice (and perhaps democracy) that are never fully decided. This does not mean that identities are simply dissolved in the face of otherness. On the contrary, it entails a recognition that it is only through otherness that a given identity is born. In an important sense, seeking out otherness is a practice of freedom, and a special feature of just and democratic solidarities (Derrida, 1997).

Indications

As discussed, when appropriated by the new communitarians and other community advocates, the idea of community may not embrace the totalitarian images of other formulations. Nevertheless, they do privilege unifying strategies to enunciate ontologically stable images of the community, define its essence through exclusionary practices and locate their primary responsibility to a predefined membership. By granting such a privilege, community advocates do not watch against the dangers of parochial self-definitions leading to totalitarianism, hostile exclusion and an obsession with community defence. As argued, a reading of Derrida's deconstructive approach could signal dissociative discursive strategies designed to counteract such dangers. By embracing the spirit (rather than trying to enunciate an ontology) of solidarity, this approach dissociates given identities instead of gathering them into a necessary or finite being. In so doing, it encourages hospitality (rather than hostility) towards otherness, and locates the prime responsibility of any collective pattern to those who are excluded. It recognises that the quest for collective solidarity is never given, fixed or absolute; but is always on the way. Calculations of such solidarity are without end.

What does all this mean for the idea of community? For some, such as Young (1990), the idea of community is too limited by its medieval, fortress-like identity to do justice to the complex 'politics of difference' facing us nowadays. As such, it ought to be replaced with a political concept more capable of pursuing social justice in contemporary settings. By contrast, others argue that deconstructive strategies could recover a radical reformulation of community politics:

> ... the question of politics ... becomes a question of how the community can remain a place for communality while at the same time being an open, interrupted community that is respectful of difference and resists the closure implicit within totalitarianism and immanentism. (Critchley, 1992: 219)

Corlett (1989) therefore proposes a 'community without unity' as a way of retracing dominant images of community, and forcing a reconsideration of liberal democratic politics. For Nancy (1991), the idea of an 'inoperative community' could connote open-ended collective calculations. Such approaches align well with this view:

There is doubtless this irrepressible desire for a 'community' to form but also for it to know its limits – and for its limit to be its *opening*. Once it thinks it has understood, taken in, interpreted, *kept* the text, then something of this latter, something in it that is altogether *other* escapes or resists the community, it appeals for another community, it does not let itself be totally interiorised in the memory on the present community. The experience of mourning and promise that institutes that community but also forbids it from collecting itself, this experience stores in itself the reserve of another community that will sign, otherwise, completely other contracts. (Derrida, 1995: 355)

One might, however, ponder the value of deferring again to the term 'community'. I prefer to leave open the question of whether solidarity is best understood as a spirit of community. Indeed, from what precedes, it may be more important to focus on strategies by which we calculate the spirit of spontaneous collective solidarity. Why? Avoiding totalitarian exclusions in calculations of solidarity is the goal – not in preserving a given concept of community as such. On this basis, one could make much more of an attempt to separate the notion of 'community' from a wider spirit of spontaneous collective solidarity.

Echoing a Derridian (1992) concept of justice, this spirit of solidarity may be regarded as a forever-elusive promise of unpremeditated collective togetherness. If such a thing exists, solidarity might be calculated through memories of spontaneous, peaceful and autonomous association; in turn, this invites reconsideration of collective images like 'community', or 'society'. There is no reason to privilege the association that now exists between new communitarian images of community and the spirit of spontaneous collective solidarity. Moreover, by separating the promise of collective solidarity from its calculation through images of community (or even society), the status of any calculation can be neither necessary nor fixed. As such, notions of community are fairly exposed as contingent constructs; enunciated by specific discursive strategies that rely upon, and are shaped by, complex socio-political negotiations in particular contexts. This is not to say that such negotiations do not profoundly affect the ways in which we are governed, conceive of ourselves or come to relate to one another. On the contrary, when successful, the effects of particular calculations of collective solidarity can be enormously significant – as is evident from the ways that notions of a unified community now dominate our regulatory environments.

However, it is important to remember that these reckonings are always recursive creations, deployed and developed within specific patterns of association. That is, the calculations emerge from, and simultaneously shape, associative arrangements between socio-political subjects at a given moment. The echoes of community that resound in new communitarian discourses are not so much reflections as achievements, spoils of today's power-knowledge contests. If we use community as a means of calculating solidarity, we express conjunctural decisions, not incontrovertible necessities. Such an insight might alert us to the possibility of calculating the elusive spirit of spontaneous collective solidarity without recourse to the duplicitous force of a unified community, with all its totalitarian possibilities.

CHAPTER 5

The Crime Victim Movement as a Force in Civil Society

Heather Strang

In late 1987 Mrs Cameron's 14-year-old son was beaten to death at a Canberra spring school fete. His 17-year-old assailant was charged with murder but pleaded guilty to manslaughter. He was convicted, sentenced to six years' imprisonment, and served 21 months. Mrs Cameron described the treatment that she and her husband received from the justice system as 'just horrific – we had no support whatsoever ... we felt so alienated'. She said that they felt so distressed by the way they were dealt with that they scarcely had time to think about their son's death.

In early 1988 the young daughter of another Canberra citizen was murdered. Soon afterwards, Mrs Cameron wrote to the father asking if she could help. In late 1988 the victim movement came to Canberra when the Victims of Crime Assistance League (VOCAL) was formed by these two people and 24 others who had suffered criminal victimisation of some kind and who lived in the same community. Their objectives were primarily to provide support and assistance to victims of all crime in their community. Later they became important players in the struggle for recognition of the rights of victims to be treated as legitimate participants in the criminal justice process.

Like similar organisations around the world, the victim movement in Canberra was shaped by the individuals who established it and by the culture in which it grew. In the first part of this chapter I want to discuss the different forms of the victim movement in different places, its impact on the administration of justice and its effectiveness in advancing the victim's cause. I will then take the Canberra movement as a 'case study' to explore the resonances between a non-punitive model of victim advocacy and restorative justice values as we described them in Chapter 1.

The Victim Movement

The 'victim movement' is a social movement which takes many forms
world-wide, ranging from a support-focused openness to restorative
alternatives through to an extreme rights-focused retributiveness. Varied
as these forms have been, the characteristic they have in common, not
only across this movement but in common with the other great social
movements of the past century, is a shared sense of injustice. Frank and
Fuentes (1990) suggested that this concern with injustice refers largely to
'us', so the movement serves both as a vehicle for working against the
oppression 'we' experience, and as a means of re-affirming the identity
of those working in the movement – and legitimating their concerns.
They also argued that 'what most characterises social movements is that
they must do their own thing in their own way' (p 141) and, classically,
do so outside existing institutions.

Movements do, however, often profit from support from existing institutions and even the state, but by doing so may risk being co-opted. This
is a special risk for the victim movement because of its attractiveness to the
'law and order' lobby. Elias (1990) went so far as to say that the victim
movement in the United States today could no longer be classified as a
social movement at all, so completely had it been corrupted by right-wing
political forces. Co-option can take other forms as well. For example, Victim Support in England and Wales, a non-government organisation lobbying for victims and providing assistance services as well, has increasingly
been seen as an adjunct to the formal justice system because of its success
in securing a place at the centre of government policy, casting other victims' groups such as rape crisis centres to the margins (Crawford, 2000).

Scheingold et al (1994) observed that it is relatively easy to put waves of
public indignation at the service of punitive policies. Cynical politicians
responding to community outrage over particular horrific events can easily channel such feeling into cries for retributive policies. Reeves and Mulley (2000) described how victim issues, as a popular political cause, have
been used to support various criminal justice agendas: 'Campaigners for
tougher sentences have used statements made by individual victims of
crime as if they represent the views of "all" crime victims. In fact, victims'
views on sentencing appear to be as varied as that of any other cross-
section of the general public' (p 142). On a hugely magnified scale we have
seen this phenomenon at work in Rwanda and Cambodia whose peoples
were co-opted into genocide. Balint (forthcoming) found that what actually happened in these and other episodes was that those with political
power, or those with aspirations, fomented sometimes dormant racial divisions to assist their political ambitions. Just as the racist vengeance of

ethnic division can be captured and magnified by power-hungry leaders (Kuper, 1981; Prunier, 1995), the vengeance of crime victims has sometimes been captured by politicians with their own retributive agendas.

To understand the nature of the victim movement as it exists today, it is important to realise that 25 years ago there was no movement at all. For centuries victims had been the forgotten third parties in a justice system which conceives of criminal behaviour as a matter between the offender and the state, with no formal role for the individuals who suffer the crime. As Geis (1990) remarked, looking back now it seems extraordinary that it took so long for the wrongs experienced by victims to be recognised: 'Their condition for centuries aroused little comment or interest. Suddenly, they were "discovered", and afterwards it was unclear how their obvious neglect could have so long gone without attention and remedy' (p 255).

Concern for victims was starting to emerge as an issue in the 1970s in Britain (Maguire & Corbett, 1987) and Continental Europe (van Dijk, 1988), but it was really in the United States that the 'movement' had its genesis. Among the most important factors which contributed to its emergence as a social force was the exceptional rise in crime rates experienced through the 1960s by the United States and other Western democracies, turning 'law and order' into a major political issue. Suddenly there were many more victims around; and many more than anyone, including politicians, had realised until the advent of victim surveys. These surveys gave an insight into the low regard for the justice system felt by crime victims, many of whom turned out to be reluctant to report even quite serious crime and extremely unwilling to act as prosecution witnesses (Biderman et al, 1967).

The American civil rights movement became a model for the early victim movement, inspired by its progressive, humanitarian ideals (Viano 1987). However, its success in improving the treatment of defendants in the criminal justice system was perceived in some quarters in the United States as further disadvantaging the interests of victims. Even at this early stage, those on the political right were portraying these developments as moves in a zero-sum equation where any protection of offender rights assumed a diminution in the rights of the victim (Elias, 1986).

Another factor which contributed in a particular way to the victim cause was the attention given by the emerging women's movement to the treatment that women victims received, especially victims of rape and domestic violence. Although these activists were at first perceived as radical and irrelevant to the mainstream movement, they became enormously effective in drawing attention to the plight of these victims and in setting up specialist services for them.

By the end of the 1970s, many diverse forces had converged to draw attention to the neglected role and importance of the victim in the justice system. The social movement that resulted encompassed a spectrum of activists from radical feminists to hardline law-and-order conservatives, an uncomfortable coalition whose varying priorities and philosophies were reflected in the disparate nature of the movement in different places and at different times.

Two Kinds of Victim Movement

These disparities resulted broadly in two kinds of movement: one focused on victim rights and the other on victim support. Van Dijk (1988) described it as a tension between 'being nice and being vindictive' and said it was the international hallmark of the movement. He observed that the objectives of the movement had developed in an ad hoc way without any systematic attention to victims' needs. He commented: 'Clearly the movement's demands and achievements do not flow from a well-defined victimological theory, or in fact from any social theory at all', but rather they sprang from 'ideologically inspired agendas for affirmative action' (p 115), giving rise to markedly different philosophies and objectives in different places.

Although the American movement and the European movement contain strands of both advocacy and assistance, the former is characterised principally by a rights approach and the latter by support activities. Shapland (1988) suggested the difference in approach was a result of the reliance on legislative change in the United States and that when the response to victims involved the criminal justice system, it would inevitably have the flavour of the prevailing criminal justice tradition (see also Viano, 1990). But at first sight the difference may seem strange, given the virtual unanimity in the research findings on victims' reactions to their victimisation and subsequent experience of the criminal justice system (see for example, Waller, 1989). Throughout the Anglo-American adversarial system and the inquisitorial system of Continental Europe as well, victims are consistently reported to be angry and bewildered, expecting to be able to turn to the police, to prosecutors and the courts for assistance and advice, and invariably finding that they are regarded by each of these agencies as outside of their area of responsibility (see for example, Shapland et al, 1985; Elias, 1986). As McBarnett (1988) observed:

> The state is not just the arbiter in a trial between victims and offender; the state is the victim ... If victims feel that nobody cares about their suffering, it is in part because institutionally nobody does. (p 300)

US model: rights-focused:

Geis (1990) argued that the fundamental basis of the power of the victim movement in the United States flows from the public and political perception that these are 'good' people who have suffered at the hands of 'bad' people. This view may render the cause politically irresistible, but it also works to support a narrow punitive focus. From the beginning there was a fierce retributive edge to the rhetoric supporting the interests of American victims. Carrington (1975), for example, a member of President Reagan's 1982 Task Force on Victims of Crime and other victim lobby groups, argued for a reversal of the Miranda exclusionary rule and increased use of the death penalty. He saw policy and policy-makers as occupying two distinct camps:

> In recent years the lines have been drawn generally into two schools of thought regarding the treatment of those accused, or convicted of criminal acts. The first of these is the hard-line or victim-oriented viewpoint; the second is the permissive or criminal-oriented approach. (Carrington, 1975: 124)

These views were echoed by many individuals and organisations in the United States newly interested in victims issues (Viano, 1983; Fattah, 1986; Davis et al, 1984). This 'law and order' faction was extremely influential in setting the agenda for the American victim movement and the high priority it assigned to rights – rights to be informed, rights to participate in the disposition of their case and, significantly, rights to influence sentencing decisions (Maguire & Shapland, 1990). The dominance of this approach was probably due to the much greater volume and seriousness of crime in the US than elsewhere, to differences in legal and political traditions and to a much greater degree of dissatisfaction felt by American victims with the defects of their court system. Whatever the reason, victims' organisations in the US tend to be punitively oriented and there have even been claims that the real goal of some constitutional amendments has been to advantage the prosecution rather than to establish victims' rights to participation (see Mosteller, 1998).

Pressure on American politicians to be seen to act on victims' behalf, to 'tip the balance' in favour of victims, on the assumption that offenders had too many rights, resulted in a huge volume of legislation conferring rights or benefits on victims in the decade after the President's Task Force on Victims of Crime in 1982 (Elias, 1990). Inevitably, this emphasis on achieving rights through such wholesale amendment to criminal justice processing has added to the strong retributive tone of these rights.

The retributive ideology in sections of the victim camp resonates with the 'just deserts' jurisprudence which has been so influential in sentencing systems in the United States, where the aim is to punish a crime according to a notional scale of harm which the offence has caused to society (Von Hirsch, 1976). Pressure from victims' rights advocates has resulted, for example, in the introduction of fixed sentences and the abolition of parole boards in some parts of the US (US Department of Justice, 1986).

An example of legislation introduced as a direct result of the political activism of a victim advocacy group is the *Washington State Community Protection Act* (1989) directed against sexually violent offenders. Three elements of this legislation were especially controversial: penalties were increased and their reach extended, sex offenders were required on release from prison to register with the police and the communities in which they reside were to be notified of their presence and offenders classified as 'sexually violent predators' who had served their term might be subject to civil action which could result in further incarceration.

The people working in Washington State for the introduction of these measures had suffered terribly through the death or mutilation of their children and they were not much interested in arguments about deterrence. In any case, there is a reluctance by citizens everywhere to engage in debate with people who have suffered so much, which in itself can be a serious impediment in moderating victims' demands. Scheingold et al (1994) discussed this issue and saw victims generally as problematic contributors to the crime debate because they tend to be incident-driven in their activities. They observed that the precipitating condition for victim advocacy was usually an especially horrifying or aberrant crime which stirred a moral panic in the community, and the atmosphere generated by these events, as well as the attitudes of the victims concerned, was likely to be overwhelmingly punitive. Reiss (1981) expressed concern about policy being formed on the basis of misconceptions derived from the aberrant, while the just deserts theorists are anxious about victims' influence resulting in disproportionate sentences in particular cases (Ashworth & Von Hirsch, 1993; Ashworth, 2000).

However, as we shall see, it is not axiomatic that all victims want punishment, no matter how much they have been hurt (see Cunneen, this volume). In fact, Scheingold et al noted that the victim advocacy groups observed in Washington State were actually not unremittingly punitive and short-term in their concerns and were interested in policies directed to crime prevention and the treatment of offenders as well. But local politicians chose to respond only to the punitive part of their agenda. Scheingold et al concluded that retributive attitudes expressed by victims who had suffered especially horrifying crimes left their communities vulnerable to manipulation by forces specifically concerned to introduce more punitive policies, even if retribution was only half of what victims say they wanted (see Morrison, this volume).

Elias (1990) has been especially pessimistic about the consequences of the appropriation of the American victim movement by the far right. He saw the strident rights-based approach perpetuating a concept of victimisation limited to 'street' crimes, with no room for 'suite' crimes, while the kinds of victims identified as the beneficiaries of these activities were likewise narrowed to those who 'deserve' them. In his view, the movement itself is conservative and manipulated, never likely to substantially improve the lot of victims because it is incapable of recognising the relationships between criminal victimisation and abuses of power. He concluded that victims in the United States

> have gotten far less than they were promised. Rights have often been unenforced or unenforceable, participation sporadic or ill-advised, services as have been introduced precarious and underfunded, victim needs unsatisfied if not further jeopardised and victimization increased, if not in court, then certainly in the streets. (1990: 242)

European Model: Support-Focused

By contrast, the emphasis in Europe has been far less on victim rights and much more towards victim support (Maguire & Shapland, 1990; Mawby, 1988). Organisations in these countries developed in the tradition of community-based voluntary associations whose objectives were primarily to alleviate suffering, and only secondarily to lobby for better treatment and more legal rights. Maguire and Shapland (1990) commented that outside the United States 'relying on victims rights to speed change is considered impractical, unlikely and even scandalous' (p 221). These victim support groups have deliberately avoided political activity or open campaigning and in particular have consistently refused to comment publicly on sentencing policy. Their aim had been to be seen as politically neutral, thus maximising their pool of volunteers and ensuring cross-party support (Zedner, 1994). Activities involving support and assistance to victims tend to share similar characteristics across nations, probably because they have developed outside the ambit of criminal justice agencies or government generally and have their roots in their communities. Shapland (1988) argued that the similarity of victim assistance services in different countries is a result of their separateness from their respective criminal justice systems.

Underlying much of the activity of European victim organisations, as well as the American movement, is the assumption that victims are the virtuous 'us' and the offenders the culpable 'other'. But victims' organisations are well aware that victimisation surveys routinely find that young men are the most victimised segment of the community (van Dijk et al,

1990). In fact victims and offenders are often indistinguishable from one another (Hindelang, 1976; Fattah, 1993). Not all victims are 'good', or in Christie's (1986) word, 'ideal', whom he characterised as respectable, weak and unblameworthy, and this reality is recognised in Scandinavia where crime victims are not treated in any special way but are supported under the general provisions of the welfare state. Such an approach may not address the special difficulties many victims face in recovering from the loss of social trust and sense of violation resulting from their victimisation, but it is unlikely that any rights-focus could help here either. What seems to be needed for all victims, the virtuous and the culpable, is what van Dijk called 'an expression of care and solidarity by the community whose integrity is at stake' (p 126).

How Useful, How Effective?

Rights Groups

The effectiveness of rights-focused advocacy groups, which have dominated the American picture, is far from clear. There is no doubt about their success in raising the profile of crime victims, but much remains undone in giving victims the voice they believe should be heard in the justice system. The prior issue may be whether they have tested the limits of the capacity of the traditional justice system to fulfil their objectives. The 'noise level' they have generated, especially in the United States, has probably contributed in a positive way to drawing attention to the condition of crime victims and in bringing about some necessary reform, but by doing so has made the movement vulnerable to appropriation by retributive conservative forces.

Support Groups

In terms of effectiveness for the welfare of victims, these groups, which have sprung up in great numbers around the world, are very popular and there is evidence of high levels of client satisfaction (Maguire, 1991). However, the question of whether they are either appropriate or effective in the services they provide has been the subject of a great deal of research with contradictory and inconclusive findings.

In terms of appropriateness, research has found that there may be a mismatch between the services offered and the needs of the victims. Several studies (Brown & Yantzi, 1980; Friedman et al, 1982; Skogan et al, 1990) found that property crime victims most often wanted practical help with repairs, security, insurance claims and financial assistance, services not often provided, at least in the United States, by victims' organisations. They tended more often to be offered professional counselling, usually some considerable time after the incident. Skogan et al (1990) suggested that the emotional support provided by family and friends was extremely important, but these connections were less likely to provide the practical help that victims needed.

In Britain, Maguire and Corbett (1987) also found that victims needed both emotional and practical support and that often they regarded the emotional impact of the crime as its worst aspect. Maguire (1991) suggested that British support organisations may be more successful than their American counterparts because they stressed in their training that emotional support was enhanced through practical help and that the time of greatest need for help of all kinds was within two days of the crime.

In looking at the effectiveness of victim support groups, the evidence is mixed. When victims are asked whether victim assistance works, they tend to be very enthusiastic. For example, in Maguire and Corbett's (1987) study, 87 percent of victims interviewed made positive comments. Similar results were also reported by Chesney and Schneider (1981), Norquay and Weiler (1981) and Skogan et al (1990). But despite the positive views expressed by victims, no study has been able to demonstrate that these services are effective in actually assisting recovery from the effects of victimisation (Maguire, 1991).

In sum, the success of victim assistance groups is difficult to assess. But perhaps civil society is strengthened in any case when the motivation for such activity is primarily to demonstrate that 'someone cares' (Gay et al, 1975; Holtom & Raynor, 1988) and to help restore victims' faith in others. As van Dijk (1986) argued, it may be that 'a community that supports its crime victims does not offer charity, but makes an investment in its own survival' (p 126).

A Third Way for Victims? Canberra as a Case Study

An influential framework for thinking about criminal policy during the last half of the twentieth century has been Herbert Packer's (1968) distinction between the crime control model and the due process model. The crime control model was based on the traditional assumption that crime was controlled by the criminal law, prosecutions and punishment. Until relatively recently, the extent of unreported crime was unmeasured and the deterrent effect of penal sanctions was unchallenged, so the justice system could be imagined as an assembly line processing the guilty and ensuring they received their just deserts. The 'due process' model, which emerged in the 1960s, was primarily concerned with offender rights, and turned the system into an 'obstacle course' (Roach, 1999) which held that the factually guilty should be acquitted if their legal rights had been violated.

Unsurprisingly, it was assumed that the crime control model was the one of greater appeal to victims. Indeed, the crime control model replicated the assumptions of the victims' rights view that the criminal law controlled crime. However, it is not inevitable that victims' legitimate grievances can only be addressed, or even best addressed, through a model of justice focused purely on the criminal sanction. Roach (1999) showed how the claims of women, children and the disabled who experienced often unreported sexual and domestic violence, as well as the struggles for justice of Indigenous peoples around the world, have resulted in an important blurring of Packer's distinctions. He suggested that victims' rights more broadly defined to encompass these previously ignored segments of the community were important new considerations in criminal justice debates and ensured that justice could no longer be defined as purely a matter between the accused and the state. He concluded that

> [T]he failure of the present system to include and protect victims could inspire a progressive approach which places less emphasis on the prosecution and punishment of crime and more on crime prevention and restorative justice. (p 4)

Canberra is not an important location in world victim politics, but it has been the setting for as vigorous debates as anywhere on issues such as the treatment of rape victims, the establishment of women's refuges, the pros and cons of victim impact statements and the like. The Canberra victim movement provides an interesting case study in which many of the competing forces in the wider movement have been played out, but which seems to have escaped the narrow choices, in philosophy and objectives, accepted by broadly similar groups in the United States on the one hand and Europe on the other. In fact, it may exemplify Roach's hopes for a 'progressive approach' which sees victims' rights as extending far beyond the frame of punishment and retribution.

Like a number of other grassroots victims' groups, the Canberra organisation, known as VOCAL (Victims of Crime Assistance League), was formed as a result of local tragedies, as already described.[1] At first glance, one would imagine that this would render it vulnerable to the extreme punitiveness described by Scheingold et al in the Washington State movement. But though individual members may have angry and vengeful feelings, overall the organisation does not have a retributive character. The founders of VOCAL recall that from the outset they decided the organisation needed a moderate, responsible style because neither the Canberra community nor the government would be sympathetic to a radical, rights-focused approach. They agreed that reason, calm and equanimity were the qualities needed in discussions to be held with politicians, police, the judiciary and civil servants to explain their case for reform. None of the members who met with judges, negotiated with the bureaucracy or appeared before committees of inquiry had ever taken part in public life before. But to the surprise of some, their actions were largely well received. As Mrs Cameron said: 'It was almost as if the world was waiting for victims to stand up', echoing Geis' (1990) comment on the self-evident justness of the victim cause, once the time was right. Contrast this with the painful feelings of victim advocates in Washington State, where Scheingold et al saw victims placing the blame for their situation on 'a callous and unresponsive state. They believed that much of their suffering was gratuitous, the result of the state placing its own bureaucratic concerns ahead of public safety' (p 14).

The two founders of Canberra VOCAL and its present chair all told me that the organisation saw its objectives as both the advancement of victim rights and the enhancement of victim assistance services and perceived no clash of interests between these advocacy and support roles. Both are informed by a restorative, non-punitive approach which puts less emphasis on adversarial conflict and more on community participation and reconciliation. What they say they want from the justice system echoes the views of victims world-wide (see, for example, Shapland et al, 1985; Mawby & Gill, 1987; Waller, 1989): they want a less formal process in which they can participate and their experience of victimisation be taken seriously; they want to be better informed about their case and to be treated fairly and with respect; they want material restoration and, especially, emotional restoration, including an apology.

Mrs Cameron, for example, described the pain of confronting her son's killer in the small area outside the courtroom, where everyone was required to wait together, and of finding herself face to face with his mother. She described how difficult it was to listen to character witnesses giving statements on behalf of the defendant while she had to remain silent about her son, and being told that she ought not to be in court and so running the risk of hearing the distressing evidence presented. She said that people did not understand that 'the not knowing is worse than the knowing'. Mrs Cameron said that any feelings she and her husband had towards the defendant were completely overshadowed by their anger towards what she referred to as 'the system'. They were given no information about when court hearings would take place and only found out through their son's friends who were subpoenaed to appear. Finally, she reflected on the emotional pain caused by the defendant not showing any remorse for his crime: 'He never said he was sorry. If he had it would have been so much easier on us, if he could have said he didn't mean to do it.'

Given that the restorative justice conferencing program operating in Canberra attempts to deliver most of the needs that victims themselves

have identified, it should come as no surprise to find a very high level of
support for the program among members of the movement. This program brings offenders and victims together with the objectives of discussing the crime and its consequences, requiring offenders to take
responsibility for their actions, and working out what is needed to repair
the harm experienced by the victim. VOCAL perceives the program as
resonating with their view of how criminal justice should be reformed to
meet victims' needs: rather than being focused on the criminal sanction,
they put more emphasis on crime prevention and making amends, with
less control by the criminal justice professionals who dominate the formal
system. On more than one occasion, VOCAL has publicly supported the
program when it has been under fire in the media. For example, when the
outcome of a poorly run conference was that the young offender should
walk through the shopping mall where he had shoplifted wearing a T-shirt
saying 'I Am a Thief', VOCAL thought the program should be defended,
not because they approved of this stigmatising outcome but because they
saw it as a mistaken outcome in a fledgling program.

Roach (1999) suggested that

> ... less formal proceedings seeking restorative justice could empower crime
> victims, as well as offenders, their families and communities, to the detriment
> of the professionals such as police, prosecutors and defence counsel, [and]
> include victims in decision-making without relying on increased punishment.
> ... Less punitive approaches can give those who have been victimised in the
> past more power and justice than crime control measures which, increasingly
> undertaken in the name of victims, often affirm the powers of criminal justice
> professionals and frequently collide with due process claims. (pp 4, 13)

In contrast to the punitive victims' rights approach, where the only
action available is appeal to politicians, the judiciary and the bureaucracy, who retain all the real power, the restorative approach allows victims to play a central role in the disposition of their case. In theory,
through their participation in the process they should be able to get the
information they say they want, contribute towards the resolution of their
case and obtain the reparation they seek. Indeed, results from the Reintegrative Shaming Experiments (Sherman et al, 1998; Strang et al, 1999),
a randomised controlled trial comparing the effectiveness of the Canberra restorative conferencing program with normal court processing,
support Roach's propositions. Victims who took part in conferencing
were much better informed about their case, had the opportunity to participate directly in resolving their case and obtained material and emotional restoration more often than their counterparts whose cases were
dealt with in court.

It seems that Canberra may be a rather good example of how victims
can begin effectively claiming back from the state their rightful role in

the justice system. Historically, victims have had their conflicts taken from them (Christie, 1977) – and no doubt were sometimes glad to be rid of them. But now many of them want them back. Perhaps, as victims in Canberra seem to feel, they are there for the asking if conditions are right on both sides. On the victim side mature, responsible leadership is needed. On the side of the state there must be a recognition of the necessity for change: a responsive state that is willing to treat its citizens as adults with legitimate grievances. But at the same time VOCAL recognises both the achievements of the organisation and the limitations that conventional law reform places on its capacity to make a difference. Certainly victims in Canberra are treated more seriously than they were ten years ago and are not as vulnerable to the sort of casual humiliations that they suffered then, but there have been limits to the improvements brought about by lobbying and legislative reform. To succeed beyond this may require the direct participation of victims, which only the restorative approach provides.

Conclusion

The victim movement world-wide has been enormously influential over the past 25 years in bringing to the attention of politicians, legislators and the communities of which they are a part, the needs and desires of victims of crime. Whether it has reached the limits of the capacity of the traditional formal justice system to give victims what they want is an important question. Shapland (2000) believes that in reality there has been little substantive change over this period, with victims still perceived as separate from the criminal justice system, '... a rather annoying group which stand apart from justice, but to whom we now need to consider creating some kind of response and making some concessions. ... There is little idea that victims are fundamentally woven into justice – that justice incorporates both victims and offenders' (p 148). She identified the difficulties that victims still contend with as being characterised by the need for justice agencies 'to reach out and respond to victims' (p 148), a task in which they have self-evidently failed. To succeed requires much greater appreciation of the legitimacy of the participation by victims in the disposition of the crimes they have experienced. This view is shared by Erez (2000) who commented that '[C]ourt inertia seems to result from the legal professionals' strong resistance against accepting victims as a legitimate party in the proceedings and practitioners' reluctance to recognize any value in victim input' (p 178). Whether restorative justice can provide a better response to those needs and desires is a question not yet fully answered. But both on theoretical grounds and on the basis of what we have learned so far from empirical research, there is room for optimism on this front.

Note

1   Information about the Canberra Victims of Crime Assistance League dis-
    cussed in this chapter is partly based on interviews conducted with the two
    founders of the organisation and its present chair. Although these three
    members are not necessarily representative of the views held by all the mem-
    bership, they have largely shaped the philosophy and the objectives of the
    organisation as a whole. I am most grateful to them for their time in talking
    to me.

CHAPTER 6

Reparations and Restorative Justice: Responding to the Gross Violation of Human Rights

Chris Cunneen

Reparations, Human Rights and Restorative Justice

This chapter considers the relationship between reparations for the gross violation of human rights and restorative justice. It does so broadly through a consideration of the international movement to provide reparations for the victims of human rights abuses. Its primary concern is, however, to specifically place the recommendations of the Australian National Inquiry into the Separation of Aboriginal and Torres Strait Islander Children from Their Families (NISATSIC – the Stolen Generations Inquiry) into a context of restorative justice. The importance of discussing human rights abuses within a context of restorative justice is manifold. It demands that we rethink the links between restorative justice, civil society and the state. When the state has been the perpetrator of crime then the restorative justice view that the crime must be returned to the community for resolution may be misplaced. Civil society will still play a fundamental role in identifying the crimes of the state and may well play a fundamental role in forcing the state to acknowledge and respond to its own wrong-doing. Yet where there have been large-scale abuses of human rights it is also the case that the state through the allocation of its own resources will play a pivotal role in the process of reparations for the harm which has been caused. Working through the issues associated with reparations for the gross violation of human rights enables us to broaden our vision of restorative justice beyond a concern with individualised concepts of crime and criminal responsibility.

The existing literature which analyses potential connections between human rights abuses and restorative justice is sparse. Van Ness (1996: 29–30) is one of the few writers in the field of restorative justice who has looked for links with international human rights norms. He finds that in

83

five areas there is substantial consistency between international standards and restorative justice theory. These include the requirement that states must balance the interests of victims, offenders and the public; the requirement that victims and offenders must have access to formal and informal dispute resolution mechanisms; the requirement for comprehensive action in regard to crime prevention; the requirement that governments provide impartial, formal judicial mechanisms for victims and offenders; and the requirement that there must be help for community reintegration of victims and offenders.

The problem with Van Ness' approach is that it narrowly restricts the discussion on human rights to particular issues relating to criminal justice norms and standards. Human rights are clearly far broader than this and relate to such areas as rights of particular groups, including women, children and minorities, and as freedom from and protection against a range of behaviours, including discrimination, arbitrary and unlawful treatment, and genocide. The narrow discussion provided by Van Ness means that one of the thorniest issues which restorative justice proponents must tackle is avoided: how to consider the relationship between restorative justice as a remedy for the gross violation of human rights when the offender is the state and its agents.

A similar problem can be seen in discussions of the application of restorative justice approaches to criminal justice process. Galaway and Hudson (1996) have argued that there are three elements which are fundamental to restorative justice definition and practice.

> First, crime is viewed primarily as a conflict between individuals that results in injuries to victims, communities and the offenders themselves and only secondarily as a violation against the state. Second, the aim of the criminal justice process should be to create peace in communities by reconciling the parties and repairing the injuries caused by the dispute. Third, the criminal justice process should facilitate active participation by victims, offenders and their communities to find solutions to the conflict. (Galaway & Hudson, 1996: 2)

The relationship between restorative justice remedies and the relative role of victims, offenders, community and the state in the Galaway and Hudson formulation becomes far more complex when it is the state which is responsible for criminal harm. This is clearly not merely a side issue when we consider the widespread role of the institutions of the state, often sanctioned by law, as the perpetrators of some of the greatest crimes against humanity. The modern political state has been integral to the commission of genocide and other human rights abuses. At least in Bauman's (1989) view, genocide and modernity have gone hand in hand. As Balint (1994: 13) has noted, the law was crucial to the Holocaust. 'It was law which provided the genocide with its order, it was law which legitimated it. ... Legislation defined the Jew and removed the Jew from the common world.' In South Africa it was the laws of apartheid which defined 'coloured' groups along territorial, residential, political, social and economic lines (Boraine, 1999: 469). In the Australian context it was the law which defined the 'Aborigine' and the half-caste, which drew the boundaries around those defined as 'quadroon' or 'octoroon'. It was the law which was to provide the operational framework for the ideas of Chief Protectors such as Dr Cecil Cook:

> Generally by the fifth and invariably by the sixth generation, all native charac- teristics of the Australian aborigine are eradicated. The problem of our half- castes will quickly be eliminated by the complete disappearance of the black race, and the swift submergence of their progeny in the white. ... The Aus- tralian native is the most easily assimilated race on earth, physically and men- tally. The quickest way is to breed him white. (Quoted in Markus, 1990: 93)

Internationally there has been growing acceptance that governments acknowledge and make reparations to the victims of human rights abuses. There has been widespread acceptance of the principle of repa- rations, including a variety of methods of redress; the importance of pub- lic acknowledgement of wrong-doing and apology for harm; the importance of participation of victims in the process of acknowledge- ment; and the acceptance of internationally accepted human rights norms as a basis for reparations (Human Rights and Equal Opportunity Commission (HREOC, 2000: iv). The principles of restorative justice are not foreign to public international law. Brownlie (1998: 460) notes that reparation is a broad term covering a variety of measures which might be expected of a defendant state, including restitution, compensation, an apology, punishment of the individuals responsible for the actions, steps undertaken to prevent a recurrence of the offence, and other forms of satisfaction. Satisfaction can involve any measure undertaken as part of reparation and may include an acknowledgement of wrong-doing.

What can restorative justice offer in the development of responses to the systematic abuse of human rights? In the first instance, it is worth recognising that the rebuilding of societies torn apart by systematic human rights abuses has involved processes of truth, justice and reconcil- iation. In some cases there have been ad hoc international criminal tri- bunals, however there has also been a reliance on various types of truth commissions in South Africa and in South America. In other countries there have been processes for reparations and reconciliation put in place.

In 1996 the Canadian Royal Commission on Aboriginal Peoples released its five-volume final report. Two years later the Canadian Gov- ernment responded to the Commission's findings with a report *Gathering Strength* (Canada, 1998). The Government report has a Statement of

Reconciliation which acknowledges past injustice and includes an apology to Indigenous peoples, particularly in relation to the effects of the residential school system. The Canadian Government has acknowledged the long-term inter-generational effects of removals through the residential school system and has provided a $350 million fund to support initiatives for Indigenous people affected by removal.

Also, the federal Law Commission of Canada (2000) has recently released a report which deals with the means of responding to the harm caused through the institutionalisation of children, including Indigenous children. In terms of our discussion of the needs of people who have been the victims of systematic human rights abuse and criminal injury, the report discusses the needs of survivors.

> The Commission was able to identify certain recurring themes in the manner these needs were expressed. Survivors seek: an acknowledgement of the harm done and accountability for that harm; an apology; access to therapy and to education; financial compensation; some means of memorialising the experiences of children in institutions; and a commitment to raising public awareness of institutional child abuse and preventing its recurrence. (Cited in HREOC, 2000: 62)

In October 1998 the South African Truth and Reconciliation Commission (1998) published its five-volume report. In its approach to reparations the Commission noted that

> if we are to transcend the past and build national unity and reconciliation we must ensure that those whose rights have been violated are acknowledged through access to reparation and rehabilitation ... without adequate reparation and rehabilitation measures, there can be no healing and reconciliation, either at an individual or a community level. (Cited in HREOC, 2000: 68–69)

The South African Truth and Reconciliation Commission was established to uncover the truth about past violations of human rights to enable the process of reconciliation and national unity to progress (Lyster, 2000). The Commission had six purposes including the generation of a detailed record of the extent, nature and causes of human rights violations in South Africa, to name those responsible for the violations, to provide a public forum for the victims to express themselves, to make recommendations to prevent future abuses, to make reparations to victims, and to grant amnesty to those who made full disclosure of their involvement in such violations. Indeed, Bishop Desmond Tutu has characterised the Truth and Reconciliation Commission as working within the paradigm of restorative justice, in contrast to approaches that rely on the prosecution of war criminals through special tribunals (*Sydney Morning Herald*, 27 November 1999, p 7).

In New Zealand the Treaty of Waitangi provides the framework for the recognition of Indigenous rights and reparation for past harms. From the early 1990s the New Zealand Government began to negotiate settlements of Maori treaty claims. Settlements are implemented through acts of parliament and may include land, compensation and a formal apology for past abuses and wrongful acts.

In September 1999 the Danish Prime Minister apologised to Inuit people who had been relocated in northern Greenland during the 1950s. A new agreement was signed between the Prime Minister and the Premier of Greenland strengthening the provisions of the *Greenland Home Rule Act* (1978) which provides a political and legislative framework for self-rule and reconciliation.

In October 1997 the King of Norway publicly apologised to the Sami people for the injustices brought about by the Norwegian state particularly through the policies of assimilation. In December 1999 the Norwegian Prime Minister apologised to the Sami people and in early January 2000 announced a fund to be established to promote Sami languages and cultures as a form of collective reparation and compensation.

In the United States, President Clinton apologised to African-Americans who had been victims of medical experimentation in Tuskegee, Alabama. Between 1932 and 1972 some 400 African-American men had been left untreated for syphilis after they had been offered free medical care. They were non-consenting participants in an experiment by the US Public Health Service. As Clinton acknowledged the federal government 'orchestrated a study so clearly racist' (cited in HREOC, 2000: 73).

There are many other examples where victims of human rights abuses have received public acknowledgement and reparations including Romany children forcibly removed in Switzerland, victims of the Nazi regime and victims in Chile, Argentina, Honduras and Kuwait (Orentlichter, 1994; Brooks, 1999; Barkan, 2000). It is not my purpose here to discuss whether these specific responses have been adequate – rather I wish to indicate the important contextual similarities in process and values.

At a basic level we can see some of the similarities between the role of reconciliation processes, reparations tribunals and truth commissions and restorative justice, at least in the broad emphasis on establishing truth as a way of resolving conflict, of providing the opportunity for reintegration of victim and offender, and on developing the principles of reparation, restitution and compensation. Both the emphasis in restorative justice and processes of reparations has been to adopt an approach which breaks down the divisions between civil and criminal wrongs, and instead prefers to consider the broader issue of individual and community harm. Restorative justice and reparations for human rights abuses are clearly identified as both a process and a set of values (Braithwaite &

Strang, this volume). As a process both bring together those affected to establish truth and provide the framework for reconciliation. As a set of values or principles both are concerned with healing and reconciliation between parties. As Alex Boraine noted in relation to South Africa, the Truth and Reconciliation Commission was established in the context of 'the compelling need to restore the moral order which was put in jeopardy by the abdication of the rule of law and gross violations of fundamental human rights' (Boraine, 1999: 469).

The National Inquiry into the Separation of Aboriginal and Torres Strait Islander Children from Their Families: The Principle of Reparations

I would now like to turn to a more specific discussion of the National Inquiry into the Separation of Aboriginal and Torres Strait Islander Children from Their Families (the Stolen Generations Inquiry) to explore the link between reparations and restorative justice. I also indicate how the failure of the Australian federal government to respond to the recommendations and findings of the Inquiry have stalled the reconciliation process at least at the level of state relations. In contrast, reconciliation as a process in civil society has grown dramatically.

From the late nineteenth century until at least the mid-1960s, large numbers of Indigenous children throughout Australia were removed from their families to be raised in institutions and by foster parents. The justifications and policy motives behind the practice varied but were broadly the result of theories such as eugenics and assimilation which assumed the biological and cultural inferiority of Indigenous peoples. The ultimate goal of these policies of removal was the 'absorption' of 'mixed race' children into the European community.

In May 1997 the Australian Government tabled the report of the National Inquiry. The Inquiry found that basic safeguards which protected non-Indigenous families were cast aside when it came to Indigenous children. The main components of the forced removal of Indigenous children were deprivation of liberty, deprivation of parental rights, abuses of power, and breach of guardianship duties. The report identified at least three ways in which guardianship duties and statutory duties had failed with Indigenous children. Firstly, there was a failure to provide contemporary standards of care for Indigenous children to the same level as non-Indigenous children. There were appalling standards of care, brutal punishments, cold, hunger, fear of sexual abuse, etc. Secondly, there was a failure to protect Indigenous children from harm, from abuse and exploitation: many of the children were verbally, physically, emotionally or sexually abused. Thirdly, there was a failure to consult or involve parents in decisions about the child. Many children were falsely told their parents were dead.

In relation to international human rights the main obligations imposed on Australia and breached by a policy of forced removals were the prohibitions on racial discrimination and genocide. The policy continued to be practised after Australia had voluntarily subscribed to treaties outlawing both racial discrimination and genocide. The legislative regimes created for the removal of Indigenous children were different and inferior to those established for non-Indigenous children. They were racially discriminatory and remained in place until as late as 1965 in Queensland.

In summary, the Inquiry found that the policy was contrary to prohibitions on racial discrimination and genocide. It was contrary to accepted legal principle found in the common law. Finally, the removals had led to other forms of victimisation and those removed had been subject to a range of criminal and civil wrong-doing. The Inquiry found that the policy adopted by governments which led to the forcible separation of Indigenous children from their families and communities constituted gross violations of human rights. The Inquiry also made a range of recommendations consistent with international remedies for human rights abuses.

In line with submissions to the Stolen Generations Inquiry, the approach of the Inquiry was to consider international provisions for responding to and redressing gross violations of human rights (NISAT-SIC, 1997: 278–280). When formulating its recommendations, the Inquiry considered the van Boven principles.[1] These principles have been accepted by the United Nations Sub-Commission on Prevention of Discrimination and Protection of Minorities as a synthesis of international practice (Pritchard, 1997: 28). Van Boven recommended that the only appropriate response to people who have been the victim of gross violations of human rights is one of reparation involving a range of methods of redress. The Inquiry agreed and recommended a broad ranging response to the stolen generations.

The Inquiry's recommendations centre around the principle of reparation. This is a much broader concept than simply compensation and can be seen as consistent with the values and principles of restorative justice. Reparations are to include five components: acknowledgement and apology; guarantees against repetition; measures of restitution; measures of rehabilitation; and monetary compensation. The Inquiry also recommended that reparation be available for all who suffered because of forcible removal including individuals removed, family members who suffered, communities that suffered cultural and community disintegration, and the descendants of those forcibly removed. In other words, the harm arising from the forced removal of Aboriginal children is seen as affecting communities and it is communities that need to be healed (see also McDonald & Moore, this volume).

There is a consistency between the van Boven principles and the principles that are usually seen to underpin restorative justice, such as recognition of wrong-doing, recompense through restitution or reparation, and reassurance that the offending behaviour will cease (Braithwaite, 1989). Importantly, however, reparations for human rights abuses involve a fundamental move beyond individual responsibility to collective responsibility for wrong-doing.[2] Thus thinking about reparations for the gross violation of human rights enables us to broaden the concept of restorative justice. It is important to acknowledge Blagg's (1998) point that restorative justice must not be narrowly defined to simple notions of individual crime. As noted above, perhaps the greatest crimes in the twentieth century causing direct human harm have been committed by governments. Again this poses a challenge for the development of restorative justice, because the state as perpetrator is also ultimately responsible for ensuring reparations. The absence of the state as an offender is not particular to restorative justice discourse. Even the international law definition of genocide is limited by the absence of reference to the role of the state (Tatz, 1999).

A fundamental principle of restorative justice is reconciliation: reconciliation between the offender and victim, between offender and community. Yet reconciliation is also a much broader collective and political process. For restorative justice to have resonance in the political process of reconciliation between Indigenous people and the Australian nation, then it must be contextualised by the recognition and implementation of the political and legal rights of Aboriginal peoples (Cunneen, 1998). The recommendations of the Stolen Generations Inquiry provide an important framework for reconciliation through reparation for past harms and recognition of contemporary Indigenous rights to self-determination. I want to now discuss in more detail the recommendations from the Inquiry, and to draw some comparisons with other processes for reparations internationally.

Reparations for the Gross Violation of Human Rights

Acknowledgement and Apology

The Inquiry recognised the need to establish the truth about the past as an essential measure of reparation for people who have been victims of gross violations of human rights. The Inquiry was told of the need for acknowledgement of responsibility and apology in many of the submissions from Indigenous organisations and the personal testimonies of individuals. Like victims of other crimes, people who have been subjected to the gross violation of their human rights want public recognition of the harm they have suffered – they are not necessarily vengeful (see Strang, this volume). Further, the Inquiry also recognised that commemoration was an important part of the reparation process. Commemoration allows both mourning and the memory to be shared and to be transformed into part of the national consciousness.

The importance placed on acknowledgement and apology is consistent both with the principles of restorative justice as well as the recommendations and processes of other commissions into human rights abuses. The South African Truth and Reconciliation Commission placed a great deal of importance on the process of acknowledgement. Acknowledgement provides a type of 'healing' truth where there is a full and public record of the victim's pain. As one of the Commissioners has noted the process is 'central to the restoration of the dignity of the victim' (Lyster, 2000). In the South African context, a public record and public acknowledgement of the past abuses is central to the process of reconciliation. Similarly in Canada, acknowledgement, apology and commemoration are seen as key components of reconciliation with Indigenous peoples.

In Australia the 'apology' continues to be the major public expression of support for the findings of the Inquiry and a continued point of pressure on the Commonwealth Government. It is clear that is has achieved a resonance with many people, and it does provide the opportunity for a personal and public display of at least some level of commitment to acknowledging and, by implication, remedying human rights abuses against Indigenous people in Australia. Indeed, the widespread public support by signing Sorry Books is itself an important phenomenon – particularly considering that it has been a response to community initiatives in the context of the Commonwealth Government refusal to acknowledge and apologise for the harm caused. To allay ongoing criticism, the Prime Minister introduced a 'motion of reconciliation' into Federal Parliament on 26 August 1999, where he expressed 'regret'. He actually described it as a 'generic' regret for past practices which were never named. Such a response provides little in developing a national context for reconciliation or for providing an environment for victims to feel their grief and loss has been acknowledged. Not surprisingly, many key Indigenous and non-Indigenous groups have not accepted the 'statement of regret' as an apology to the Stolen Generations.

The issue of the apology shows the importance of civil society in both achieving some level of reconciliation independent of government, and importantly in this context, of placing considerable pressure on government to achieve a moral as well as a political and legal solution to the issue. The broad-based social movement for reconciliation has seen apologies to the Stolen Generations from the fullest range of institutions within civil society: churches, educational groups, local community groups, trade unions and so on (see Cunneen & Libesman, 2000a). There are two interrelated points about the role of civil society and social movements that can be drawn out in this context. First, a strong social movement may well be a necessary prerequisite for bringing the state into a restorative justice process under conditions where it has responsibility for repairing the damage it has caused or contributed to. Indeed some commentators in the US have argued that a strong 'redress movement' (i.e., social movement demanding redress by the state) is what differentiates successful and unsuccessful claims for reparations for past human rights abuses (Brooks, 1999: 7). Second, the role of a strong social movement in pressuring the state reverses the concerns of some commentators that restorative justice may simply provide the opportunity for further penetration of the social world (through the rhetoric of 'community') by the state.[3] Social movements in this context are resisting state definitions of harm and redefining the role of reparations/restoration. In other words they provide *both* moral and political leverage against a recalcitrant offender.

Guarantee Against Repetition

The Stolen Generations Inquiry recognised that guarantees against repetition were an important part of the reparation process and there are recommendations which deal specifically with this issue. These recommendations refer to the need for compulsory educational modules in school education on the issue of the Stolen Generations. They also require the Commonwealth to legislate the Genocide Convention for effect in domestic law. This recommendation is based on the fact that although Australia ratified the Genocide Convention it has not passed domestic legislation which would give effect to international law. Implementation of the Genocide Convention in domestic law would create a criminal offence of genocide within Australia.

The concept of a 'guarantee against repetition' can be seen within the values of restorative justice. Such a notion is basically a reassurance to the community that future harmful acts will not occur. Clearly, such a reassurance is more difficult in cases where the state has been the perpetrator rather than an individual offender. The Australian Government has refused to introduce domestic legislation outlawing acts of genocide. It has done so on the convoluted logic that genocide has not occurred in Australia because the legislation which enabled the forced removal of Indigenous children did not display the necessary 'intent to destroy' the racial group as such. The historical evidence presented by the Inquiry seriously challenges this view. We might want to consider the way other states have used similar arguments to deny genocide against Indigenous peoples. Both governments in Paraguay and Brazil have denied that genocide occurred against Indian peoples because there was no intent to destroy the people. As Balint (1994: 36) has noted, 'this type of analysis removes the victim from the equation of genocide. It also denies a broad notion of intent, including negligence or recklessness.'

Some form of guarantee against repetition is a necessary component of international redress for human rights abuses, as well as a key value shown in the restorative justice literature. Some form of guarantee against the repetition of an offence is necessary before the process of healing for all parties can begin and the reintegration of the offender back into the community can occur. Perhaps the acknowledged difficulty of this process is made even more complex and more imperative when there are multiple victims and offenders and the offending behaviour has at some time received legitimacy and support from the state institutions.

Measures of Restitution and Rehabilitation

'The purpose of restitution is to re-establish, to the extent possible, the situation that existed prior to the perpetration of gross violations of human rights' (NISATSIC, 1997: 296). The Inquiry recognised that 'children who were removed have typically lost the use of their languages, been denied cultural knowledge and inclusion, been deprived of opportunities to take on cultural responsibilities and are often unable to assert their native title rights' (NISATSIC, 1997: 296). As a result the Inquiry made a number of recommendations concerning support for people returning to their land and the communities receiving them, the expansion of funding to language, culture and history centres to ensure national coverage, and funding for the recording and teaching of local Indigenous languages where the community determines this to be appropriate. The Inquiry also made recommendations to assist in re-establishing Indigenous identity and funding for Indigenous community-based family tracing and reunion services, as well as the preservation of, and Indigenous access to records. Measures for rehabilitation were also an important component of the reparations package. The Inquiry was made very aware of the long-term problems caused by forcible separation. It made significant recommendations in relation to mental health care and assistance in parenting and family programs.

Again there are clear parallels with the recommendations from other international commissions. The South African Truth and Reconciliation Commission (1998) recommended five components to a reparations and rehabilitation policy, which included urgent interim reparation for those in urgent need; individual reparation grants for individual victims; symbolic reparation measures (national remembrance days, memorials, monuments, museums, etc.); community rehabilitation programs to establish community-based services; and institutional reform to prevent the reoccurrence of human rights abuses. In Canada the Government has responded to the findings of the Royal Commission on Aboriginal Peoples with a fund to support Indigenous people who were forcibly removed.

Restitution and rehabilitation for victims have been considered an important component of restorative justice. In general terms the principle has been identified as repairing the harm caused to victims through some form of recompense, involving where possible restitution, compensation and reparation (Pettit & Braithwaite, 1993). Healing and making amends are common restorative justice values referred to in other chapters in this volume (see for example, Braithwaite & Strang).

Monetary Compensation

The Stolen Generations Inquiry recognised that the loss, grief and trauma experienced by those who were forcibly removed can never be adequately compensated. However, the submissions to the Inquiry also demanded some form of monetary compensation for the harm that had been suffered – particularly as a form of recognition of the responsibility for the causes of that harm. The Inquiry recommended that monetary compensation should be payable for harms and losses where it was not possible to make restitution. Following both the van Boven principles and submissions to the Inquiry, it recommended ten heads of damage for compensation: racial discrimination; arbitrary deprivation of liberty; pain and suffering; physical, sexual and emotional abuse; disruption of family life; loss of cultural rights and fulfilment; loss of native title rights; labour exploitation; economic loss; and loss of opportunities.

The Inquiry recommended that a National Compensation Fund be established to provide an alternative to litigation. The Inquiry recommended a Board to administer the fund and that it be comprised of a majority of Indigenous people. The procedural principles applied to the Compensation Fund should be culturally appropriate, expeditious and non-confrontational. The principles should include widest possible publicity; free legal advice and representation for claimants; no limitation period; independent decision-making including participation of Indigenous people; minimum formality; not bound by rules of evidence; and cultural appropriateness. Credible claims of forced removal should be compensated for by a minimum lump sum. The burden of proof should be on Government to rebut otherwise credible claims. Further compensation should be available where claimants can prove on the balance of probabilities that particular harm or loss was suffered.

The Inquiry's approach to compensation is consistent with the views expressed in other commissions of inquiry into gross violations of human rights and is consistent with international law. The South African Truth and Reconciliation Commission recognised that many people wanted financial compensation for their losses and felt that this was an appropriate and just response. The Commission recommended that the South African Government not take a narrow and legalistic approach to the question of compensation. International obligations for adequate compensation for people who have been subjected to human rights violations arise from Article 8 of the Universal Declaration of Human Rights, Section 3 of the International Covenant on Civil and Political Rights and the Convention against Torture and Other Cruel, Inhuman and Degrading Treatment.

The Australian Government had ruled out compensation even before the Inquiry had finished its deliberations and presented its final report. The Government has consistently and unashamedly sought to trivialise the issue of compensation for Aboriginal people affected by removal, and deny the validity of harm which has been caused. By way of contrast, both the South African and Canadian governments have recognised that compensation is an important part of the process of reparation and reconciliation and that contemporary governments must shoulder the responsibility of the actions of previous governments.

Contemporary Removals

A substantial part of the Inquiry was concerned with issues relating to the contemporary separation of Indigenous children and young people. The Inquiry extensively examined the range of factors through which Indigenous children and young people are removed from their families. Many Indigenous people speaking to the Inquiry noted the links between child welfare and juvenile justice. The outcome of whatever legislation their children are removed under is the same: the children and young people are lost to their communities. While legal, policy and analytical distinctions between child welfare and juvenile justice can be drawn, it is also important to consider the continuum of intervention which occurs with families and children. Most importantly the evidence showed the inter-generational effects of previous removal and current interventions by welfare and criminal justice authorities. The trauma caused by colonial policies was still clearly impacting today (Cunneen & Libesman, 2000b).

The Inquiry noted the widespread desire of Indigenous people in Australia to exercise far greater control over matters affecting young people as reflected in many written submissions and evidence presented at hearings. Many submissions from Indigenous people and organisations to the Inquiry called for transfer of control of child welfare matters to Indigenous communities. These submissions also referred to Canadian and US models where native peoples had been able to exercise greater control over child welfare through the *Indian Child Welfare Act* 1978 (US) and the Canadian First Nation Peoples Children's Services. The recommendations from the Inquiry stress the importance of self-determination, as well as greater Indigenous controls over decision-making in the juvenile justice system and matters relating to child welfare.

The issue of responding to contemporary removals of Indigenous children poses a particular set of problems which advocates of restorative justice must squarely confront. The inter-generational effects of colonial policy mean that Indigenous children are massively over-represented in child welfare and juvenile justice systems. This problem is not particular to Australia. One important implication of this is that restorative justice advocates must allow their own practices to contextualise the contemporary effects of past policies. We have discussed more fully elsewhere the way many welfare and juvenile justice officers often have little understanding of what we have termed 'postcolonial trauma' (Cunneen & Libesman, 2000b: 114). The individualisation of family problems through child welfare casework or criminal justice notions of individual responsibility provide virtually no framework for a contextual understanding. It seems to me that restorative justice advocates can make a real contribution in this area by supporting welfare and justice practices which allow for the deeper meanings of harm and responsibility to emerge.

Indigenous self-determination poses a related set of issues for restorative justice. Self-determination may involve the devolution of power to community or regional structures. It certainly involves a move away from the centralised authority of the nation-state. At least at this level it is consistent with the broad philosophy of restorative justice, which advocates a return of conflict from the state to the parties and communities involved. Certainly Indigenous organisations see self-determination in the context of the devolution of power and authority from the (colonial) state to the organisations of (Indigenous) civil society. Unfortunately, much of what has passed for restorative justice in practice, at least in Australia, has not led to any real devolution of power to Indigenous communities (Cunneen, 1997, 1998). In this context restorative justice advocates need to go well beyond simply holding up Indigenous dispute resolution mechanisms as a form to be adapted or adopted, to actually advocating for the rights of Indigenous peoples to exercise jurisdiction.

Conclusion

Much of the struggle by minority groups has been expressed in terms of international human rights, and this is nowhere more the case than with Indigenous minorities. Some within the restorative justice movement might feel uncomfortable with what they see as an over-emphasis on claiming rights and a lack of emphasis on restorative values of healing and reconciliation. In my view this is a misconceived dichotomy. There are several reasons for this. First, we need to realise why claims to international rights have been so important for Indigenous peoples. They are often referred to as 'entrapped nations' or 'nations within nations'. The implications of this are that historically they have been unable to expect protection from nation-states, and indeed as the case studies referred to in this chapter have shown, it is the nation-state that has been the perpetrator of the worst crimes against Indigenous and other minority groups. It is not surprising then that there is an appeal to standards and mechanisms beyond the state.

A second reason relates to the values which are embodied in internationally accepted human rights. Both restorative justice and the demands for reparations for past abuses are about responding to the claims of injustice. An obvious issue is how do we define 'injustice'. For those seeking redress for historical injustice, internationally accepted human rights norms provide the basis on which claims can be developed (Brooks, 1999: 7). They provide a framework through which the demands for specific types of reparations can be made. Perhaps more importantly, the core international human rights provide a moral framework through which we can assess and evaluate the behaviour of governments. This moral framework is not an arbitrary collection of disparate behaviours which are disapproved. International human rights law provides us with the means to place content into fundamental notions of human injustice. Certainly many of the crimes to which Indigenous peoples have been subjected are covered by *jus cogens*, customary international law. When the Stolen Generations Inquiry stated that the main international human rights obligations imposed on Australia and breached by a policy of forced removals were the prohibitions on racial discrimination and genocide, we know that the behaviours referred to deserve the widest condemnation as morally and legally repugnant.

An issue related to this discussion of human rights is the question of reconciliation. Perhaps the advocates of restorative justice and the advocates of human rights can both learn from their potentially differing interpretations of this concept. In broad terms, reconciliation is about healing, about bringing together warring parties, about ending conflict. Yet reconciliation cannot be achieved without justice to the aggrieved party. This issue was clearly recognised in Australia by the Council for Aboriginal Reconciliation. While the Council was at the forefront of making reconciliation a social movement, it was also a consistent advocate for reparations and social justice for Indigenous people – and much of this claim derived from an understanding of Indigenous demands in the arena of international human rights.

In general terms, the reparations packages that have been advocated for victims of human rights abuses are consistent with the values and processes of restorative justice. The van Boven principles centre around the concept of reparations and use a language familiar to restorative justice: acknowledgement and apology, restitution, rehabilitation, compensation and reassurance against future acts. Indeed, this is the approach which has been adopted in South Africa and Canada, and recommended in Australia. In South Africa, the Truth and Reconciliation Commission consciously referred to the notions of restorative justice as characterising their approach.

The outcomes of the Stolen Generations Inquiry in Australia, also highlight some of the political problems which arise when there is a recalcitrant government which *refuses* to acknowledge responsibility for past actions. It highlights the central problem of power imbalances where the offender simply denies responsibility to the victim. Rather than seek a restorative justice approach the Australian Government has been content to allow the victims of human rights abuses to proceed individually before the courts for civil claims. Impacting on the government's recalcitrance, however, has been a powerful social movement for reconciliation. This raises a further issue and requires some rethinking for restorative justice advocates. How can civil society through social movements force the state to take responsibility for its past harms? Restorative justice requires the devolvement of ownership of the conflict back to the parties involved. In this case one of the parties involved is the state and as a perpetrator must be held responsible for its actions.

Notes

1   Basic Principles and Guidelines on the Right to Reparation for Victims of Gross Violations of Human Rights and Humanitarian Law (NISATSIC, 1997: Appendix 8).

2   This is not to deny that holding individuals responsible for particular crimes (such as sexual assault or physical abuse) arising from the forced removal of Indigenous people may be important.

3   I would also include myself in this group, see Cunneen, 1997, and also Pavlich in this volume.

CHAPTER 7

Restorative Justice and Civil Society in Melanesia: The Case of Papua New Guinea

Sinclair Dinnen

A Crisis of Governance

The threat of violence is a fact of daily life for many Papua New Guineans, especially town residents. While notoriously unreliable, reported rates of criminal violence, including robberies and rapes, have risen sharply in recent years (Levantis & Gani, 1998). Concern with personal safety is reflected in the elaborate security surrounding urban homes and commercial premises, a reluctance to visit certain areas or venture out after dark. Gangs of young men, known locally as *raskols*, are viewed as the main perpetrators of violent crime. As a result they have become a source of great personal insecurity, as well as a major target of reactive policing.

Escalating lawlessness and the inadequacies of state controls have been portrayed as part of a larger crisis of governance facing many of the young Pacific Island countries. This crisis manifests itself in the deterioration of essential government services, growing levels of corruption, political instability, ready resort to violence by aggrieved groups, and the proliferation of micro-nationalist tensions, as on the islands of Bougainville and Guadalcanal. Against such a background, the need for fundamental institutional and policy reform, including reforms in the area of law and justice, is widely accepted.

Civil Society and Restorative Justice

In Papua New Guinea (PNG), 'civil society' is the term commonly used to refer to those associations occupying the intermediary space between the state, on the one hand, and the most localised entities of tribe, clan, language group, and family, on the other. Civil society comprises organisations that transcend parochial loyalties while remaining independent of the state. It includes trade unions, professional associations, student groups, non-government organisations, churches, and the media (Haynes, 1996: 32). Civil society, in this sense, remains relatively undeveloped in PNG. This is a consequence of historical factors, shared with many other ex-colonies, as well as of the extraordinary social diversity of this Melanesian country. The most significant agencies of civil society in both colonial and post-colonial periods have been the churches and missions.

Although not a familiar term in PNG, the idea of restorative justice appears to sit well with some older Melanesian approaches to conflict resolution. It is, moreover, consistent with the emphasis on community empowerment and decentralisation in current debates about public sector reform. Advocates of restorative justice in the developed countries often draw inspiration from what they view as traditions of conflict resolution in small-scale, Indigenous societies. Restorative practice, it is argued:

> involves returning to the ancient view that redefines crime more as an injury to the victim and the community than as an injury to the government. It views criminal justice as involving the victim, the offender, and the entire community in its processes. Above all, it views the proper response to crime as 'community building'. Everything that is done should be designed to restore the fabric of the community. (Hahn, 1998: 133)

While providing an appealing rationale, the justice practices of so-called traditional societies are rarely as straightforward or homogeneous as implied in such depictions. In equating restorative justice with 'traditional' approaches to conflict, the tendency has been to misrepresent, over-simplify or romanticise the latter.

This chapter looks at the prospects for restorative justice in modern Papua New Guinea – a country in which the legacies of small-scale societies remain strong. Beginning with an introduction to Melanesian society, there follows an account of the impact of colonial intrusion upon social control at local levels. The growth of crime and deficiencies of state responses in the period since Independence are followed by discussion of a number of recent restorative initiatives.

Melanesian Societies[1]

Australia granted Papua New Guinea independence in 1975. Twenty-five years later, PNG remains one of the most socially diverse and fragmented countries in the world. Over 800 languages (about two-thirds of the world's languages) are spoken among a population of 4.7 million people. The country's territorial boundaries comprise the eastern half of New Guinea, the world's second largest island. They encompass a varied topography, ranging from the high valleys of the central Highlands, vast tracts of lowland swamps, to numerous low-lying islands and scattered coral atolls. Approximately 85 percent of the population are subsistence farmers living in rural villages.

Melanesian societies were traditionally small-scale and insular, often consisting of less than a thousand people. Political units consisted of those groups within which organised warfare did not usually occur (Chowning, 1973: 21). Social relations were essentially kinship relations. Reciprocal obligations were a significant feature of Melanesian morality. Reciprocity was embodied in the ceremonial exchange of food and gifts. These practices sometimes evolved into complex trading partnerships over considerable distances as, for example, in the elaborate inter-island 'Kula ring' documented famously by Bronislaw Malinowski (1972). Gift exchange was a means of maintaining social control, a vehicle for trade, a way of demonstrating leadership, and a strategy for consolidating alliances between groups.

Melanesian societies were 'stateless' in the sense that they had no centralised political or administrative organisation equivalent to a government that could weld together those sharing a common language and culture. Civil society, in its current Western usage, was the only society. Legitimacy was dispersed widely, at least among all adult males. Prominent males, the so-called Melanesian 'big-men', led traditional polities (Strathern, 1971). Subject to considerable variation, leadership status was more usually achieved than inherited, often through individual prowess in warfare, organising trade, or ceremonial exchanges. Warfare was endemic in many places (Berndt, 1962). In practice, war was typically followed by elaborate forms of peacemaking between the various parties. The complex cycles of war and peace characteristic of the New Guinea Highlands[2] complicate a dichotomous view of the relationship between violence and non-violence. They also challenge views of the former as inherently abnormal or pathological. Anthropologists argue that violence and non-violence need to be analysed in terms of the whole range of social relationships in these societies. Speaking of the Mount Hagen area of the Western Highlands, Marilyn Strathern states that:

> The mediation of conflict through wealth exchanges (compensation) of the Hagen sort cannot be taken simply, then, as non-violent solutions to potential or actual violent eruptions ... Reciprocity involves a constant strain towards balancing or out-balancing exchanges. Added to this, the mediatory character of wealth allows the inflation of emotions to collective dimensions; it thus sustains the circulation of violent as well as non-violent interchange. (1985: 129)

Violence and peacemaking were 'normal' and integral parts of the same political process that regulated relations between adjacent groups, essentially two sides of the same coin.

No separation existed between law and politics, or law and morality. There was no distinct idea of crime, no criminal code, nor any special body charged with enforcing customary norms. Melanesian institutions and systems of social regulation were based on different principles from those of European society. Lawrence (1969) identifies three important dimensions of the relationship between morality and social control in Melanesian societies. First, the rule of reciprocity governing relations between individuals provided the essence of self-regulation or of those forces preventing wrong-doing. Cooperation between members was essential for the survival of both the individual and the group. Secondly, morality was not conceived as universalist, as in Western society, but was restricted to a particular social range. This range, which varied from society to society, was based on kinship or other close, personal affinity. No obligation was owed to those who fell outside these social relations. Finally, this process of self-regulation was not a separate institution within the total social order. It was an essential and indivisible part of it.

Self-regulation included both retributive and restorative elements. Threats of violent retaliation or 'payback' figured prominently in the repertoire of 'traditional' sanctions (Taylor, 1982). Ostracism, exclusion from rituals and, very rarely, outright expulsion from the group provided other options. Likewise with gossip, shaming and ridicule. Sorcery was another important strategy of social control.

The Colonial Experience

The colonial state was, by definition, an external creation. It was imposed arbitrarily on existing Melanesian social and political groupings through an incremental process of 'pacification'. As elsewhere, the politics of colonialism in PNG were inherently undemocratic. The impacts of colonial incursion on Indigenous societies, however, were neither monolithic nor uniformly disintegrative.

The timing of colonial encounters varied enormously between different groups and parts of the territory. Some coastal and island communities had a long history of engagement with the outside world, often pre-dating formal colonial annexation in 1884. By contrast, in parts of the New Guinea Highlands, the most densely populated region, encounters with Europeans did not take place until 70 years after annexation (a mere 21 years before Independence). Colonial influence was extended in a piecemeal fashion. European patrol officers, known as *kiaps*, established government stations and set out on foot with armed police to pacify local peoples. *Kiaps* sought to stop inter-group fighting, conduct censuses, and collect head tax. They also presided over ad hoc courts administering a body of paternalistic 'native regulations'. In practice, government by patrol often meant little more than a couple of visits a year for villages close to administrative centres, a single visit every one or two years for more distant villages, and even rarer visits in less accessible areas.

Indigenous institutions were interfered with only when it was considered necessary, as when they were perceived as a threat to colonial authority. Otherwise customary forms of self-regulation prevailed, as adapted to the opportunities and constraints of externally induced change. For most of the colonial period there was no discrete system of criminal justice. Instead, the policing, judicial and penal powers of the colonial regime were parts of an undifferentiated system of 'native administration'.

The suppression of inter-group fighting was perhaps the most lauded achievement of the Australian administration. *Pax Australiana* did not, however, eventuate as a result of the destruction of Indigenous social regulation. Local actors were never merely passive objects in a top-down process of external imposition. Colonial peace was achieved with Melanesian acquiescence. For many local groups, cooperation with Europeans was a convenient way of securing powerful new allies in continuing struggles against traditional rivals, a means for developing trade, or acquiring new forms of wealth and knowledge (Reed, 1943).

Colonial justice was accepted largely because of its limited capacity to displace Indigenous institutions or control local politics. There was no colonial presence in most villages on most days. When present, it was often susceptible to appropriation by local actors. The *kiap* court provided an additional forum that could be incorporated into a rich repertoire of indigenous strategies for dealing with conflict. Parties could add these new courts to available options, thereby enlarging the scope for 'forum shopping' (Oliver, 1955: 326). These interactions between Indigenous and introduced legal systems served to reinforce, rather than undermine, each other.

Until comparatively late, the colonial state evinced only a desultory interest in 'development', placing more value on stability, the conservation of 'traditional' society, and the gradual extension of government authority. This was not an environment conducive to the growth of a vibrant civil society. Beyond the family, clan and tribe, civil society consisted almost exclusively of mission and church organisations. These organisations, in turn, were often active agencies of the colonial state.

Institutional Modernisation

An acceleration in the pace of socio-economic change from the late 1950s contributed to the emergence of new social tensions and divisions. These developments, in combination with growing international pressure, weakened the legitimacy of the colonial project.

Australian authorities embarked belatedly on a process of institutional modernisation aimed at laying the foundations of a modern nation-state. The 1960 Derham Report presented the blueprint for a centralised system of law enforcement and judicial administration that was to be bequeathed, albeit in incomplete form, to Papua New Guinea at Independence. The colonial system of district administration was to be replaced by a modern criminal justice system with a separate court hierarchy, police force and prison service.

These reforms contributed to the weakening of social controls at local levels. This can be best appreciated by contrasting them with the colonial system they replaced. Under the former, the juridical powers of the *kiap* could be supplemented by powers issuing from his various agency functions (Gordon, 1983: 220). These included a range of discretionary strategies for inducing behavioural change among individuals and groups. Punishment was merely one option. The decisions of the *kiap* could, moreover, be enforced immediately, with minimal formality or delay.

By contrast, a formidable array of rules and regulations limited the discretion of the *kiap*'s successor, the professional magistrate. Western justice took longer, entailing a cumbersome and formalistic process. Growing levels of dissatisfaction among Indigenous litigants accompanied these changes. Concern with due process, a focus on individual responsibility, and the neglect of victims, offended local perceptions of dispute management. Speaking about the Mount Hagen area of the Western Highlands, Strathern claimed that:

> The Kiap's handling of trouble cases in the past combined both a concern for public order and a capacity to deal with minor offences. In fact, these derived from different aspects of his roles (administrator and magistrate), but it meant that he 'settled disputes' roughly along lines familiar to Hageners. The paradox is that although the modern official courts are ostensibly concerned with law and order, they fail in Hageners' eyes to take cognisance of matters directly related to both of these elements. (1972: 143)

Police authority also suffered. The formerly powerful and prestigious agents of pacification were now subject to regular and humiliating 'defeats' in court, often on baffling technical grounds.

Ironically, the colonial system provided greater scope for deliberation and participation by Indigenous parties. *Kiaps* could use positive and negative sanctions and could address the social context of wrong-doing, thereby conforming more closely to local perceptions of appropriate conflict resolution. Moreover, while the *kiap* brought the colonial system to the village, the system that replaced it was urban-centred and inaccessible to many villagers. One response to the weakening of social controls was increasing resort to older methods of self-regulation. These included the revival of so-called tribal fighting, made more deadly through the introduction of modern firearms.

Independence and the Growth of Crime

When Australia relinquished control in 1975, Papua New Guinea inherited arbitrary colonial borders and the hastily assembled framework of a modern nation-state. There had been no unifying anti-colonial struggle and, indeed, many Highlanders had strongly opposed Independence (Dorney, 1990: 49). The 'nation' that came into being on 16 September 1975 was, in many respects, the embodiment of Benedict Anderson's 'imagined community' (1983). Micro-nationalist movements emerged in the more developed areas (May 1982), there was little sense of shared identity beyond a small urban elite, with the primary allegiances of most 'citizens' remaining firmly implanted in local societies.

The institutions of the modern state, including the criminal justice system, existed alongside hundreds of local systems of self-regulation. Nationalist rhetoric and the Constitution promised a legal system in which indigenous customs would play a prominent role. Despite early efforts by the Law Reform Commission, relatively little progress was made in integrating national law and local custom. Twenty-five years after Independence, the institutional framework of law and justice, with the notable exception of the Village Courts, remains essentially that introduced in the twilight years of colonial administration (Dinnen, 1995a).

Previously negligible crime rates began rising in the late 1960s. Urban growth precipitated the emergence of juvenile delinquency. The abolition of colonial restrictions over Indigenous movement had opened up the towns, formerly European enclaves, to migration from rural areas. Port Moresby, the national capital, experienced a 12.2 percent growth rate between 1966 and 1977 (King, 1992) and doubled again in size in the first decade after Independence (Dorney, 1990: 229). The legalisation of alcohol in 1962 provided another catalyst for crime.

The evolution of Port Moresby gangs has been depicted as one of progressive organisational sophistication (Harris, 1988). The first gangs were primarily mechanisms for managing the personal adjustments facing young male migrants new to the urban environment. Criminal organisation became more sophisticated as gangs spread their activities from the settlements to the more respectable suburbs. Better-educated members enabled a 'process of vertical integration of gangs into larger criminal networks' (Harris, 1988: 13). Gangs were becoming an important vehicle for material and personal advancement. By the late 1980s, Port Moresby gangs were:

efficient criminal organisations which operate with little fear of apprehension. ... They have strong links with other criminal groups in the country for the distribution and sale of stolen goods; they are heavily involved in the drug trade; and they have close links with some politicians and businessmen who use them for political purposes and to 'payback' their enemies. (1988: v–vi)

The proliferation of firearms has added greatly to the menace of *raskolism* in recent years. Weapons include high-powered automatic rifles, homemade guns, and even grenades (*Post-Courier*, 22 August 1996). Shoot-outs between police and criminals are reported regularly. In December 1999, police killed five suspects who had hijacked a helicopter in a spectacular attempted bank robbery in downtown Port Moresby.

At a macro level, the rise of *raskolism* is symptomatic of the growing marginalisation of large numbers of PNG's young people. In the monetised town environment, there is little subsistence base to fall back upon for the basic necessities of life. Urban crime is an employment category in its own right, constituting an important element of the informal economy. Recent estimates suggest that 18 percent of the urban labour force resort to crime as their main source of income (Levantis & Gani, 1998: 91). The ties binding rural youth to their villages are also under intensive pressure from the forces of modernisation and globalisation. Urban drift continues unabated, as does the spread of *raskolism* to many rural areas.

While *raskolism* is associated with contemporary processes of socio-economic change, there are also continuities linking it to older social traditions. The warrior ethos and antagonism towards women suggest that it is also a means for constituting male identity among young men caught in the ambivalent space between town and village, tradition and modernity. *Raskolism* may, in part, be an alternative to the older rituals of male initiation that have disappeared in most places. The social organisation of *raskolism* and, in particular, the relationship between criminal leaders and their followers suggest that crime is an important way of building individual prestige and standing. A sizeable proportion of the proceeds of acquisitive crime is distributed strategically to promote the reputation and following of individual criminal leaders. In this respect, the dynamics of criminal leadership resemble more enduring patterns of Melanesian leadership, whereby strategic gifting was an important mechanism for constituting big-man status. Today's criminal leader can, in this sense, be viewed as a 'big-man' of crime (Goddard, 1992 & 1995).

State Responses to Crime

Public debate on law and order in Papua New Guinea has been a familiar Western one, entailing demands to strengthen the police, increase penalties and provide more secure prisons. Despite the rhetoric, crimi-.

nal justice agencies have not been equipped to meet the challenges of burgeoning crime. Lack of institutional capacity has facilitated the growth of *raskolism*. On the one hand, weak state controls account for the relative ease with which criminals have been able to evade apprehension, accentuating the already low levels of deterrence attaching to the criminal justice process. In the late 1980s, only five percent of stolen property was recovered, while just seven percent of stolen vehicles and three percent of break-and-enters resulted in arrests (Harris, 1988: 25). A recent estimate claims that the typical probability of being arrested for crimes of larceny remains at just over three percent (Levantis, 1997). On the other hand, the deficiencies of law enforcement provide the pretext for increasing reliance on militarised responses to crime. These strategies, in turn, have had distinctly counter-productive outcomes in practice.

Reflecting its colonial origins as a force concerned primarily with extending government control rather than the control of crime, police performance has been consistently poor in the prevention and investigation of crime. Police coverage at Independence extended to only 19 percent of the total land area and 40 percent of the population (Dorney, 1990: 296). A modest increase in the size of the force since has failed to match the demands of a growing population and escalating lawlessness. Many rural areas have little, if any, permanent police presence. Police vehicles are often immobilised temporarily owing to lack of funds for fuel or maintenance. Related difficulties affect other parts of the criminal justice system. Prisons are notorious for their inability to provide secure custody. Mass escapes occur regularly, generating local outbreaks of crime.

Emergency measures have become normalised as routine responses to crime. States of emergency, curfews, and special police operations have been used to restore order in high-crime areas. They involve restrictions on movement, police raids, and orchestrated displays of militaristic strength that belie the actual capacity of the security forces to contain disorder on a significant scale.

While militaristic policing helps restore confidence among some groups, it undermines it for others. Police raids often end up as indiscriminate 'fishing expeditions'; property that cannot be accounted for by receipts is confiscated or stolen. Such strategies are deliberately punitive and aimed at coercing acquiescence on the part of targeted communities. They inevitably lead to a further deterioration in relations between these communities and the police. An obvious irony is that the post-colonial state is drawing on old colonial strategies of pacification as the foundation for its modern crime control tactics.

Militaristic strategies reinforce the integration between criminals and their residential communities by compounding their shared sense of grievance. Allegations of human rights abuses invariably follow such operations, as do civil actions against the state for monetary compensation. While providing short-term relief, curfews are expensive and have had no lasting impact. Once lifted, crime rates begin to rise again. Curfews lose their deterrent effects if used too frequently. Wanted criminals are likely to move to areas not covered by the restrictions, thereby contributing to the further dispersal of criminal networks.

Violent encounters between police and suspects constitute an important aspect of *raskol* induction. Stories about state violence allow criminals to build their reputations among peers, as well as eliciting sympathy from the wider community. Incarceration is another source of prestige and standing in the *raskol* world. Bomana, the large prison outside Port Moresby, is referred to colloquially as 'the college', a place where inmates graduate with enhanced criminal skills and contacts.

Aspects of the aggressive masculinity of *raskolism* are present in police culture. Adversarial relations with 'suspects' and the ethos of the tough cop are widely emulated. Senior officers regularly issue (illegal) orders to 'shoot-and-kill'. Cultural stereotypes are used to legitimate coercion against particular groups. In the Highlands, militaristic policing is justified by reference to the 'fact' that Highlanders respect demonstrations of superior strength. Violence employed against criminals attracts an uncritical, often celebratory, domestic press. The underlying message is that might is right and that violence constitutes a legitimate solution to problems. An already high tolerance of violence is further entrenched. In practice it becomes increasingly difficult to distinguish between the violence of criminals and police, as each side is drawn further into a spiral of retributive violence.

Towards Restorative Solutions

As violent crime has grown, politicians have demanded more and better-equipped police, more prisons and harsher penalties. In recent years there has been a growing chorus of voices calling for qualitative criminal justice reform. This has often included a call to mobilise informal controls existing at community levels. Such an approach was advocated by some observers at Independence:

The family structure, the older web of obligations, the status within a tribal group, and the expectations of neighbours or friends may have to be used in new ways to ensure the effectiveness of social if not legal control far beyond the standards possible in the so-called advanced countries. Ridicule, shame, ostracism and sanctions still often available to the developing countries remain powerful in shaping conduct (Clifford, 1976: 82).

An important impetus to criminal justice reform in PNG in recent years has been the need to develop more socially appropriate responses to crime. Many citizens have felt increasingly perplexed and dissatisfied with the workings of the formal system. Growing interest in community structures in Western crime prevention debates has struck a chord in Papua New Guinea. An obvious source of appeal lies in the relative strength of local organisations in PNG, as well as the rich traditions of self-regulation.

The task of reform along these lines is extremely challenging. Local structures have inevitably been touched by the larger transformations of recent PNG history. The ideas and practices of Christianity, Western education, urbanisation, and global culture have all affected traditional authority. Even were it possible to turn back the clock, not all 'traditional' values and practices are consistent with the laws of the modern nation-state. The status of women, to take one example, remains a critical area of tension between 'traditional' and 'modern' spheres. Violence, as noted earlier, was an important and legitimate strategy of conflict resolution in Melanesian societies. It was integral to the cycles of war and peace that characterised relations between different societies. An uncritical attachment to 'traditional' or 'community' values can inadvertently promote the continuation of older forms of injustice.

The performance of the Village Courts, the most consciously adapted institution in the modern judicial system, provides insight into both the potential and limitations of community revivalism in PNG. Legislation providing for the establishment of Village Courts to settle minor disputes in accordance with local customs was enacted in 1974. They have since become the busiest and most numerous of PNG's courts, operating in both rural and urban settings. An important part of their rationale is to provide an accessible forum for dealing with minor disputes and infractions, one that is responsive to the particular needs and expectations of local communities. In some places they appear to work extremely well (Goddard, 2000). This is particularly the case in many coastal, island and urban communities. In other places, however, notably parts of the Highlands, there have been many complaints. These relate in particular to the role of the Village Courts in reinforcing the subordination of women and children (Garap, 2000). In such places, Village Courts have been susceptible to capture by local big-men in pursuit of their own personal and political agendas, rather like the *kiap* courts of the colonial era. The problem here is that these courts have been too responsive to local power structures. In the process they have often compounded the grievances of subordinate groups. Similar issues have been raised by other restorative initiatives, including community policing and a variety of youth mobilisation programs (Dinnen, 1994). While ostensibly addressing the inadequacies of the Western model, these initiatives generate their own set of problems.

Ironically, some of the most innovative restorative initiatives have come from criminals themselves. These often involve strategies for exiting crime. A key feature has been the manner in which they seek to address issues of social and economic marginalisation underlying contemporary criminality. They also provide important clues as to how PNG's relatively weak civil society can be more effectively mobilised in the management of crime and conflict. In essence, they constitute a set of creolised strategies that engage creatively with a mixture of traditions, old and new, indigenous and foreign. Like *kiap* justice, they often entail extensive negotiation between the different parties to conflict. As such, they resonate with older Melanesian forms of deliberative democracy. While providing insight into the potential direction of restorative reform in PNG, these initiatives also have their shortcomings. Prominent among these is their failure to satisfactorily address the grievances of the victims of crime.

Mass surrenders are the most intriguing example of homegrown restorative strategies. The surrender of self-professed criminals has become a regular occurrence in different parts of the country (Giddings, 1986). Between 1991 and 1994, for example, local newspapers reported 13 surrenders, comprising a total of 913 'criminals' (Dinnen, 1995b). A typical surrender involves a group of young men confessing publicly to past crimes, explaining their reasons for engaging in criminal activities, expressing contrition, and seeking assistance for their chosen reform strategy. Individuals are likely to express a variety of reasons for leaving crime. These might include: a desire to break out of the cycle of violence; becoming a 'born again' Christian; acquiring family responsibilities; and aspirations to engage in legitimate economic activity.

Surrenders often follow protracted negotiations between criminal leaders and brokers from civil society, often a pastor, a church or community group. They sometimes occur in the course of evangelical crusades. Their form reflects the significant role of Christianity in Papua New Guinea. The term 'rehabilitation' has become a euphemism for spiritual rebirth. Conversion to Christianity is advocated as an individual solution to crime. For convicted criminals, professions of born-again faith often precede re-entry into the law-abiding world. Mass baptisms sometimes occur at the larger surrenders, adding to the poignancy and symbolism of the occasion. The language and ritual of being 'saved', 'forgiven' and 'born again' express the symbolic passage from criminality to reform, as well as appealing to older traditions of reconciliation.

Surrender ceremonies are public occasions, usually occurring in town. Members of the surrendering group will give speeches, outlining their criminal pasts, reasons for abandoning crime, and aspirations for a non-criminal future. Weapons and other implements of crime are formally handed over. This symbolises the abandonment of crime and also implies reciprocal obligations on the part of those accepting the surrender. As such, it evokes older exchange traditions. The surrendering group expects some return for their actions, perhaps clemency in the case of minor offences, as well as material assistance for selected reform strategies. Surrenders are, thus, conditional. The self-professed criminals use their criminality as a means of negotiating their exit from crime and its wider context of marginalisation. Behind the commitment to reform lies the veiled threat of returning to crime if the reform conditions are not met. These conditions typically include access to micro-credit facilities, small development projects, employment openings, education and training opportunities.

Churches have also taken a lead in facilitating so-called gang retreats, where criminal leaders meet with prominent business, community and political leaders and engage in frank discussions about the genesis of 'law and order' problems. In 1985, 75 self-professed gang members attended a five-day retreat at Goldie River Army Barracks outside of Port Moresby. Discussions were held with a number of national leaders, including the Governor-General, the Deputy Prime Minister, several Cabinet ministers, as well as with business and community leaders. Gang leaders proposed a moratorium on crime in return for economic and educational concessions to a variety of 'youth groups'. Another retreat was held in 1991. Several hundred 'criminals' met with the Prime Minister and other Cabinet colleagues. Once again, lengthy negotiations took place and gang leaders sought to extract material concessions in return for abandoning crime.

The success of these strategies depends on the support forthcoming in the period after the surrender or retreat. Many fail through lack of adequate material or technical support and follow-up. Financial assistance often comes in the form of one-off payments. If funds are wasted on ostentatious consumption, beneficiaries are likely to drift back to crime after the money has been exhausted. Some cases will succeed, however, as former criminals take advantage of the new opportunities presented.

Prospects for Restorative Justice

The failings of the Western criminal justice model in Papua New Guinea are usually addressed in institutional terms. Thus, the problems of policing are attributed to factors such as lack of resources, inadequate training, indiscipline and so on. The solution therefore lies in building up the institutional capacity of the police and other criminal justice agencies. While capacity building is an important part of any solution, it is important to recognise the limitations of Western criminal justice approaches to PNG's problems of order. These problems have profound social and economic dimensions that are simply not amenable to 'law and order' solutions, whatever their practical or ideological thrust. Rising levels of criminal violence have occurred against a background of rapid and bewildering change. Violence in Melanesia is also to be understood

against a much longer history (and pre-history) of violence as a legitimate strategy of self-regulation under certain circumstances. There are
real difficulties in viewing restorative and retributive justice as mutually
exclusive practices (Daly & Immarigeon, 1998). This is particularly so in
Melanesia, given the entangled character of their relations in pre-
colonial and colonial social ordering.

These difficulties do not detract from the potential or desirability of
exploring restorative solutions in contemporary Papua New Guinea. The
need for substantive reform is largely a consequence of the patent failure
of current crime control practices. Surrenders and retreats provide
important clues on how to nurture civil society in this divided nation in
pursuit of more socially attuned responses to conflict. They encourage a
participatory process between criminals, state officials and brokers from
civil society. The process of deliberative democracy inherent in these
strategies provides an important way of building civil society. A strong civil
society will, in turn, provide an important restraint on state actions in this
area. Deliberative and participatory processes are firmly embedded in
Melanesian social traditions. The impersonal and exclusionary character
of Western criminal justice practice is one of its most baffling and unsat-
isfactory aspects for many Papua New Guineans. Whereas litigants could
engage actively in numerous ways with the old *kiap* courts, negotiation
with today's magistrates and judges is confined to the lawyers. This
appears to work out well for the small elite who can afford to pay for the
services of private lawyers. For the vast majority, however, it is further evidence of the injustices perpetrated by the modern justice system.

While surrenders and gang retreats have the potential for addressing
some of the issues of marginalisation underlying much *raskol* crime, in
practice they afford little for the many victims of *raskolism.* Restorative
approaches in PNG need to address this vital and neglected area. This is
particularly so in the case of women victims given the emphatic masculinity of *raskol* violence. One possibility might be to link surrenders and
retreats. Part of a surrender agreement could be a retreat in which
women from the relevant communities would assess how well the agreement had been honoured from their perspective. Although rarely
acknowledged as such, women have always been important peacemakers
in Melanesia. Their energy and talents in this respect are very much in
evidence in the current Bougainville peace process. Moving towards a
more restorative system of justice means drawing on this abundant reser-
voir of skills.

Like its counterparts in other parts of the world, criminal justice in
PNG is in crisis. The acuteness of that crisis is apparent in the high levels
of fear and personal insecurity. Talk of the collapse of law and order is
ubiquitous and has become a recurring theme in overseas depictions of

modern PNG, with disastrous effects on tourism and foreign investment. Instead of resorting to more of the same, ultimately counter-productive, solutions, the time is right for fundamental criminal justice reform. The most promising prospect for sustainable reform lies in drawing from the best of Indigenous and foreign experience and deploying this in creative ways. Surrenders and gang retreats, among others, provide an idea of how such reform might look in practice.

Notes

1   The physical and cultural bounds of Melanesia are often taken to extend from the western end of Irian Jaya (West Papua) through to Fiji in the east, including the islands of the Bismarck Archipelago, the Solomon Islands, Vanuatu and New Caledonia.
2   For example, the Moka ceremonial exchanges in the Western Highlands and the Te exchanges in Enga. See: Strathern, 1971; Meggitt, 1977.

CHAPTER 8

Restorative Justice in Everyday Life

Ted Wachtel and Paul McCold

In most of the essays in this volume, restorative justice is conceived as an innovative way of dealing with crime, delinquency or bullying. This essay expands the relevance of restorative justice practices – such as conferencing and circles – beyond their limited use in criminal justice systems. Used widely, restorative practices can significantly contribute to the grander project of enhancing the civility of society. By involving all of those affected by a specific offence, conferences and circles enhance democratic processes by moving responsibility for decision-making away from judges and lawyers and giving it to those citizens with a direct interest at stake (McCold, 2000). But the potential of restorative practices goes beyond resolving specific incidents of wrong-doing to providing a general social mechanism for the reinforcement of standards of appropriate behaviour. Restorative practices demonstrate mutual accountability – the collective responsibility of citizens to care about and take care of one another (Pranis, 1998).

The state, under the guise of caring for its citizens, steals their conflicts and hands them over to courts. In doing so, government deprives its citizens of direct participation in the resolution of those conflicts, thereby undermining society's capacity for civility (Christie, 1977). People need involvement, both on a practical and emotional level, so that the harm done by the offence is fully addressed (Crawford et al, 1990). Christie (1977) explains that a state monopoly on resolving conflict represents a loss for both the victim and for society – a lost opportunity to deal with the anxiety and misconceptions produced by the offence and to repair civility.

If we are serious about conceiving of taking responsibility as a democratic virtue, then it will not be enough to cultivate restorative practices in formal criminal justice institutions. Restorative justice concepts '... are directly relevant to the harms suffered in the course of everyday life and routine conflict, and where the event is not classified as a crime' (Peachey, 1992: 552). People also need this kind of involvement in disputes in schools, workplaces and elsewhere in the community. How can society move beyond current formal restorative rituals to incorporate restorative practices into everyday life?

Before demonstrating how attributes and partial elements of formal restorative processes can be used in our daily interactions, it is necessary to review the variety of approaches to the social control of misbehaviour. We suggest that most of modern Western thinking has been largely limited to rationales and justifications of punishment, prohibiting a more realistic consideration of the policy options available.

Beyond the Punitive–Permissive Continuum

Punishment is the prevailing mode of social discipline today, not just in criminal justice but throughout society. Retribution is assumed to be the most appropriate formal or informal response to crime and wrong-doing in communities, schools, families and workplaces (Newman, 1978; Marongiu & Newman, 1987).

Being 'tough on crime' is not a new phenomenon. Bernard (1992) identified a 'harsh–liberal' cycle of juvenile justice policies, which has been repeated three times in the last two hundred years. The liberal reform cycle begins when justice officials and the public are convinced that juvenile crime is exceptionally high, so there are many harsh punishments but few lenient treatments for juvenile offenders. Eventually, forced to choose between harsh punishments and doing nothing, reforms are enacted to provide non-punitive treatment alternatives. After some time, however, justice officials and the public blame these lenient treatments for perceived high crime rates. This leads to a narrowing of lenient treatments and expansion of harsh ones (repressive reform). Then the cycle is set to begin again. Society finds itself trapped on a punitive—permissive continuum (Figure 8.1).

The United States now seems poised for the liberal part of such a cycle, as the public becomes increasingly disillusioned with harsh penalties. In a recent survey of households in eight northeastern states, 75 percent of the public agreed that the entire criminal justice system should be completely changed (Schulman et al, 1999). If Bernard is correct, we

punitive   permissive

Figure 8.1 Punitive–Permissive Continuum

will soon begin a new round of liberal rehabilitative reforms. Is there an enlightened public policy alternative that can prevent history from repeating itself in endless repetition of reform and counter reform in our approach to social discipline?

Reconsidering Social Discipline Policy

We can construct a more useful view of the social discipline choices by looking at the interplay of two more comprehensive continua – control and support. Control is defined as the act of exercising restraint or directing influence over others (Black, 1990: 329). Clear limit-setting and diligent enforcement of behavioural standards characterise high social control. Vague or weak behavioural standards and lax or non-existent efforts to regulate behaviour characterise low social control. Support is defined as the provision of services intended to nurture the individual (Black, 1990: 1070). Active provision of services and assistance and concern for individual well-being characterise high support. Lack of encouragement and minimal provision for physical and emotional needs characterise low support.

For simplicity, we limit these continua to the extremes of 'high' or 'low'. In Figure 8.2, we combine a high or low level of control with a high or low level of support to reveal four general approaches to social discipline and the regulation of behaviour. We call these four approaches or policy models *punitive, permissive, neglectful* and *restorative*.

The punitive approach (upper left of Figure 8.2) is comprised of high degrees of control but little individual support or nurture, while the permissive approach (lower right of Figure 8.2) is comprised of low control and high support, a scarcity of limit-setting and an abundance of nurturing. Thus four policy options become apparent, revealing the punitive–permissive continuum as a false forced choice.

Development of the Social Discipline Window

The origin of this contingency approach to group dynamics began with the research of Kurt Lewin (Lewin et al, 1939; Lewin, 1943, 1948) who defined three basic behaviour patterns distinguished by the degree to which leaders allow subordinates to participate in decision-making: *authoritarian, democratic* and *laissez-faire* (Luthans, 1985: 476).

Stodgill and Coons (1957) and Blake and Mouton (1964) independently isolated two primary dimensions of behaviour related to leadership effectiveness. Respectively, the first dimension was *consideration* (for employee needs) or *employee-centred*. The second dimension was called *initiating structure* (the degree to which the leader defines and organises

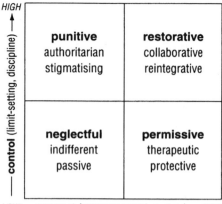

Figure 8.2 Social Discipline Window

tasks for subordinates) and *production-centred* (the degree to which the leader is task-oriented). These two-dimensional approaches led to one of the best-known leadership models, the 'managerial grid', which identifies four styles of management: *authority compliance, country club, impoverished* and *team style.*

Glaser (1969: 289–297) published a similar grid to describe parole officer behaviour. He used the same people-oriented dimensions as Blake, which Glaser called *support* (provision of services to clients) and *control* (concern for public safety through supervision). He identified four behaviours that he labelled *punitive, welfare, passive* and *paternal.* Duffee et al (1978: 396–400) expanded upon Glaser's model to describe general organisational models of correctional policy, re-labelling the two dimensions as *concern for the individual offender* and *concern for public safety.* These authors called the four policy approaches *reform, rehabilitation, restraint* and *reintegration.*

All of these two-dimensional typologies grew out of empirical studies and all have been empirically validated and replicated. However, Glaser's interpretation of the second dimension as control is more useful for the purpose of generalising to the social discipline of misbehaviour. Notice that all of these models agree that the HIGH–HIGH corner of the diagram captures Lewin's dimension of participation. By contrasting control and support, the social discipline window classifies individual, organisational and other approaches to formal and informal social discipline in a broad range of settings. These settings include parenting children, teaching students, supervising employees, regulating corporations and responding to international conflicts (Braithwaite, forthcoming).

The Punitive Approach

The punitive approach (upper left of Figure 8.2), is high on control of behaviour but low on supporting and nurturing the individual – the traditional 'spare the rod, spoil the child' approach to social discipline. Schools, employers and courts in the United States and other countries have increasingly embraced the punitive approach, suspending and expelling more students, reprimanding and dismissing more employees, and imprisoning more citizens than ever before. The theoretical history of the punitive approach dates back to the mid-eighteenth century to Cesare Beccaria and Jeremy Bentham in what is called the classical school of criminology. Bentham saw all behaviour as reducible to the pursuit of pleasure and the avoidance of pain and felt punishment could be used as a deterrent. Both felt that punishment should fit the crime, defined crime in legal terms and emphasised offender free-will. They viewed punishment as a necessary evil to regulate civil society.

Duffee et al (1978: 398) and Glaser (1969) describe this approach in correctional settings as highly moralistic. This approach assumes offenders willingly committed their offences. It treats all offenders alike using 'firm but fair' rhetoric. Convicted offenders are seen to have privileges, not rights, which should be granted to those most compliant. The emphasis is on community safety with a high level of supervision intended to catch violators and enforce rules.

Max Weber (1864–1930) first articulated the classic approach to administration. He assumed that people are basically lazy and untrustworthy. The purpose of discipline in bureaucracies is to maintain order through clear lines of authority and rules, strictly enforced by a system of punishments and rewards (Souryal, 1995: 42). Taylor (1913) advocated designing work 'scientifically' in such a way that the human element had minimum influence on production, and both Weber and Taylor favoured an authoritarian approach to organisational management.

Redeker (1989) describes the modern version of bureaucratic authoritarianism as the 'progressive' model of employee discipline – progressive because it involves a graduated series of punitive responses for minor misbehaviour. For theft, assault, intoxication or criminal offences, summary dismissal without opportunity for redemption is deemed appropriate (Redeker, 1989: 70, fn 5).

Nelsen (1996) refers to this approach to parenting and teaching as strictness, involving excessive control of children. In its extreme form, there is order without freedom, no choices or explanations – 'You do it because I said so.' Punitive parenting is adult-centred, and children are not involved in the decision-making process.

Cameron and Thorsborne (this volume) report that school administrators' approach to staff discipline tends to be no less punitive than the discipline policy used for students. While it is rare for staff to be terminated, they say 'current formal procedures for resolving diminished work-performance issues, and grievance processes, for example, if not wholly punitive, are extremely punishing emotionally, with the system paying the price through absenteeism, sick leave and resignations'.

The Permissive Approach

In many ways the permissive approach is a mirror opposite of the punitive. The positivist school of criminology rejects a legal definition of crime, focuses on the act as a psychological entity, emphasises determinism over free-will, and holds that punishment should be replaced by a scientific treatment of offenders in a way that protects society by curing the cause of the misbehaviour (deviance). The positivist view blames imperfect social systems or individual pathologies (Duffee et al, 1978: 258). In either case positivists tend to excuse the offender from personal responsibility and call for active social programs to prevent and treat crime.

Duffee et al (1978: 398–399) describe this approach as *rehabilitation*, where the source of criminality is assumed to be within the person or their reaction to social influences (Johnstone, 1996). The correctional system is seen as a hospital where therapy is provided for improper socialisation, poor family experiences and other social maladies. The emphasis is on treatment and self-expression with correctional officers acting as therapeutic professionals.

The humanistic or human relations approach to management traces its beginning to Elton Mayo (1880–1949) and the Hawthorne experiments of the 1920s and 1930s, which investigated worker productivity. Mayo concluded that resolving social problems faced by workers increases their productivity and that inspiration and motivation are basic needs of workers. Herzberg's (1968) research found dissatisfaction related to unfavourable working conditions such as strict policies, low pay, inferior status and inflexible supervision. Satisfaction related to motivators that include individual achievement, recognition, responsibility, growth and work itself. Likert (1961, 1967) argued that no organisation can maximise its production potential without concern for employee motivation.

McGregor (1960) also studied worker productivity and postulated Theory X and Theory Y as opposites on a continuum. Theory X is the classical perception of humans, implying that management must constantly control, punish and manipulate the worker. Theory Y envisioned workers as willing to work and failing to be productive only when management

failed to provide the proper motivators. Factors found to produce satisfaction in workers were the work itself, a friendly atmosphere, personal
recognition and acknowledgement of achievement, professional growth,
work challenge, accomplishments, responsibility and discretion. Thus,
from a human relations perspective the essential task of management is
to arrange conditions and operations optimally for the people who work
for them.

Blake and McCanse (1991: 29) refer to this style of management as
country club management – high concern for people and low concern for
production. Thoughtful attention to the needs of people leads to a
friendly organisational atmosphere and a comfortable work tempo.

Nelsen (1996) describes this approach to parenting and student discipline as no limits – freedom without order, unlimited choices, a 'you can
do anything you want' approach. Parenting is child-centred and misbehaviour is excused or not believed. ... There are no rules: 'I am sure we
will love each other and be happy, and you will be able to choose your own
rules later.'

The Neglectful Approach

An absence of both limit-setting and nurturing is neglectful (lower left of
Figure 8.2). One can hardly talk about a body of literature advocating
neglect as an intentional policy approach to social discipline, although
there are a few such theories (e.g., Schur, 1973). However, we know that
growing up is the single most effective cure for crime and misbehaviour.
Left alone, the vast majority of misbehaving children eventually become
productive members of society (Hirschi & Gottfredson, 1983).

Gabor's (1994) review of a wide range of self-report surveys of average
citizens from the United States, Canada, England and Sweden all consistently showed that most, if not all, people break the law at one time or
another. Cohort studies also consistently report that between one-third
and one-half of all males will be arrested at least once during their life-
times (p 56). Gabor concluded that criminal behaviour is widespread in
society and not limited to 'deviants'; yet, only three to four percent of
crimes in Canada and well under one percent of crimes in urban areas of
the US lead to the punishment of the offender (p 287). In this sense,
'doing nothing' is the most common response to crime in society.

Relying solely on government to respond to criminal behaviour, without individuals or communities themselves taking any responsibility, is in
itself neglectful. It is made doubly so 'by the community in leaving crime
matters entirely in the hands of statutory agencies, and by the latter in
considering that when a culprit has been adjudicated guilty and allotted
a punishment that is the end of their responsibility' (Marshall, 1992: 25).

The Restorative Approach

The fourth possibility is restorative (upper right of Figure 8.2), the approach to social discipline and control of behaviour that is the focus of this volume. In this chapter we define restorative justice as a process where those primarily affected by an incident of wrong-doing come together to share their feelings, describe how they were affected and develop a plan to repair the harm done or prevent a recurrence (see Braithwaite & Strang, this volume; see also McCold, 1996, 2000). The essence of the restorative approach is a collaborative problem-solving response to misbehaviour. Restorative approaches simultaneously exercise high control and high support, confronting and disapproving of wrong-doing while supporting and acknowledging the intrinsic worth of the wrongdoer.

In a community or family group conference, those who admit what they have done are usually diverted from formal processing. The offender meets with the victim(s) of their actions and the families and friends of both victim and offender, and all are encouraged to tell how they were affected by the behaviour. Nathanson describes the affects or emotional dynamics of a conference:

> The initial response of the perpetrator is often indifferent and unconcerned. Yet as the conference runs on and both family groups begin to speak about their estrangement from the perpetrator, that individual comes swiftly to learn that the love of the community is a deeply missed and quite important part of his or her world. With such recognition comes an avalanche of shame, after which the individual is likely to express remorse, accept the forgiveness of all concerned, and sign a document pledging to work in some way to repair or undo the damage produced by the antisocial act. (1998: 85)

Braithwaite (1989) called this process reintegrative shaming, where disapproval is expressed within a context of care and concern. As an approach to crime, Braithwaite likened it to the family model of discipline, where disapproval and control of behaviour are possible while maintaining bonds of respect.

Charles (1985) summarised developments in educational discipline across seven recent models (Kounin, Neo-Skinnerian, Ginott, Glasser, Dreikurs, Jones, Cantner). All seven models include restorative themes: all students seek belongingness and success; misbehaviour is a choice which has consequences; the teacher best achieves discipline by modelling good behaviour and demonstrating persistence, consistency, follow-up and genuine caring; the response to misbehaviour should redirect the student and encourage self-control; effective school discipline requires collaboration from the whole school community including students and parents (Charles, 1985: 205–207).

The restorative approach to parenting and classroom control has been called positive discipline (Nelsen, 1996). 'You can choose within limits that show respect for all' (pp 7–8). Nelsen suggests that adults and children decide on rules for their mutual benefit, choosing solutions to problems that are helpful to all concerned.

Effectiveness of the Approaches

Meta-analyses of the research are unanimous in their findings. McLaren (1992) concluded that interventions that expose offenders to harsh or rigorous regimes rarely result in reduced reoffending. MacKenzie (1998) concluded from the research that deterrence programs that increase the punitive impact of the sentence, such as Scared Straight – where young people are taken to prisons where inmates tell them of the horrors of prison life – or shock probation, do not reduce crime and have been associated with increases in the later criminal activities of participants. Snyder and Patterson (1987) concluded that delinquents who engaged in overt aggressive behaviour came from families that were more punitive. Braithwaite (1989) argued convincingly that stigmatising misbehaviour through punitive responses can produce deviant subcultures and organised efforts to circumvent official controls.

Reviews are also consistent in findings about permissive approaches. Gendreau and Ross (1983) found that unsuccessful delinquency programs included the use of counselling procedures which depended primarily on open communication 'friendship' models, were non-directional or involved self-help groups in which the offenders themselves were in charge of the program. Also, programs based on a 'medical model' disease conception of anti-social behaviour have not been fruitful. McLaren (1992) concluded that interventions based on a 'medical model' are even less likely to be effective than punitive, deterrence-based approaches. Gottfredson (1998) concluded that for juvenile justice and non-juvenile justice interventions alike counselling interventions are among the least effective for reducing delinquency. MacKenzie (1998) concluded that meta-analyses of rehabilitation continually show these programs are not effective in preventing crime. Baumrind (1971, 1978) concluded that the loving laissez-faire style of child-rearing is very ineffective, while Snyder and Patterson (1987) found that delinquents who demonstrated covert anti-social behaviour (e.g., lying, stealing) had families characterised by lax and permissive discipline.

Very little research has been conducted on the effects of neglect as a deliberate strategy. Most young people will mature out of criminal behaviours as they assimilate into adult society, with the attendant responsibilities for work and family. West and Farrington's (1977) Cambridge

longitudinal study of delinquency found boys who were equally delinquent but escaped apprehension had better long-term outcomes than
boys who were caught. Box's (1981) review of research on the effects of
labelling found a majority of the studies supporting the conclusion that
punishment can lead to deviance amplification among those punished
(also see Braithwaite, 1989).

We have known since Kurt Lewin first told us in 1939, that the
amount of participation that the 'changee' feels is the most important
factor in behaviour change. Collaboration works better than other
approaches to achieve the goals of organisations (Likert, 1961; Stodgill,
1974; Bowers & Seashore, 1966; Blake & Mouton 1964; Glaser, 1969).
Both Baumrind (1978) and Braithwaite (1989) interpret the empirical
research on the effectiveness of child-rearing as showing that authoritative or reintegrative parenting, setting limits with love, is the most effective. Gendreau and Ross (1983) found that successful criminal justice
programs had characteristics that distinguish them from their less successful counterparts, including client participation in resolving personal or social difficulties and interpersonal relationships between
client and staff marked by empathy and trust. McLaren (1992) identifies
a small number of effective programs that had distinct characteristics:
relations between staff and offenders characterised by empathy, trust
and open communication; offenders trained in practical, personal and
social problem-solving skills; and offenders involved in planning interventions. Sherman (1998b) claims that while there may be disagreement over the exact causes of crime, there is widespread agreement
about a basic conclusion – strong parental attachments to consistently
disciplined children in watchful and supportive communities are the
best 'vaccine' against street crime and violence.

The authoritarian–punitive approach to social control and discipline
of behaviour appears always to lead to backlash, at least in its most
extreme forms. Totalitarian regimes create their own pressure for popular rebellion. Harsh and stigmatising punishments eventually produce
resentment and a desire for revenge and can lead to organised groups
actively working to circumvent authority. Without concern for the emotional and physical conditions of those subject to control, it is question-
able whether even a moderate level of punishment can produce more
compliance than deviance amplification (Wilkins, 1966).

If we have been waiting for the research to prove restorative practices
work, we need wait no longer. Collaborative, problem-solving approaches
have a history of success in families, communities, organisations and international relations. The social science research is overwhelming, consistent and clear. In the vast majority of situations, restorative practices work
better than punishment or treatment approaches.

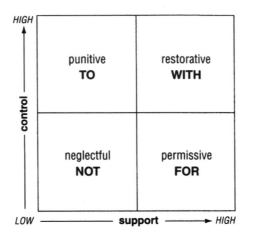

Figure 8.3 Simplified Social Discipline Window

Summary of the Models

The Community Service Foundation (CSF) is a non-profit, non-governmental organisation that works with troubled youth in southeastern Pennsylvania. Staff at CSF's six alternative schools and 12 group homes have been using restorative practices since 1977 (Wachtel, 1998). At a management retreat supervisors identified four key words as a shorthand method to help CSF staff distinguish the four approaches contained in the social discipline window: NOT, FOR, TO and WITH (Figure 8.3).

If staff were to be neglectful towards youth in the agency's programs, they would NOT do anything in response to inappropriate behaviour. If permissive, staff would do everything FOR the youth and ask little in return, making excuses for behaviour. If punitive, staff would respond by doing things TO the youth, scolding and handing out punishments. Responding in a restorative manner requires that staff work WITH the young people in their care and engage them directly in the process of holding them accountable. A critical element of this restorative approach is that, whenever possible, WITH also includes victims, family, friends and community – those who have been affected by the offender's behaviour.

We see this as fundamental democratic practice. NOT is the world of passive citizenship, of alienation. TO is the world of tyranny. FOR is the world of paternalism. WITH is the practice that nurtures democratic citizenship. Becoming a democratic citizen who is actively responsible is not something that just happens (Barber, 1992). Democratic citizenship is something we learn WITH others. Sadly most social discipline is in the worlds of TO, NOT and FOR.

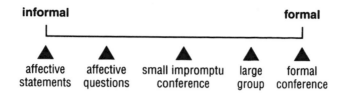

Figure 8.4 Restorative Practices Continuum

The Restorative Practices Continuum

Although the restorative approach to social discipline expands available options beyond the traditional punitive–permissive continuum, the implementation of restorative justice to date has been narrowly restricted. The concept of restorative justice is usually confined to a few programs like community service projects designed to reintegrate offenders and formal rituals such as victim–offender mediation, sentencing circles and family group conferences or community conferences.

The term 'restorative practice' includes any response to wrong-doing that falls within the parameters defined by our social discipline window as both supportive and limit-setting. By way of illustration, examples from CSF schools and group homes have been placed along a 'restorative practices continuum' (Figure 8.4). Moving from left to right, the restorative interventions become increasingly formal, involve more people, more planning, more time, are more complete in dealing with the offence, more structured and, due to all of those factors, may have more impact on the offender.

The most informal is a simple affective statement in which the wronged person lets the offender know how he or she feels about the incident. A staff member might say, 'Jason, you really hurt my feelings when you act like that. And it surprises me, because I don't think you want to hurt anyone on purpose.' If a similar behaviour happens again, the staff member might repeat the response or try an affective question, perhaps asking, 'How do you think Mark felt when you did that?' and patiently wait for an answer.

In the middle of the continuum is the small impromptu conference. Brenda Morrison in her work in Canberra schools (see Morrison, this volume) refers to this as 'corridor conferencing'. Our residential program director was awaiting a court hearing about placing a 14-year-old boy in a CSF group home. The boy's grandmother told the director how on Christmas Eve, several days before, her grandson had gone over to a cousin's house without permission and without letting her know. He did not come back until the next morning, just barely in time for them to catch a bus to her sister's house for Christmas dinner. The program director got the grandmother talking about how that incident had affected her and how worried she was about her grandson. The boy was surprised by how deeply his behaviour had affected his grandmother. He readily apologised.

Close to the far right of the continuum is a larger, more formal group process, still short of the formal conference. Two boys got into a fist-fight, an unusual event at CSF's schools. After the fight was stopped, their parents were called to come and pick them up. If the boys wanted to return to the school, each boy had to phone and ask for an opportunity to convince the staff and his fellow students that he should be allowed back. Both boys called and came to school. One refused to take responsibility and had a defiant attitude. He was not re-admitted by the group. The other was humble, even tearful. He listened attentively while staff and students told him how he had affected them, willingly took responsibility for his behaviour, and got a lot of compliments about how he handled the meeting. He was re-admitted and no further action was taken. The other boy was put in the juvenile detention centre by his probation officer. Ideally, he would be a candidate for a formal family group conference.

Informal restorative interventions often simply involve asking offenders questions from the scripted formal conference. 'What happened?' 'What were you thinking about at the time?' 'Who do you think has been affected?' 'How have they been affected?' Whenever possible, we provide those who have been affected with an opportunity to express their feelings to the offenders. The cumulative result of all of this affective exchange in a school is far more productive than lecturing, scolding, threatening or handing out detentions, suspensions and expulsions (see also Morrison, Cameron & Thorsborne, this volume). Interestingly, CSF's staff rarely hold formal conferences. They have found that the more they rely on informal restorative practices in everyday life, the less they need formal restorative rituals.

Restorative Contagion

Restorative justice is a philosophy, not a model, and ought to guide the way people act in all of their dealings in everyday life (see Braithwaite & Strang, this volume). In that spirit CSF uses restorative practices in dealing with its own staff issues and strives for an atmosphere in which staff can comfortably express concerns and criticisms directly to supervisors and to each other. Several CSF employees became engaged in a squabble that was disrupting the workplace. A conference was convened with no clearly identified wrongdoer. The participants were asked to take as much responsibility as possible for their part in the problem and were assured that everyone else was being asked to do the same. Not only did a great deal of healing take place during the conference, but several individuals made plans to get together one-to-one to further resolve their differences. The conflict is now ancient history and no longer a factor in the workplace.

Restorative practices are contagious, spreading from workplace to home. A CSF employee described how she, her husband and her younger son restoratively confronted her young adult son, who had just entered the world of work. The parents expressed their embarrassment that their son had been late to work at a company where they knew a lot of his co-workers. They insisted that they were stepping back from the situation. If their son lost his job, it was not their problem, but his. As a result of the informal family group conference, the young man now sets three alarm clocks and gets to work on time.

A police officer who was trained in conferencing shared how he confronted his little boy, who had torn off a piece of new wallpaper, with questions from the conference. The youngster became very remorseful and acknowledged that he had hurt his mother, who loved the new wallpaper, and the workman he had watched put up the new wallpaper. Dad felt satisfied that the intervention was far more effective than an old-fashioned scolding or punishment.

A police officer ran a variation on a family group conference with a dispute between neighbours about a barking dog; another held an impromptu conference on the front porch between a home-owner and an adolescent prankster who stole a lawn ornament. Still another police officer held a conference for the families of two runaways, helping the teenagers' understanding of how hurtful their actions were, although they had not committed a criminal offence that would typically require the officer's involvement. An assistant principal made two teenagers, on the verge of a fight, tell each other how they were feeling and quickly resolved the dispute. A correctional officer addressed an inmate's angry outburst with a conference. A social worker got family members talking to each other in a real way about a teenager's persistent truancy and got the youth to start going to school.

Principles of Practice

The examples in the last section, and others like them, suggest six simple principles of practice:

1. *Foster awareness.* In the most basic intervention one may simply ask a few questions of the wrongdoer which foster awareness of how others have been affected. Or one may express one's own feelings to the offender. In more elaborate interventions one provides an opportunity for others to express their feelings to the offenders.

2. *Avoid scolding or lecturing.* When offenders are exposed to other people's feelings and discover how victims and others have been affected by their behaviour, they feel empathy for others. When scolded or lectured, they react defensively. They see themselves as victims and are distracted from noticing other people's feelings.

3. *Involve offenders actively.* All too often one tries to hold offenders accountable by simply doling out punishment. But in a punitive intervention, offenders are completely passive. They just sit quietly and act like victims. In a restorative intervention, offenders are usually asked to speak. They face and listen to victims and others whom they have affected. They help decide how to repair the harm and must then keep their commitments. Offenders have an active role in a restorative process and are truly held accountable.

4. *Accept ambiguity.* Sometimes, as in a fight between two people, fault is unclear. In those cases one may have to accept ambiguity. Privately, before the conference, one encourages individuals to take as much responsibility as possible for their part in the conflict. Even when offenders do not fully accept responsibility, victims often want to proceed. As long as everyone is fully informed of the ambiguous situation in advance, the decision to proceed with a restorative intervention belongs to the participants.

5. *Separate the deed from the doer.* In an informal intervention, either privately with the offenders or publicly after the victims are feeling some resolution, one may express that he or she assumed that the offenders did not mean to harm anyone or that he or she was surprised that they would do something like that. When appropriate, one may want to cite some of the offender's virtues or accomplishments. The goal is to signal recognition of the offenders' intrinsic worth and disapprove only of their wrong-doing.

6. *See every instance of wrong-doing and conflict as an opportunity for learning.* The teacher in the classroom, the police officer in the community, the probation officer with his caseload, the corrections officer in the prison all have opportunities to model and teach. One can turn negative incidents into constructive events – building empathy and a sense of community that reduce the likelihood of negative incidents in the future.

Conclusion

We know the world will change only very slowly and very imperfectly. We cannot afford to be unrealistic or utopian. We must be flexible and experimental. In implementing restorative practices we must allow ourselves to move beyond the limited framework of the criminal justice system and recognise the wider possibilities.

Most of our current practices are not only ineffective in changing negative behaviour, but they undermine democratic citizenship. They teach punitive or permissive approaches to problem-solving by doing things TO and FOR people, rather than engaging WITH them in a way that asks individuals to take responsibility for their own choices. If systems are not inherently restorative, they cannot hope to effect change through an occasional restorative intervention. Restorative practices must be systemic, not simply situational. You can't just have a few people running conferences and everybody else doing business as usual. You can't be restorative with students but retributive with staff. You can't have restorative police and punitive courts. To reduce the growing negative subcultures inside and outside corporate life, to successfully prevent crime and to accomplish meaningful and lasting change, restorative justice must be perceived as a social movement dedicated to making restorative practices integral to everyday life.

CHAPTER 9

Community Conferencing as a Special Case of Conflict Transformation

John M. McDonald and David B. Moore

This essay is a contribution towards a broader theory of transformative justice and of *conflict transformation*. We present it in a spirit of dialogue with others interested in similar ideas and practices. The essay is based on our experience as principals of Transformative Justice Australia (TJA). In this capacity, we have run training workshops for justice system practitioners in many jurisdictions. We have also applied a theory of conflict transformation in workplaces ranging across mining, manufacturing, health, education, retail, media and many other sites in civil society. As TJA sees it, the process we call conferencing remains the major reactive intervention based on a theory of conflict transformation.

Community Conferencing

Both in its community and workplace variants, conferencing involves a group of people affected by a specific case of conflict. Most or all of them are brought together by a conference facilitator, whose role is to referee the ensuing conference, not to become a player in it. To referee fairly, the facilitator must judge whether participants are playing by the agreed-upon rules.

We believe that the guiding rules or principles of the conferencing process must be fundamentally democratic. That is to say, a conference must satisfy the precepts of participation, deliberation, equity and non-tyranny (Fishkin, 1995). Thus, a facilitator must identify the full list of people affected by the conflict, invite them to attend, and so satisfy the precept of *participation*. (The length and complexity of preparation will depend on the nature of the case and the supporting program.) The precepts of *deliberation* and *equity* are satisfied by having participants speak in an appropriate sequence, prompting them with open questions, and allowing adequate time for them to speak and be heard. Finally, a facilitator may need to use subtle intervention techniques to prevent one or more participants from using their position, personality or political ideology to exercise excessive power over other participants. In this way, the facilitator upholds the precept of *non-tyranny*. In short, the facilitator must ensure that:

- everyone affected should be encouraged to attend;
- everyone in attendance should be given the opportunity to speak and be listened to;
- each issue should be given adequate consideration.

To fulfil these precepts, a conference facilitator:

- identifies sources of conflict in a system of relationships;
- brings the people in that system of relationships together in a circle;
- asks questions of participants in a scripted sequence;
- begins with open questions about incidents and/or issues that contributed to the conflict;
- then asks questions that foster acknowledgement and greater understanding of the present effects of the conflict;
- referees the process as participants experience the transformation of conflict into cooperation;
- assists with the negotiation of an agreement on ways to repair past harms and to minimise future harm.

Early Theory

The origins of the conferencing movement are usually traced to New Zealand and with good reason. The 1989 legislation of an Indigenous process into a national common law justice system was a highly significant event. The next stages in the story have been the interpretation of that event outside New Zealand, and attempts to adopt the conferencing process in the context of broader movements for justice reform (Hudson et al, 1996).

In Australia, the first structured pilot program of conferencing began in 1991 in the rural New South Wales city of Wagga Wagga (McDonald & Moore, 1995). The title of the first major article analysing that program, 'Shame, Forgiveness, and Juvenile Justice' (Moore, 1996a), carried deliberate echoes of John Braithwaite's (1989) influential *Crime, Shame and Reintegration*. This book had been a starting point for theoretical debate about conferencing in the Australian pilot program.

The title of the article also highlighted what we considered to be the key psychological and sociological elements of a juvenile justice system built around conferencing. As we saw it then, shame was the key psychological element. Forgiveness was the crucial sociological element. We now qualify those judgements.

We still feel that the expression of shame occurs at a turning point in the conference. We still feel that the offer of forgiveness can be a very important reaction – or interaction. But we now emphasise that a significant part of the experience of shame seems to be *collective*. We emphasise that, in the emotional dynamic of a conference, individual and collective *emotional transformation* seems more significant than does the experience and expression of any specific emotion. And we describe forgiveness as much a process of *transformation* as of reintegration. These changes may seem subtle, but we consider them to be highly significant criminologically, psychologically, philosophically, and politically.

The political impetus for conferencing programs was clear enough. Critics had identified and denounced various structural problems, various injustices, of the justice system. Collectively, the constructive critiques called for a model that could:

- increase diversion from courts;
- reduce recidivism;
- increase participant satisfaction with the official response to the incident;
- foster collective solutions to harm minimisation; and
- engage the emotions which guide the moral values linked to justice.

A key *political* question in the Wagga program of conferencing was one of strategy. What was an appropriate way to introduce conferencing into the criminal justice system? We distinguished at the time between central and local implementation strategies, between a model of the 'scientifically guided society' and a model of the 'self-guiding society'. In the former model, solutions are imposed by a central technical elite. In the latter, the opinions of experts are consulted and considered, but the aim is to reach mutually satisfactory arrangements through broader political debate (Lindblom, 1990). We favoured something closer to the model of the self-guiding society as a strategy for introducing conferencing into the justice system.

The Wagga program seemed consistent with this model. A rural city police patrol was using a conferencing process within existing administrative guidelines. Hence the formal title of the program: 'effective cautioning using family group conferencing'. The program had the imprimatur of the local (civilian) police consultative committee; it was administered by a community policing unit; it was evaluated from the local university campus. Thus, the program appeared to devolve administrative responsibility for dealing with crime to the lowest appropriate levels.

Within the framework of *criminology*, conferencing seemed to:

- move beyond retributivist and rehabilitationist models;
- offer more than the minimalist search for situational prevention and opportunity reduction; and
- accommodate reintegrative shaming practices without undermining the hard-won safeguards provided by a liberal legal system.

We considered at the time that conferencing was the most prominent practical example of the theory of reintegrative shaming. The practice of reintegrative shaming required more than an explanation within the framework of criminology. It also required justification. This seemed a task better suited to moral psychology and moral philosophy, disciplines more obviously concerned with values such as mutual respect, civility and reciprocity.

It was precisely these psychological and philosophical aspects of our account about which we were least confident at this time. The theory of reintegrative shaming derived from points of agreement in key schools of criminology. The theory made important predictions about what the experience of shame could do. It said less about what shame is. And questions about the nature of shame soon became politically important because of the close connection between the theory of reintegrative shaming and the practice of conferencing. Accordingly, in the Wagga program, a great deal of effort was devoted to seeking an adequate understanding specifically of the emotion of shame.

The Emotion of Shame and the Sequence of Community Conferences

The literature on emotions considers shame – together with pride – to be a key 'emotion of self-assessment'. The classical and modern literature on these emotions of self-assessment generally holds that shame and pride:

- are both inward- and outward-looking;
- can be generated by internal and external sources;
- influence behaviour in a way that maintains equilibrium between perceptions of the self and the perceptions of others.

This regulatory function is understood to be evident at both the individual level and at the broader cultural level. There is an historical dimension to this. External sources of shame and pride are said to:

- be learned;
- change over time;
- perform a social regulatory role across a whole culture (Elias, 1978/82).

Clearly, then, the emotions of self-assessment are complex. It seems inadequate to analyse them as purely physiological, purely psychological, or exclusively socio-cultural phenomena. But many studies seem to have over-simplified in just this way. Furthermore, some of the literature on emotions and social regulation adopts the simple dualism of cognition and emotion common to much psychological theory (See Damasio, 1994; Ramachandran & Blakeslee, 1998). Thus, the significance of emotions as regulators of social conduct has been understated. Insufficient attention has been paid to mechanisms for learning, practising and strengthening social or moral responsibility.

There is another dualism in the literature. Some accounts emphasise the internal sources of moral motivation. Other accounts emphasise the external forces for social conformity. Some promising attempts to synthesise these internalist and externalist accounts deal with specific phenomena, such as the act of apology (Tavuchis, 1991). Yet even the more insightful works tend to focus primarily on *what* was happening between parties to an exchange of apology and forgiveness. They focus less on *why* this was happening.

Writers dealing specifically with shame tend to distinguish shame from guilt. Guilt is said to be felt in anonymity; shame requires an audience. Guilt is said to be felt only by the transgressor; shame can only be felt vicariously. Guilt involves a distinction between act and actor; shame does not. And guilt protects the self because it allows a person to distance themselves from their unworthy actions (Taylor, 1985).

But again, the *mechanisms* by which emotions were generated remained unexplained. An exception is the 'microsociology' of Thomas Scheff (1994). This work came closer to explaining the generation of these emotions, and thus to explaining the motivation for people to engage in apologetic exchanges. Scheff and Retzinger's (1991) work on relationships suggested that guilt was a cognitive rationalisation of the basic emotion of shame. Moore (1996a) took this argument a step further, distinguishing guilt as *legal culpability* from guilt as *feeling*. And if these two manifestations of guilt are distinguished, the feeling of guilt can indeed be identified as one manifestation of the basic emotion of shame (see also Hepworth & Turner, 1982: 160–161).

Modern Western legal systems seem to have separated guilt as legal culpability from guilt as feeling. While the state makes technical judgements about culpability, communities make judgements about morality. Institutional separation may have enabled psychological separation. A person's acceptance of technical guilt for their actions might be separated from possible feelings of guilt about their moral status in community. The rationalised legal system may thus make possible 'rationalisation' in the psychological sense of 'self-absolving justification'.

Some classics of developmental psychology contain similar arguments (Miller & Swanson, 1960). Guilt can correlate with:

- inner conflict;
- constricting anxiety; or
- empathy.

This last phenomenon, empathic guilt, can be a healthy phenomenon. It can encourage a person to criticise their own actions in the interest of interpersonal relations. Empathic guilt is very different from guilt that 'rationalises' behaviour to protect the self but thereby makes others even more indignant. And if empathic guilt or shame is consciously acknowledged, indignation can be transformed into something positive. In short, it seems that the expression of shame, followed by the ritual of apology and forgiveness, offers the clearest escape from the anger of collective moral indignation.

The sequence in which conference participants speak is of crucial importance here. The conference sequence is the map that helps guide participants to move beyond anger. (And since the Australian pilot conferencing program was located in the justice system and dealt with incidents of undisputed harm, we used the shorthand labels of victims and offenders when designing this map.) Offenders speak first. Their account is followed by the victim's account. In early 1993, we still thought it appropriate that the offender's supporters should be next to speak. Thus, the sequence in which conference participants were invited to speak was:

(i)   offender(s),
(ii)   victim(s),
(iii) offender's supporters,
(iv)   victim's supporters.

Our reasoning from that time still sounds plausible. We argued that offenders are encouraged by the vicarious shame of supporters to feel and acknowledge shame and then to express remorse. Victims are encouraged by their supporters to regain some sense of self-respect and then to be more readily forgiving. So the logic of the sequence seemed clear. Remorse is followed by forgiveness. So, too, the offender's (remorseful) supporters should speak first. The victim's supporters should follow.

And yet, in practice, this arrangement did not prove as satisfactory as having victims' supporters speak before offenders' supporters. By the middle of 1993, on the basis of observation and intuition, we had switched to the alternative sequence of:

(i)   offender(s),
(ii)   victim(s),
(iii) victim's supporters,
(iv)   offender's supporters.

Collective Vulnerability

An adequate explanation for the greater efficacy of this sequence was first clearly articulated early in 1995, during discussions with colleagues in North America, particularly those affiliated with the Philadelphia-based Tomkins Institute. Yet an adequate personality theory should have alerted us earlier to the reasons why this sequence worked so well. Briefly, these reasons are as follows:

Offenders generally seem to express a sense of shame most strongly when everyone has spoken. This is the moment when the extent of the harm has been most thoroughly communicated. As the primary cause of that harm, offenders are now at their most vulnerable.

Precisely at this moment, a relationship common to all participants comes to the fore. There may be an echo of everyone's original indignation. But there is also a shared sense of relief at having spoken. Above all, there is a sense of what a Canadian colleague has called 'collective vulnerability'. (The physiological manifestation can perhaps be better described as 'deflation'.) At this moment, for the first time, all participants have explained how they have been affected. Collectively, they have 'painted a picture' of what happened, and what has happened since. There is shared reflection on the damage that has been done to relationships. Participants sense that they are a community of people. Every one of them has been affected by conflict in the wake of the incident.

This moment of collective vulnerability comes just before the coordinator moves to the final stage and asks the victim(s) what they would like to see come out of the conference. In short, this is the turning point of the conference. And in retrospect, the 1993 article had spelled out clear reasons why the words of the *offender's* supporters should be echoing at this moment.

An offender feels on the verge of rejection or acceptance at this moment, and most needs support. Supporters of the offender are best placed to provide that support. They are generally closest to the offender. They tend to be most aware of injustices and mitigating circumstances within the private sphere of family and friends. They are best able to strike a balance between the partiality of love and the impartiality of justice.

In contrast, the supporters of the victim tend to display indignation at the offence. Their indignation is strengthened by concern for the victim. But they are not in a position to offer forgiveness. So it is appropriate for them to speak for the first time immediately after the victim has first spoken. It is inappropriate for them to be prompted to speak again until the final stage of the conference.

When they do then speak, supporters tend to demand material reparation on behalf of the victim. They are well placed to make some initial claim for reparation. In contrast to their supporters' claims for *material* reparation, victims themselves tend to place more value on *symbolic* reparation. An apology and other symbolic reparative gestures from the offender are generally seen as the crucial offerings.

All this offers a purely *rational* account of why it might be in the interest of victims to be forgiving. Yet the responses of conference participants consistently appeared to be *intuitive* or *emotional*. People's intuitive responses appeared to work in their own best interests, and also in the interests of the group as a whole. Thus, it seemed that the configuration and format of the conference prompted effective intuition, both individual and collective. The empathy generated by the whole process seemed to benefit all participants. Empathy seemed to lay the basis for the gradual restoration of trust in the affected community.

Indeed, the most striking general impression from watching, audio-recording and analysing dozens of conferences was that the power of each conference derived from the collective emotional transformation of participants. Some of us involved in the operation and/or evaluation of the Wagga conferencing program became sensitised over time to this phenomenon. A clear illustration came from an early publicity exercise.

In 1992, film crews from two of Australia's main commercial television networks filmed drama students from Charles Sturt University role-playing a typical community conference scenario. The students' acting was impressive, and on first viewing the general result seemed highly realistic. Viewed six months later, however, the filmed role plays seemed far less realistic. There was a clear reason for this: the actors' individual emotional expressions were not synchronised. In contrast, the emotional expression of real-life participants seems to become increasingly synchronised in the course of the conference.

The drama students seemed to be working with an overly cognitive theory of psychology as they deduced how their characters ought to feel in light of what they had experienced. But cognitive theories of psychology did not seem to accord with the collective experience of participants in real conferences. In conferences of various sizes, dealing with a range of offences, and with participants from a host of different cultural and ethnic backgrounds, very similar patterns had been observed. So what was clearly needed was a model of emotionality that explained:

- emotional 'contagion';
- the consistency of emotional sequence in each conference;
- the power of feelings to influence thinking;
- the apparent universality of basic emotional experience and expression.

The model of personality offered by Silvan Tomkins and other theorists of personality subsequently helped to answer many of our questions

(Moore, 1996b, 1996c; Nathanson, 1992; Demos, 1994). (Conversations in 1995 with Lauren Abramson, of Johns Hopkins University, helped us better to articulate this emerging model of connected emotional transformation.) The model identifies the underlying emotional dynamic of the generic conference. Four general stages of emotionality can be identified:

- a stage marked by contempt, anger and fear, directed at *individuals*, as a result of their actions in the past;
- a stage marked by disgust, distress and surprise, evoked by *present* revelations about those *actions*, and associated *thoughts* and *emotions*;
- a *transitional* stage of shame, experienced individually as deflation, and collectively as vulnerability, once the group has a fuller picture of how they have all been affected;
- a stage marked by interest and then by relief, as *plans* for the *future* are developed.

The collective sense of vulnerability, the collective experience of shame or deflation, marks the transition from the negative second stage to the positive fourth stage. Importantly, this transitional collective experience of shame is not simply negative.

The affect auxiliary of shame is essentially a brake on the positive affects of interest and enjoyment (or relief). Thus, there is a neutral aspect to this collective experience: shame is an absence of the positive, rather than something negative in its own right. And there is even a positive aspect to the experience. The collective experience and expression of shame is a visceral reminder: participants can experience positive emotions in each other's company. This experience sets the stage for reaching a constructive agreement and then for implementing it.

In other words, the crucial dynamic is not that *one* conference participant expresses shame, and thereby clears the hurdle beyond which reintegration can occur. Rather, the crucial dynamic is that *all participants* experience a sense of shame, and this experience marks the transition from a generally negative emotional climate to a generally positive emotional climate. The collective experience of shame marks the transition from conflict to cooperation.

This psychosocial account of conference dynamics turns out to have political consequences. The origins of the theory of reintegrative shaming are in theoretical criminology. But, through no fault of its author, the language of reintegrative shaming has been open to misinterpretation when theory has been put into practice. Most obviously, the meaning of 'reintegrative shaming' has tended to change as the phrase passes through the interpretative frameworks of legalist and welfarist ideologies. Thus, the phrase reintegrative shaming has come to be (mis)understood as:

- *punishment* imposed on an individual by the *state*, or
- *therapeutic treatment* imposed on an individual by the *state*, or
- punishment or therapy imposed on an individual, by a *collectivity*, on behalf of the state.

Our interpretation differs from all of these. To reiterate: the conferencing process is a means by which a group of people, affected by conflict, may begin to understand themselves as a community with a common concern. (Although all our original applications of conferencing dealt with conflict arising from acts of *undisputed harm*, this proves not to be essential to the definition of the generic process.)

The collective experience of shame marks the transition from a focus on problems in the past and present, to a focus on possibilities in the future. Reaching this point of understanding-that-runs-deeper-than-cognition involves individual and collective emotional transformation. Personal emotional transformation is interwoven with the interpersonal transformation of relationships.

Refining Practice

The implications of this evolving body of theory have since been worked into the practice of TJA. Thus, we have now moved from explaining community conferencing primarily as:

- an example of reintegrative shaming

to understanding conferencing more generally as:

- a mechanism by which the negative emotions associated with conflict can be transformed into the positive emotions associated with cooperation.

This may seem a simple and inconsequential reformulation. It is not. We have found it to have widespread implications and to broaden the applications of conferencing. We have summarised briefly some of the philosophical and psychological reasoning behind the reformulation. The reformulation was also prompted by our gradual recognition that:

- the language of 'victims', 'offenders' and 'bullying' is inadequate or inappropriate in many cases that are otherwise suitable for conferencing;
- situations where all conference participants have known each other for some time tend to be more complex than situations where those who caused harm were not previously known to those they harmed;
- in situations where participants have known each other for some time, conflict often results from the cumulative effect of many minor disputes, rather than from any single incident;

- in situations where participants have known each other for some time, conferencing design principles need to be derived more obviously from politics and systems theory than from criminology and welfare;
- programs using 'family group conferencing' (FGC) in still essentially punitive systems are being distinguished from programs using FGC as an extended version of a welfare case conference. To mark this distinction, the term 'family group decision-making' (FGDM) is emerging for applications of conferencing in welfare systems. Particularly in North America, FGC and FGDM seem to be informed respectively by a (misunderstood) theory of reintegrative shaming and by family systems theory. In short, for want of adequate theory, a traditional distinction between justice- and welfare-oriented programs has reasserted itself;
- conferencing is being compared increasingly with victim–offender mediation, circle sentencing, and other processes with related origins and/or goals and/or a categorisation as 'restorative'.

In light of these developments, we considered more carefully the first principles guiding conferencing practice and developed a broader interdisciplinary theory. A series of analytical distinctions led us to our current formulation of conferencing as a process of *conflict transformation*. The theory centres on a distinction between minimising, maximising and transforming conflict (Moore & McDonald, 2000), and we summarise it in the following way.

Disputes and conflict can be resolved by an *adversarial* process such as in court, or by a *non-adversarial* process. It is less well understood that there are two distinct categories of non-adversarial process. Processes such as mediation are designed to deal with specific disputes. Conferencing is designed to deal with general conflict.

In an adversarial court system, the adjudicator considers arguments from both sides, then imposes a judgement. The dispute is declared resolved. But adversarial dispute resolution has many costs. It is expensive, it is time-consuming, and it has a damaging side-effect: *adversarial dispute resolution tends to maximise the conflict between disputants.*

'Alternative Dispute Resolution' (ADR) emerged in response to these problems. ADR has come to have two distinct meanings. As a general category, ADR refers to non-adversarial processes. But ADR is also applied to a specific non-adversarial process, sometimes called 'interest-based mediation', which seeks to:

- separate the people from the problem;
- focus on interests, not positions;
- invent options for mutual gain;
- insist on the use of objective criteria (Fisher & Ury, 1991).

When disputants *agree to disagree*, a mediator can follow these rules of non-adversarial negotiation to *minimise the conflict* while the disputants search for common ground.

In many cases, however, people will not even agree to disagree. They will simply disagree. Mediation is not the optimal process here. Mediation deals with disputes, but when people cannot agree to disagree, their primary problem is not a dispute; it is conflict. And although disputes and conflict often occur together, they are different phenomena. Disputes tend to be about specific contested facts. Conflict tends to be general and defined by negative feelings. People may experience a dispute without any significant conflict. Indeed, mediation works best in such situations. Conversely, people may experience conflict:

• after some undisputed harm,
• with no specific dispute between individuals, but conflict between groups to which they belong, or
• with many disputes, most of which are merely symptoms of the conflict.

When conflict is associated with no dispute or with many disputes, dispute resolution informed by the principles of successful negotiation cannot readily be used. By definition, people in conflict tend to:

• identify the other people as the problem;
• cling tenaciously to their own positions;
• see no possibility of mutual gain, feeling they can only win if the others lose.

Indeed, if dispute resolution is used with people in conflict, it can actually make matters worse. It can purify the fuel for the fire of conflict. Before people in conflict can negotiate constructively, they require a process to acknowledge and *transform the conflict*. The *workplace conference* process is gaining recognition as an exemplary process for conflict transformation (Moore, 1998a). Workplace conferencing allows participants gradually to shift their focus from the past, to the present, to the future. As they do so, they shift their emotional state from conflict to cooperation. Then they can negotiate.

The Present

There are many civil societal applications of this conferencing process. TJA has worked, and continues to work, with sporting bodies, churches and ethnically based organisations. Our original involvement with the government sector continues through work with education, police, justice agencies and public sector unions. We are helping develop fairer and more effective procedures for dealing with internal disciplinary matters within the Australian Defence Force. Additional military applications in peacemaking and peacekeeping are also being considered.

A novel recent development has been the opportunity to work with the Australian playwright David Williamson. The premiere production of David's play *Face to Face*, which is based on the work of TJA, ran in Sydney for an extended season from March through May 1999 (Williamson, 1999). It received consistently glowing reviews, prompting an Australian national tour during the first half of 2000.

For David, our work in organisations has provided an unusual entree to some dramatic scenes in Australian workplaces. For us, a wide audience for plays in the radical naturalist style may help solve a problem that has limited access of the theory and practice of conflict transformation to workplaces. We call this problem the gatekeeper's paradox. It is the paradox that a workplace conference cannot occur until approved by a key decision-maker or gatekeeper in that workplace. Yet it is difficult for gatekeepers to grasp the potential impact of a workplace conference unless they have observed or participated in a properly facilitated conference ... which they are unlikely to do unless a conference is held in their workplace.

We anticipate that *Face to Face* and other dramatic studies of conflict transformation will provide gatekeepers with an opportunity to observe an ideal–typical workplace conference. They should then be better placed to evaluate the benefits of a transformative approach to conflict in their organisation.

This experience of dramatising ideal–typical conferences in workplace and other community settings has prompted us to reflect on lessons that might be drawn from each stage of practice thus far: about the conferencing process; about conferencing programs; and about pedagogy. How is our own evolving understanding of conflict transformation best passed on?

In retrospect, the strongest part of the Wagga program of conferencing may have been the program itself, rather than the process or our pedagogy. The chosen site was a good-sized city, large enough to contain a broad range of talents, small enough to have extensive but visible community networks. And sufficiently removed from Sydney headquarters that it could flourish independently long enough to become established and publicised.

Ongoing dialogue between police, policy officers, officials from other state government agencies, academics, local government officials and others fostered mutual adjustment of theory and practice. There were, of course, problems with the program. Its early strengths became weaknesses. For instance, it relied on the drive of a few individuals, and so did not achieve sufficient structural support. It would have benefited from more support horizontally – across the patrol, other agencies and community groups. It lacked sufficient support vertically – at the level of district, regional and central command. The role of police officers as facilitators and program coordinators was also criticised. The resulting defensiveness meant that perspectives from other agencies were less readily accommodated.

As it happens, a program that used police officers to facilitate conferences made possible more experimentation with the process than might otherwise have been possible. This experimental approach to procedures was a strong point of the program, though this source of strength later proved a weakness. With one lead facilitator and only a handful of supporting facilitators, it was possible to have in-depth discussions about techniques, procedures and principles. But this also sometimes made it difficult to determine whether the success or failure of some technique or method was due to a facilitator's individual style or because the facilitator was applying some general principles.

Similar strengths and weaknesses subsequently emerged in the pedagogy that emerged from this program. Its strongest point was probably our training manual. The manual articulated principles distilled from careful observations of the process, rather than from some overt ideology, or from procedures developed in some other forum and rigidly adhered to. Furthermore, the manual offered answers to as many of the questions about process and program as we could recall and record.

However, once we had developed a standard set of principles and procedures, we may have become overly prescriptive. This was a problem of both tone and content. We still have a general preference that one person facilitates a conference, not two, and that the same person prepares the conference as facilitates it. We believe we have good reasons for these preferences. However, we no longer discourage people from experimenting with different arrangements. We are less prescriptive about issues such as seating positions, or the degree of preparation and follow-up.

Most problematically – and ironically – our tone in broader conversations about conferencing was inconsistent with the philosophy guiding the process. We too readily took an adversarial, combative or divisive approach to the political strategy of reform. This contrasted with the search for common ground through dialogue. Now, in the spirit of that search for common ground, we conclude this summary of current projects by raising issues with which we are currently grappling. Most notably, we are grappling with issues of coordination, facilitation and education.

Coordination, Facilitation, Education

The issue of coordinating conferencing programs arises from the apparent dangers of relying on a single agency, particularly in state politics.

First, this reliance tends to turn discussion about conferencing into debates about the relative powers of various agencies. It also tends to limit the application of a theory that should have many applications. The Canberra conferencing program offers an interesting case study here. Because of the size and significance of the evaluation (the Reintegrative Shaming Experiments, or RISE), the ongoing dialogue between the police agency and the evaluation team may produce interesting and unexpected results. Developments in Queensland are also of interest. There the Department of School Education was the first agency to establish a coordinated program, and so conferencing is less obviously associated with the justice system (see Cameron & Thorsborne, this volume).

In North America, there is a proliferation of programs with varying degrees of coordination. In Canada, they range from the most remote rural settlements to the most cosmopolitan boroughs of metropolitan Toronto and Vancouver. There is similar diversity in the United States, ranging from Minnesota, which seems to have been the first state to fund a coordinator of restorative justice programs, through Vermont, to Pennsylvania and Maryland. Various models for sponsoring and for evaluating programs have emerged. Our most recent work has been in Baltimore, where support for conferencing has come from the Governor's Office on Crime Control and Prevention, and also from George Soros' Open Society Institute.

Again, these programs all raise questions of coordination. Is some central or regional coordination necessary, and, if so, how can this be achieved without developing cliques, stifling initiative, or freezing people and programs out for political or commercial reasons? In our experience, collection of basic information about numbers and levels of participant satisfaction should be centralised. Information about resources for facilitators and program coordinators might also be centralised, as part of general quality assurance. An alternative or supplement to this option is a rating system, such as is now being developed by various agencies in the United States. Beyond these minimal activities, it is difficult at this stage to say whether centralised coordination is likely to help or hinder the establishment of viable programs offering a transformative approach to conflict.

A related issue with which we are currently grappling concerns facilitation. Most notably, we are wondering whether there is an optimal professional background or set of personal qualities for conference facilitators. We have encouraged maximum diversity of agency and background among participants in our community conferencing facilitators' workshop. And many participants bring a mix of skills appropriate for a conference facilitator.

One contrast we have noticed both in North America and in Australia is between workshop participants who think of themselves as mediators or counsellors, and those who consider that they use processes such as mediation. Is mediation an identity or an activity? This is much the same distinction as between being and doing, between an actor and their actions, that is frequently made in conferences. In our experience, those who describe themselves as mediators, or as counsellors, have found it more difficult to play the role of neutral referee in a conference. Those whose identity is not tied to a single process have generally been more flexible. They have been quicker to adopt the skills required to facilitate a conference.

We have also been grappling with issues of education – in two senses of the word. First, we have sought effective means of education, defined as the dissemination of useful information. We are still struggling to refine the way in which we converse with decision-makers about the transformative approach to conflict and the particular process that we call community conferencing. It seems one needs a kitbag of metaphors and analogies appropriate to each industry and sector to communicate most effectively.

Second, we have been working with the education industry (Moore, 1998b). Of the big bureaucracies, education has generally been quickest to hear the distinctions we draw between restoration and transformation, between disputes and conflicts, between mediation and conferencing. This may be because the more astute decision-makers in education are primed by the tripartite authoritarian–permissive–authoritative distinction from child psychology. They may be open to the critique of the behaviourist–cognitive psychological admixture that guides so much 'school behaviour management'.

When decision-makers have heard these distinctions, and can arrange for frontline support staff (such as social welfare officers) to attend a community conferencing facilitators' workshop, some of those staff do have the inclination, the ability, and somehow also the time, to prepare and facilitate conferences (see Morrison, this volume). A program currently running in New South Wales is illustrative. TJA was asked by the NSW Department of Education to design a training workshop for educators in schools. Our proposal was presented to principals, teachers and administrators in one education district and it was accepted. We subsequently ran workshops in three more districts, followed by supplementary workshops for district education officers from around the state. Taking a structural approach to implementing conferencing in an organisation as large as the New South Wales Department of Education requires constant adaptation to the requirements of that organisation. But it can be done, and done successfully.

The general point here is that governmental reform seems to have been blocked less by any inadequacies in the conference process or by the lack of bureaucratic resources to deliver it. Rather, it seems generally to have been blocked by the difficulty of gatekeepers to acknowledge that there is a different approach to conflict. Without that acknowledgement, co-option of the conferencing process occurs quite naturally – usually without malice or even design.

Thus, there seems to have been a tendency in the mediation and welfare industries to devolve conferencing back into a process of conflict minimisation (avoidance). Conversely, justice system legislators have tended to devolve conferencing back towards conflict maximisation (amplification). Nevertheless, we remain confident that the general principle of the self-guiding society can work as a political strategy for promoting a transformative approach to conflict. The application of this philosophy is, after all, a good part of the reason why conferences are effective; the facilitator only guarantees the process; participants generate the outcome.

Future Projections

We have shown a preference for programs that are self-guiding and self-organising. We have experienced a great deal of chance in reform. So it would be inconsistent for us to make any detailed predictions here. Nevertheless, we have experienced some obvious pitfalls, and are guided by some apparently helpful principles.

The most obvious pitfalls relate to strategies for promoting theories of justice and practices such as conferencing. These are the pitfalls of zealotry and the temptations to seek monopoly. Zealotry occurs when enthusiasm for one's message overrides empathy for the intended recipient(s). In this area of reform, zealotry might best be avoided by aiming for consistency between the philosophy of conferencing and the strategies used to promote conferencing and related processes. Another pitfall seems to us to be any temptation to seek some monopoly on conferencing, either by attempts to license the process commercially or to legislate restrictions on individuals and agencies who can facilitate community or workplace conferences. The reverse of seeking monopoly control over the process or programs is to seek maximum promotion of the fundamentals and then to focus on expanding the number of ways in which those might be applied.

A related principle is that new applications of general principles seem often to develop through symbiosis between two existing products. (A recent industrial example is a seminar combining methodologies for continuous quality improvement with work on transformative approaches to conflict.)

These sorts of symbiotic relationships illustrate a third general principle that currently guides the work of TJA. This is to seek associations of mutual interdependence with other independent contractors and so assiduously to avoid any semblance of the master–servant relationships that prove so debilitating in so many workplaces.

It seems to us that these pitfalls and principles point to a deeper issue concerning the rules that guide commercial and government agencies. This has been an increasingly important issue for those of us in TJA who have moved from government sector employment to self-employment, but work now quite deliberately across the community, government and corporate sectors. A particularly useful guide to navigating this territory has been Jane Jacobs' 1993 *Systems of Survival*.

This unusual work is written as a dialogue on a distinction made by Plato in *The Republic*. Plato warned that mixing different areas of work can be dangerous. Most notably, he warns against mingling between those he calls guardians and those who produce and trade other goods and services. The participants in Jacobs' dialogue revisit this insight with a knowledge of modern sciences. They find a key to understanding contradictions in the moral systems of working life: as a species we live by taking and guarding territory. But we also live by trading.

As Jacobs sees it, systems of taking (and then defending) and systems of trading operate according to two sets of moral rules, which she calls the guardian and the commercial syndromes. (There is a loose correspondence here with the values of government agencies and the values of small- to medium-size commercial organisations.)

The syndromes are internally morally consistent, but are mutually contradictory. So particular care needs to be taken when theories and practices are moved between government, commercial and community sectors. The cautionary note applies to conflict transformation through community and workplace conferencing. In working across these sectors, we must deal continually with the different value systems of guardians and traders. It remains a balancing act.

Citizens of a complex democratic society need not be permanently confined to the caste of guardian or the caste of trader. They should be capable of using both syndromes well, adopting different roles at different times according to the principle of knowledgeable flexibility. But this first requires that we understand the inherent logic of the guardian syndrome and the commercial syndrome, and remain aware that corruption lies in the simultaneous mixing of guardianship and trading.

So, to the extent that we can make predictions or projections about TJA and other organisations working in conflict transformation, we predict that the complicated relationship between the guardian and commercial syndromes will remain a prominent issue. Further experimentation is required to determine the most appropriate and effective mechanisms for promoting conflict transformation within the government sector, the commercial world and civil society. Jacobs suggests that a symbiotic relationship would see the guardian syndrome discourage fraud and unconscionable greed in commerce, while the commercial syndrome encourages the guardian agencies of government to respect private plans, private property, and personal rights. These are admirable goals, and we would be delighted if the work of conflict transformation could assist organisations to achieve them.

As a summary of our current thinking, then: we have suggested that community conferencing in justice systems can be understood as a special case of conflict transformation. Conferencing is appropriate when people are in conflict as a result of an act of undisputed harm that is defined as criminal. Accordingly, we suggest a change in the formula that so influenced our original work in this area.

A reformulation should make both theory and practice more widely applicable. It should give *programs* currently guided by this theory further guidance on *process* dynamics. And it should make justice programs using conferencing more consistent with the republican political theory that informs related work. Thus, we suggest that the phrase *Crime, Shame and Reintegration* might be usefully (re)formulated as: *Conflict, Acknowledgement and Transformation.*

CHAPTER 10

Restorative Justice and the Need for Restorative Environments in Bureaucracies and Corporations

James Ritchie and Terry O'Connell

> What holds civilised societies together is the capacity to
> make a distinction between what belongs, in the way of
> loyalty, to clan or sect or family, and what we owe to
> neighbourliness; what belongs to our individual and
> personal lives and what we owe to *res publica*, or
> commonwealth, the life we share with others.
>
> *(Malouf, 1998)*

Introduction

David Malouf's proposition raises an interesting set of questions of relevance to restorative justice advocates. What do we owe to the life we share with others? More particularly, to what degree are our relational obligations and opportunities reinforced or undermined by bureaucratic and corporate life? To what degree are institutional and bureaucratic arrangements a significant barrier to achieving the optimum in a civil society? As a great deal of the life we share with others involves us in corporate/bureaucratic arrangements either as producers or recipients of goods and services, observing corporate/bureaucratic life through a restorative justice lens might provide an opportunity for restorative justice to make a considerable contribution to civil society through bureaucratic reform.

The reason restorative justice can make a significant contribution to reform effort is that learning acquired through various restorative justice interventions and practices delivers reflective benefits which extend beyond the core actors to touch a much wider community. These broader benefits include increased optimism for peripheral participants, reinforcement of normative behaviour and confirmation that fair process is an attainable ideal. These benefits are real and they build confidence that workplaces can indeed be healthier environments. Such by-products contribute to rejuvenating and revitalising fractured 'communities' in the corporate and bureaucratic worlds as well as in the broader community.

These by-products are a consequence of a shift in emphasis from enforced compliance towards voluntary compliance. Therefore we might begin with our conclusion: voluntary compliance is a cornerstone of restorative justice arrangements (and the central tenet of the democratic state and a civil society) and when voluntary rather than enforced compliance informs corporate and bureaucratic life beneficial outcomes are achieved which could not otherwise be obtained. For these benefits to become widespread, restorative practice has to break out from its past communitarian boundaries to become a mainstream activity.

Mainstreaming Restorative Practices

The writers are interested in a potentially much broader role for restorative justice: a role extending beyond reactive and situational reparative arrangements to embracing a design supported by a coherent management philosophy and effective implementation strategies that is also preventative and strategic.

This presents both a developmental and expansionary dilemma for the restorative justice movement, and near boundless opportunity. The opportunity is the creation of restorative environments within which restorative practice makes sense and becomes commonplace (see Wachtel & McCold, this volume). Clearly, in this wider construction restorative practice requires a restorative environment if it is to be other than a 'boutique' activity confined within the boundaries of communitarian movements and groups.

The dilemma is precisely how such a wider construction is to be achieved. For, in order to become widespread, restorative practices will be channelled through organs of the modern state, through departments and agencies; through departments and agencies whose routine practices are not attuned to restorative values (See Cameron & Thorsborne, this volume). This challenge is all the more important if there is a need to move beyond a view of the retributive and restorative systems as antithetical to one another. Harmony of the degree implicit in such urging can be obtained only if certain environmental pressures are understood and managed for beneficial effect. A very significant factor in understanding such environmental pressures is the degree of 'addictiveness' or receptiveness of any corporation or bureaucracy.

'Addictiveness' in Bureaucratic Systems

From among a plethora of critiques of bureaucratic life we have selected Schaef and Fassell's (1997) emphasis on organisational addictiveness as a framework recognisable to readers working in government instrumentalities, especially police services and large social support agencies dealing with issues such as child mistreatment, domestic violence and youth offending.

Schaef and Fassell's central proposition is that many government departments and private corporations exhibit behaviours corresponding to those of drug-addicted individuals. These individual and collective behaviours include denial, self-centredness, widespread confusion, an overwhelming belief in resource scarcity, demands to control the uncontrollable, the demand for the ideal person to be one who is seen to be 'in control' of his/her emotions, and behaviour conducive to maintaining a closed and non-reflective environment. Schaef and Fassell's helpful framework illustrates the reality that the degree of addictiveness or good health of any operating system has a major influence on the outputs and outcomes that system is capable of delivering. This reality is of critical importance to those restorative justice practitioners who wish to see restorative justice practised beyond 'boutique' community programs. For example, the issue of addictiveness or receptiveness of processing agencies should be of critical importance to the Blair Government's crime reduction program in the United Kingdom, which has expanded restorative justice initiatives as a key component of its platform.

Addictiveness and its Effects

The effects of addictiveness can include individual and bureaucratic isolation, elephantine rates of progress, the illusion of control, unresponsiveness to mandator demand, aridity in individual workplaces and the delivery of less than optimal outcomes for participants and clients alike. A primary effect of addictiveness of relevance to restorative practice is the resort to processes of enforced compliance. Schaef and Fassell note:

> An addictive system is first of all a closed system. It is closed because it presents few options to the individual in terms of roles and behaviours, or even the thinking and perceptions a person can recognise and pursue. Basically, an addictive system calls for addictive behaviours. It invites the person into the processes of addiction and addictive thinking patterns. (1997: 61)

Compliance is routinely obtained through essentially restrictive and narrow instrumentation expressed in rules and requirements. Very limited options, in terms of roles, behaviours and thinking, are a primary output of an addictive system.

These outputs are clearly not desired by modern managers and leaders, but they are a consequence of particular control preferences in corporate and bureaucratic life. Why do processes of enforced compliance prevail over voluntary compliance in the organs of the modern state? Why do we, when constructing or reforming institutions, not begin with an overt attempt to obtain voluntary compliance before proceeding to compliance through enforcement mechanisms? If a central principle of the democratic state is voluntary compliance (expressed in social contract theory for example) then why is so much compliance sought through enforcement? Answers to these questions will present reformers with a better appreciation of the hindrances which need to be overcome if restorative practice is to become widespread. An example might illustrate the point. At its worst, addictiveness in a corporate or bureaucratic system creates an overwhelmingly toxic environment, as New South Wales Police Royal Commissioner James Wood reported:

> At the core of many of the problems that have emerged lies the traditional approach of the Service to its staff ... they have largely been developed in a conditioned, inward-looking environment which has been characterised by command and control, autocracy and suspicion of new ideas. (1997: vol. 11, 207)

Up until the late 1990s the New South Wales Police Service exhibited all Schaef and Fassell's characteristics of addictiveness. A less potent example of the effects of addictiveness, yet one which amply illustrates how addictiveness easily distracts bureaucracies and distorts their performance and deliverables, is provided by our colleague Chief Constable Sir Charles Pollard, from Thames Valley Police (this volume). Advocates of strict enforced compliance processes believe their preference is built upon the need to control for optimum outcomes, but that seems problematic if the following example is a guide :

> ... The Milton Keynes Criminal Justice Audit was an independent research project carried out by Professor Joanna Shapland of Sheffield University in 1994, on behalf of the Milton Keynes Youth Crime Strategy Group. The study investigated the cost of the criminal justice system in Milton Keynes by analysing its constituent elements. ... It found the total annual cost was in the order of 16M pounds. Most of it was spent in 'processing'. ... What was particularly revealing was that just over one percent was spent on actually working with young offenders, and less than one percent was spent on dealing with victims. These findings are conclusions of the recently published Audit Commission national report. ... Misspent Youth: Young People and Crime. (1997: 16)

Addictiveness promotes denial and dissonance around that which is demanded of a modern agency. Recent Australian research which contrasts public and practitioner expectations of the role of police, found.

The public reported that they would prefer the police to place a higher priority on a wide range of tasks, whereas the police reported that they would prefer to place a higher priority on criminal investigation tasks. ... the public prefer the police to be more than a crime fighting body. Overall, the public felt the police should take a more pro-active role. (National Police Research Unit, 1998: 5)

Distortion of the type captured in the examples immediately above occurs because the ideal which drives an institutional body is quite different to that which drives a community. Institutions create their own demands and their responsiveness is intimately connected to the addictiveness they suffer. Critically, the emphasis restorative practice places on the relational/communitarian aspects of the life we share with others is countermanded by the norms of addictive systems in which

Self-centredness is a prominent characteristic of addicts and the addictive system. The self-centredness of the addictive system is not only selfishness, it is also making the self the centre of the universe. Everything that happens is thus perceived as either an assault on or an affirmation of the self. It is 'for' or 'against' the self. (Schaef & Fassell, 1997: 63)

This is at the heart of our dilemma, and our opportunity. In order to become widespread restorative practice must attend to this critical obsession with the self in corporate and bureaucratic life. Responding to addictiveness of such magnitude demands a sophisticated and multidimensional approach. Fortunately, restorative practitioners have a number of advantages that can be employed to good effect in addressing addictiveness, thereby creating more responsive environments.

Restorative Justice, Social Assets and Trends

System addictiveness creates gaps between expectations and deliverables and one consequence is that disillusionment with bureaucracies is rife. Inglehart (1997), using 1981 and 1990 as points of comparison, employed census and research data from 21 OECD nations to determine broad movements in public sentiment. He found a steady decline over the decade in pride in nation, confidence in police services, confidence in armed forces and belief that greater respect for authority would be a good thing. By contrast, he found that interest in political debate, involvement to the point of signing a petition and belief that, generally speaking, people can be trusted, had all risen and enjoyed greater acceptance during the decade. Such research is important for it identifies the shifting values of a civil society and respondents' directional preferences (see Sherman, this volume). In these data, the relational wins out over the institutional.

Promoting Responsiveness

Building a methodology to promote responsiveness will involve at least maximising participation, shifting emphasis from formal to social controls and employing tensions creatively, all of which we now consider in turn.

Maximising Participation

Maximising participation is a sound starting point for it reflects a democratic ideal which cuts across institutional preferences for closed arrangements, central planning, exclusive licence, minimum competitiveness and at its worst excess, monopoly. Kay Pranis, reflecting on her experiences of restorative justice in communities, concludes:

> The experience with both conferencing and circles teaches us that ordinary citizens do not need complex training to be able to sort through information from a variety of perspectives and pick out the most critical issues and craft ingenious solutions. Democracy is undermined by dependence upon professional classes to analyse and solve community problems. Conferencing moves responsibility and authority back to community members, especially the victim and offender and their supporters. (1998: 48)

Employing Pranis' lead, overcoming addictiveness and its effects does not demand superhuman skilfulness, but is reliant, primarily, on effective processes of engagement – processes available to many bureaucratic participants.

Shifting Emphasis from Formal to Social Controls

All human organisation is comprised of two control systems, the formal control system of requirements, commands and instructions and the social control system concerned with treatment, a sense of collective worth, and communal expectations. Formal control system power is evidenced in the practices of differentiation and dominance. The relative importance of both systems is captured in this extract:

> Clearly, little would get done by or in organizations if some control systems were not in place to direct and co-ordinate activities ... but what control system? In designing formal control systems, we typically attempt to measure outcomes or behaviours ... however it is often the case that neither behaviours nor outcomes can be adequately monitored. These are the activities which are non-routine and unpredictable, situations that require initiative, flexibility and innovation. These can be dealt with only by developing social control systems in which common agreements exist among people about what constitutes appropriate attitudes and behaviours ... when we care about those with whom we work and have a common set of expectations we are 'under control'

whenever we are in their presence ... we want to live up to their expectations. In this sense most social control systems can operate more extensively than most formal control systems. With formal control systems people often have a sense of external constraint which is binding and unsatisfying ... with social controls we often feel as though we have great autonomy, even though paradoxically, we are conforming much more. ... (UCLA Management Review, 1989: 18)

Social control system power offers an opportunity to build implementation processes consonant with our alternate philosophy: revolving around ready acceptance of self-generated controls rather than forced compliance. John Braithwaite noted that voluntary compliance with agreements attains higher levels of implementation 'because they are agreements, not [court] orders' (1998a: 6). Further, Zaleznik (1989: 29) notes that social control methodology creates trusting environments which promote voluntary compliance as an organising principle because '... obligations are mutual and therefore one member does not ask for conduct that will create an imbalance'.

A philosophy of learning, support, reflection, repair, reconciliation, reassurance, flexible application, of employing a relational focus to build or rebuild confidence about behavioural norms – these are cornerstones of an effective social control system. It is in employing these devices that the numbers of victims and offenders can be reduced substantially (for bureaucracies produce, as an unintended consequence, victims and offenders aplenty). These processes, employing a different control power, allow movement from despair to hopefulness. Processes of voluntary compliance, based on restorative justice vision, principles and practices can deliver an institutional reform agenda which could reduce costs, improve services, and deliver more agreeable workplaces.

Employing Tensions Creatively

Restorative practitioners look at problems differently from formal control system advocates who seek the minimisation of friction, the promotion of top-down initiatives and compliance through excessive reliance on rule-driven behaviours. We tap into very different impulses – especially responsiveness, inclusion and reflection. We use knowledge in different ways. We identify with Nils Christie's (1977) view of conflict, which is the antithesis of how formal control systems seek to operate:

Highly industrialised societies do not have too much internal conflict, they have too little. We have to organise social systems so that conflicts are nurtured and made visible and also see to it that professionals do not monopolize the handling of them. ... It is an important goal for crime prevention to re-create social conditions which lead to an increase in the number of crimes against other people's honour. (p 4)

Managing crimes and infringements against other people's honour is our still unrecognised strength because restorative justice can 'add value' in ways the formal control system cannot deliver. By employing a restorative justice approach, we are able to move from being reliant on a reactive set of measures towards a comprehensive philosophy of engagement and inclusion that connects individual desire for relationship and fair process to the opportunity to make a genuine difference in our workplaces. This then is a story of restorative justice that has moved beyond interventions designed to repair harm to a philosophical framework which informs processes of practical implementation which can then construct an altogether different reality around relationships in corporate and bureaucratic life. It represents a shift that maintains the capacity for dealing with aberrant behaviour while providing the capacity for constantly reinforcing wholesome normative behaviour.

Our potential will be realised whenever we obtain a proper and effective balance between the formal and social control systems in our diverse operational realms. Crucial to such activity is the construction of a values framework directly linked to how desired outcomes can be achieved. For example, for public confidence in police to be maximised there is need to construct communities of ethical police practitioners, in which officers have made their own values explicit and identified behaviours appropriate to what is clearly the most relational of all occupations. This too is a restorative opportunity because values construction is not a top-down process; values are grown, not imposed. Wherever compliance is presently imposed, there will be found opportunities for restorative justice processes.

Three brief examples can illustrate the potential for significant change, obtainable at little cost, through the deployment of a restorative justice framework to inform and guide sound professional practice. These case studies demonstrate how a healthy and more productive alignment between the relational and institutional paradigms can be achieved using restorative justice processes.

Lessons from an Educational Setting

The first example involves a small inner-city primary school in the Sydney suburb of Lewisham. Classified as a 'disadvantaged school', its children are predominantly from non-English speaking parents (80 percent) with 10 percent from Aboriginal and Pacific Island communities. Police involvement began in 1998 as part of a joint school and community project aimed at creating 'a more exciting, interesting and relevant learning space as well as a safe recreational space for the community'. We were invited to share our experiences of restorative justice processes and how they might assist develop a safer school through the use of a relational focus.

Our involvement at Lewisham included the provision of restorative justice conference training and a series of follow-up workshops. While all the school staff (teachers and administrators) were involved, there was still a significant challenge in having teachers understand the implications of adopting a restorative justice framework (See Cameron & Thorsborne, this volume). For example, it was obvious that most teachers viewed compliance as an important end in itself. In responding to each behavioural 'incident' teachers immediately resorted to a 'quick fix' which did not draw into application their professional training about the provision of the best possible learning and developmental opportunities for students. The demand to respond within a pressured work environment overwhelmed the capacity to respond in the professionally appropriate manner (a common workplace experience). Instead of viewing each incident as a learning opportunity, incidents were viewed as a problem. In contrast, our approach was that recommended by Guy Masters who found a strong feature of discipline in the Japanese school system was acceptance that behavioural issues offer 'a short and finite opportunity for teaching' and that this attitudinal stance was acted upon (1997: 23). At Lewisham, as in many educational settings, there was a disjunction between what is known and what is practised. The values statement was one thing; operationalising it quite another matter (see also Cameron & Thorsborne, Morrison, this volume).

The central issue reduced to this: how could teachers display wholesome behaviours in a way that would breathe life into the existing values statement of 'learn, respect and be safe'? And how would better practice contribute towards enhancing the Lewisham school community? In pursuing these questions there was a need to tease out what meaning various community members would attach to these three principles. What behaviour would provide tangible expression of these values? The starting point could fairly be described as teachers having little consciousness that they themselves needed to 'model' behaviours which reflected their agreed ideals.

Lewisham teachers began 'experimenting' with restorative justice processes during 1998. Teachers designed a check list of key questions to be employed in disciplinary interactions. These questions emphasised relationship and the consequences of inappropriate behaviours. For more serious incidents, which have traditionally resulted in suspension, restorative conferences were used. The results have seen a halving of the suspension rate, and there have been fewer disciplinary incidents requiring a teacher response. In their own estimate teachers have become less confrontational and have adopted common language and practices around behavioural issues. While developments to date have been encouraging we are just beginning an evolutionary process in transforming the way in which teachers, students and parents relate to one another. Our joint next step will be to examine classroom modelling and routinised reflection as necessary elements in learning and development.

The primary lesson from Lewisham to date is how improved relational techniques promote consonance between the stated values of an institution and the actual behaviours of key institutional actors. A decent group of teachers who knew what wholesome behaviour looked like did not recognise that their own behavioural signals often contradicted the values to which they all subscribed. The needed change was accomplished by shifting their operating style from imposed compliance to the promotion of enhanced voluntary compliance processes.

Lessons from Policing

Waratah Local Area Command is a policing jurisdiction in the industrial city of Newcastle, New South Wales. Its Commander was a 34-year-old Police Superintendent John Trott, an officer with negligible police operational experience. The Command was 21 percent under its authorised strength. The Behavioural Change Program, part of the Restorative Justice Group of the NSW Police Service, was invited to assist in the development of a new policing culture in Waratah as a consequence of the Royal Commission into the NSW Police Service. We sought to directly address a classic policing problem reflected in the quotation from Justice James Wood mentioned earlier.

The Royal Commissioner's viewpoint was underlined by the NSW Police Service internal cultural survey (NSW Police Service, 1998) which showed that many police felt the Service was not an open, honest and transparent organisation. Many police did not feel valued or listened to.

Our 'reform' effort moved beyond the superficialities of re-organisation and re-structuring. Guided by our belief that police could not have healthy relationships with the public whom they serve unless they first had healthy relationships with one another we began our intervention in Waratah with an 'establishing standards' seminar. Tapping into professional frustration and aspiration (much of which had been long suppressed by the realities of a highly malevolent operating culture which placed self-protective behaviour well ahead of the demand for service delivery) we focused on police expectations of one another. We knew from police research (Bull et al, 1983) that the primary external influences on police were :

> ... co-workers, supervisors, family and friends. That is the order in which they
> were found to be effective. Co-workers appear to be about twice as influential
> as either of the other two sources. (p 136)

Beginning with relationship questions was not easy. The presenting group of police may have hated their command and control chains, and they may have held deeply felt contempt for their senior officers, but at least they were known quantities. These frustrations, and others, had long been absorbed 'givens' of institutional life, so the prospect of a viable alternate way of proceeding was greeted with great scepticism.

Yet, with persistence, we began to see a significant shift in key group actors (some simply avoided our processes) when expectations of one another were constantly brought to the foreground. Our operating framework was a standard restorative justice process: How did that make you feel? What was the hardest thing for you in that circumstance? We introduced conferencing training. When hardened police began to reflect with comments such as 'I wish I had been taught these techniques before my boys grew up. I would have been a better father', we knew we were making progress.

An early independent assessment (Collins, 1998) was made and provided a highly optimistic review in which members of the management team said the following:

Responses to being asked about changes in the way they related to others:
  'I'm more open, more truthful, more willing to listen, more tolerant';
  'I'm aware now that my view is not the only point that's relevant';
  'I take time to think about things';
  'I'm more concerned with others' welfare';
  'I challenge people to take their issues back to the person they are talking to me about';
  'I don't want them to call me sir.'

Responses to being asked about changes in how others related to them.
  'People are more civil, open minded, more positive. There is an increased sense of belonging';
  'People are more game to speak up';
  'There is more discussion going on and people seem to be more proficient at solving their own problems';
  'I feel less popular now, I'm trying to relate in a new way of doing things and I don't know how effective I am at it.'

Responses to noticed changes in the way they approach their work.
  'I question why I am doing things in a certain way';
  'I understand my role much better and like it';
  'My focus has changed to what will make a difference. ... I'm more strategic now in my thinking';
  'I don't need to see everything anymore, I'm delegating more responsibility';

'I'm interested in feedback';
'I encourage others, try to get the best out of them, let them come up with solutions.'

There was evidence of positive bias in these results so, exercising caution, we decided to test the magnitude of change by running a crime reduction operation with frontline practitioners to test whether our engagement processes could produce operational results. The operation had four significant features worth recording: a primary goal was to promote police legitimacy in the community, operations were arranged so police had to interact with shopkeepers and the public, middle management control was minimised by having teams brief one another rather than operating through coordinators, and choice was introduced where once instructions and rule-driven behaviour predominated. Officer comments included:

'Police are starting to enjoy their work again';
'Members of the public are making complimentary comments';
'Police are already starting to feel a sense of achievement';
'Arrests have been of better quality with arrests of recidivists';
'Intelligence reports have increased';
'Freeing up re-active vehicles';
'Less complaints from car crews about work loads';
'Operation a welcome change from General Duties' work';
'There has been a breakdown of sections and staff are getting on better.'

The Waratah experiment started to attract attention (some of it hostile). Other independent assessors saw very significant improvement. The Audit and Evaluation Services Unit of the Police Service noted that Waratah had satisfied three of the four corporate goals at the highest performance category and the fourth at the intermediate category. A significant increase in intelligence input to twice the surrounding Command averages was noted. This was important not only as a practical policing aid but as an indicator of professional commitment. They also noted that all staff (not only those included in the original assessment above) were 'enthused, even excited' about their work. The Police Internal Affairs Department, responsible for monitoring complaints against police, noted a 57 percent decline in complaints during the period of the Restorative Justice Group and the new Commander's involvement. (The control group – two adjacent Commands with very similar profiles – recorded an increase of 12 percent in complaints and a decrease of four percent in complaints against police in the same 12-month period.) The Minister for Police speaking in the NSW Parliament commented:

Operation Digos, which took place in the Waratah electorate, was an outstanding success. The police involved deserve praise. In July, as a result of

Operation Digos, there was a 16 per cent reduction in property theft. Break and enter offences involving residences fell by 23 per cent and break and enter offences involving business fell 52 per cent. Assaults were reduced by 20 per cent and stealing fell by 20 per cent – an outstanding result. I congratulate the members of the Police Service who are doing such a fine job protecting the community. (NSW Parliamentary Hansard, 1998: 17)

The primary lesson from Waratah is that a focus on the relational delivers tangible improvement of an order that enforced compliance cannot match. An agreed-values framework permitted new learning, adaptation, reflection and improved professional practice. This was not universally welcomed. Resistance, both overt and covert, was real, and we are far from satisfied that we have yet obtained the requisite degree of purchase for sustainable improvement. Crime has started to rise again, as the lessons slip out of the memory bank. We have to revisit so that changed behaviour becomes embedded. Acculturation processes which precipitated the Royal Commission are not altered in the twinkling of an eye.

However, the Waratah experiment has been repeated in another police command in NSW with even more dramatic results. In Shoalhaven Command on the south coast of New South Wales, crime rates dropped more than in Waratah (break, enter and steal reduced by 45 percent) and have been sustained at those lower levels for almost two years. The same improvement in morale is in evidence and complaints against police have reduced 25 percent despite an obviously increased police presence. A third example has emerged in another Command which, within five months of entering the program, reduced its crime levels to the lowest for six years. Again morale was significantly improved.

There might be a temptation to attribute all this to simple sound management. That is true to a degree, but it is sound management shaped by restorative principles. Shoalhaven and Waratah have attracted widespread international interest in the policing world. Clearly, progress to date shows that an improved relational focus employing restorative justice principles has the capacity to deliver tangible improvement and minimise dissonance between the demands of the institutional and relational paradigms. These results are a far cry from the police service Royal Commissioner Justice Wood reported upon in July 1997.

Lessons from a Correctional Setting

Our involvement within NSW Corrective Services began in 1994 and has taken place in two different, yet related ways. First, we have facilitated a number of restorative conferences for serious crime including sexual assault, home invasion, burglary, motor vehicle death, arson and more recently, murder. Secondly, we have provided restorative conference facilitator training to a group of prison officers working in a women's prison.

The initial involvement began when Cathy, a victim of sexual assault, approached us requesting our assistance in meeting her offender, David, who, having admitted to this offence, was sentenced to three years in prison. Cathy was deeply unhappy following the court process. This experience was for her one of total humiliation in which the legal process completely invalidated her experience of the crime and its broader consequences. With the assistance of Corrective Services, a restorative conference was arranged. This forum provided Cathy and her family with the opportunity to be validated, an experience which was not possible within the existing formal institutional arrangements.

The success of this conference was an important catalyst in promoting discussion on restorative justice within Corrective Services. Workshops were arranged for members of the senior executive on restorative justice's relevance in correctional settings. An internal policy document was prepared. Cathy's conference, with its relational focus, had reduced institutional rigidity to the point where senior Corrective Services officials felt confident enough to refer other incidents of serious crime for restorative conferencing.

More recently a high-profile murder case was an important opportunity to demonstrate that restorative justice processes can go some way to meeting the needs of all those directly or indirectly affected by crime. Importantly, the murder conference was filmed and shown on Australian national television. This episode has had a profound effect on participants. A spontaneous reflection after filming saw hardened cameramen, sound technicians, and film editors report on just how great were the impacts following their involvement. These words from a young technician on the project are representative:

> I learnt a great deal over the two days at Long Bay [Prison]. Perhaps the most meaningful lesson amongst all the expectation and raw humanity was just how empathic the documentary maker can and should be. That fine line between illumination and exploitation was never even close to being crossed. ... people felt safe enough to express their grief with dignity. (Personal communication)

Hopefulness, surprise – all the positive effects of conferencing – were on display, as were desolation and anger. The primary consequence of these events has been development within the NSW Department of Corrective Services of a restorative justice unit.

Trust and Balance

These case studies demonstrate that a relational focus which promotes voluntary compliance through increased depth of understanding and improved levels of empathy can deliver systems and practice improvement in bureaucratic bodies. Concentrating on the relational provides a focal point around which process, practice and behaviour might become consonant. Restorative justice processes and sound management principles combined provide a means of establishing trust where confusion or system atrophy has prevailed. Such processes call into being conversations about mutual expectations, which are precursors to performance improvement.

Seeking a balance in bureaucratic life is critical to the issue of sustainability in performance improvement. Reformist literature is full of programs that worked, for a time. Few reformers maintain 'purchase' for a sufficient time and to a sufficient degree to permit programs to reach their potential. Organic processes do not usually survive long in mechanistic structures. The relational is usually pulverised quickly in the institutional rockcrusher.

Yet, these problems can be addressed through well managed and properly implemented restorative justice processes. A strong relational focus draws on hidden capital that abides within each community, as it did in the communities around which the case studies are built. That which people own, they will honour. That which is imposed upon them, they will resist. They resist, not because the institutional objectives being addressed are not worthwhile, and not because specific tasks on which they are engaged are unreasonable in themselves, but because the mode of delivery through the addictive aspects of the formal control system invariably signals that they are not trusted sufficiently with choices, options, interpretive licence and experimentation. In such circumstances institutional life is drained of vitality. Bureaucratic participants are flogged to be creative and responsive within a framework constructed to minimise responsiveness. Furthermore, the pressure which the formal control system promotes is rarely, if ever, matched by support needed to ensure satisfactory learning and the maintenance of focus on outcomes rather than processing of the sort revealed in the Milton Keynes reference above. The absence of support turns multitudes of decent people into victims and their formal control system associates into oppressors. If that observation is generally true why would people not resist, especially insightful and creative people?

Conclusion

Today, how we live, work and relate to one another has developed a debilitating reliance on state intervention to address community problems. It has promoted the dominance of professionals in responding to societal tensions, and has created a bureaucracy for every occasion. Wherever such developments have eroded the capacity for relational processes to liberate individuals from bureaucratic and corporate addictiveness they reduce the worth of civil society. Restorative justice can assist in redressing these distortions, for agreed compliance in a restorative environment offers options for learning, growth and democracy that addictiveness and formal controls cannot provide.

CHAPTER 11

'If your only tool is a hammer, all your problems will look like nails'

Sir Charles Pollard

Caring Communities and Safety

All the old clichés about police officers 'nailing' their suspects are starting to look a little dated. Contrary to popular opinion, the police do not spend all their time 'catching criminals' (Home Office, 1993); rather they spend the bulk of their time dealing with what might be termed social conflict – nuisance and disorder incidents of the sort often laid at the door of juveniles or people on the fringes of mainstream society.

The traditional police way of dealing with those people was to 'nail' them, using the mechanisms of the criminal justice system. This is not surprising: the criminal justice system was, and to many still is, the only formal tool for dealing with social conflict in our communities. Thus all offenders are, at least in principle, treated the same. The problem is that while the criminal law may be the right tool to 'nail' the persistent burglar, it can be too heavy-handed a response to, say, a first time shop-theft offence or incivilities on the street.

The principle that all offenders are treated the same has been eroded in the United Kingdom since the introduction of cautioning in the 1970s, but the fundamental problem remains that when the only *official* tool to hand is the criminal law, police officers are inevitably driven towards its use even when it exacerbates rather than eases community tensions. In other words, over-reliance on traditional theory (the criminal law) and traditional practices (particularly the criminal trial) has conditioned them to deal with incidents of crime and disorder in pre-ordained ways.

One of the main options for the police has always been strict law enforcement. For officers faced with minor disorder and nuisance, the only viable alternative was to exercise their discretion and use negotiation

165

and persuasion to resolve the problem. This highlights a curious paradox: these informal skills are used much more often and usually with greater impact than law enforcement, yet police training has always been about how to access and use the mechanics of the *formal* criminal justice system.

Using these informal mechanisms is not, therefore, without its difficulties. In the United Kingdom, a lack of clarity about police powers together with the lack of suitable defensive equipment (police officers traditionally had only a small, ineffective wooden truncheon with which to protect themselves until the introduction recently of batons and CS spray) may have undermined officers' confidence in their ability to cope. This could mean that they sometimes backed away from minor disturbances. The apparent diffidence of individual officers, and the comparatively small number of officers available for foot patrol, may have added to the feeling among some communities that 'the streets' were no longer so safe.

For the police, the problem of striking the balance between discretion and intervention links into Wilson and Kelling's 'broken windows' theory (see Kelling & Coles, 1996). This highly influential theory maintains that the police can show too much discretion in the face of nuisance and disorder: when that happens and they appear unduly lenient, then the forces of law and order risk being seen as weak and ineffectual by some sections of the public. This is why the fad of 'zero tolerance policing' – a theory discussed across all Western democracies – has recently been in the public spotlight.

Wilson and Kelling are probably right: putting the brakes on incivilities and social nuisance is important to stop communities spiralling into crime and disorder. But they never suggested that this should be achieved by an over-emphasis on scorched earth law enforcement tactics so beloved by tabloid media and opportunistic politicians; instead they recommended a more holistic approach in which sensible law enforcement complements other *community-based*, problem-solving tactics. However, Wilson and Kelling stopped short of proposing alternative tools that police officers could effectively use in dealing with incivilities and social nuisance, and outside the formal criminal justice system.

Wilson and Kelling gave the police their grand strategy; but in the vital matter of tactics, there was still an operational vacuum. Perhaps this is why restorative justice has struck such a chord with police officers, certainly in Thames Valley. Its appeal comes from it offering the police an operational tool-bag that supports their work at the cutting edge of the criminal justice system; that allows individual officers to hone their problem-solving skills; that gives police managers a flexibility they lacked when the tools of the police trade were limited to the 'hammer and nails' of the criminal justice system. Restorative justice provides the sort of rational, problem-solving response to social conflict that is highly resilient to the demands of different policing situations, and promotes more of the human, face-to-face contact with victims and offenders that so many officers intuitively recognise as essential to rebuilding social capital and community confidence.

Restorative justice is not just about new approaches to juvenile justice, although that is of course important: it is also about shifting police culture towards a more problem-oriented, community style of policing; bridging the gap between the criminal justice system and the caring agencies; developing new ways of resolving conflict more amicably and sensitively in civil society in schools and the workplace; and, most importantly of all, providing new processes and mechanisms to help strengthen communities, rebuild emotional and physical landscapes fragmented by crime, and improve the overall quality of life.

Restorative justice also raises searching questions about the traditional criminal justice system – of the exclusionary and adversarial nature of its processes, its lack of accountability, and its failure to deliver any real community in recent times. These are the issues which need to be explored in the coming years and it is on some of these issues that I wish to concentrate in this chapter.

Policing and Problem-Solving in a Civil Society

The Buckinghamshire town of High Wycombe, with a population of 70,000, comes within the policing ambit of Thames Valley. It presents officers with a range of issues typical of modern urban areas, including a large ethnic population. A group of Asian youths had started using a privately owned shopping mall as a meeting place; they behaved uncivilly towards shoppers and were therefore banned from the mall with no right of appeal. This they saw as grossly unfair and their resentment at being excluded spilled onto the streets outside. At this point, the local police inevitably became involved. Then followed a separate incident between the police and one of the youths which escalated into more frequent and ever angrier confrontations.

In the past, this policing problem would have been curtailed, albeit only temporarily, by arresting and prosecuting the youths. We would also most probably have seen heightening tension over the following few weeks, more arrests and more complaints against individual police officers, all of which would have to be investigated. Projected six months forward, and what had started as relatively minor incidents might have snowballed into a serious policing problem and a drain on the resources of not just police, but of the rest of the criminal justice system as well. The attitudes of those involved would have hardened even further into mutual cynicism and suspicion. Race relations in the town would be the poorer, the mall and its hinterland would have acquired a reputation as a 'crime hot spot' and shoppers, fearful of crime, would stay away with consequences for local economic prosperity.

Fortunately, most of that was avoided. What happened instead was that the beat team Inspector with geographical responsibility for the town decided to convene a restorative justice conference of the kind which has been employed by the Thames Valley Police for the past several years. All that was necessary was arranged and on the day some 20 people attended the conference. The aim was to discuss the incidents and the harm they caused, to decide jointly what should be done to repair the harm and to prevent similar incidents in future. Among the participants were most of the youths, local police, security guards, shopping centre management, shop-owners and youth workers.

The conference format was highly successful in opening up channels of communication between everyone there. The retailers voiced their fears that trouble would drive local shoppers away; after listening to them, the youths conceded that they should change some of their behaviour and language. They also agreed that when on the premises they should behave as asked by the security staff; in return, the security staff agreed to make sure the youths were aware of the mall's rules, and to consider an appeals system for use when people were banned from the centre. The police in their turn agreed to look into some of the incidents about which the youths complained, and to visit their Youth Club.

A long-term and obviously deep-rooted issue which welled up time after time during the conference was the Asian youths' belief that the police were racist. The four officers attending the conference strongly disagreed with this, and cited a number of examples where they felt they had policed 'without fear or favour or prejudice' (Association of Chief Police Officers of England and Wales, 1993). Then came the surprise. One of the police officers recognised that the Asian youths' *perception* of police behaviour was not some wild allegation, but was grounded in the belief that the police did not always give them the respect they wanted; this officer also knew that members of ethnic minorities were four times more likely to be stopped and searched by the police than were other members of the community (Home Office, 1998). He told the youths he recognised and acknowledged their point of view. For this honesty and openness to be expressed reflected the civil tone encouraged throughout by the facilitator, the problem-solving ethos of the conference, and the chance it gave for the youths whose conduct was under scrutiny to air what they saw as legitimate grievances.

The conference did not provide an easy solution to the problem, but it did succeed in opening dialogue between the parties, reducing tension between them and prompting the youths to modify their behaviour in public. The local retail community benefited; shoppers no longer felt under siege from anti-social behaviour. Thus the conference made gains on two fronts: not only did it defuse a potentially serious situation, but it also opened the door on new possibilities in relations between the police and an alienated segment of the local community.

How is it then that the Inspector felt able to even consider dealing with the problem in such a radically different way? Part of the answer is that he knew all about conferencing, its utility to police work and its potential for transforming relations not just within communities but between those communities and the police. The fact that this officer in local command was empowered to use conferencing, and that the concept was already acceptable to his staff, points to something of a quiet revolution in police culture: a shift from an adversarial mentality to one of problem-sharing and problem-solving between police and local community. The speed with which restorative conferencing has made inroads into the traditional 'canteen culture' of Thames Valley Police is truly fascinating. The enthusiasm of those who have taken part in a conference fires their colleagues who in turn also want to use it in their daily routine.

Whether restorative conferencing can cut the Gordian knot of crime remains to be seen. I personally believe that restorative justice *will* impact on local rates of crime, disorder and fear – and we in Thames Valley are hoping to reduce crime further than the 25 percent cut already achieved over the last five years (Thames Valley Police, 1998). If that happens, restorative justice will have contributed in no small way. Its potential for dealing with young offenders developing a pattern of offending behaviour is widely recognised; but equally significant in the long run may be that it offers the police a range of problem-solving tools particularly suited to dealing with nuisance and disorder incidents and fixing 'broken windows'.

The Evolution of Restorative Justice in Thames Valley

In 1995, Thames Valley Police in Milton Keynes, a city of 180,000 people, facilitated the formation of a multi-agency Youth Crime group. One of this group's first priorities was to audit the cost of criminal justice in their city. The results were startling. Through an independent study by the University of Sheffield (Shapland et al, 1995) they discovered that less than one percent of the budget was being spent in the community on crime prevention and services to victims and offenders. The rest was spent on bureaucratic inter-agency communications which remained hidden from, and largely irrelevant to, those most personally affected by crime. The audit team concluded that 'much of the effort put into the system is processing with some (absolutely correctly in our view) on due process' and they added, significantly, that 'very little indeed' was spent on preventing crime or service to those most personally affected.

These findings stimulated the development of the Milton Keynes Retail Theft Initiative (RTI) for first and second time shop-theft offenders – a major problem for the communities who depended for their livelihood on the regional shopping centre based in Milton Keynes. The RTI was strongly restorative in tone, with the addition of some intervention options which could be tailored to individual needs. It also retained a punitive element through the official cautioning of the offender. The Home Office evaluation of the scheme found a reoffending rate up to two years later of only three percent compared to a rate of 35 percent for a similar group, with the added bonus of reduced police time spent on paperwork (McCulloch, 1996).

With our Milton Keynes work restricted to shop-theft offenders, we were keen to broaden this approach and in 1996 set up a conferencing pilot scheme at Aylesbury, a town with a population of 60,000. Two years later, we were in a position to start extending our conferencing program forcewide, using a model similar to those of Wagga and Canberra (see McDonald & Moore, this volume). This meant that henceforth conferencing would become a viable option for the two million people living within the Thames Valley Police area. All conferencing is overseen by a headquarters-based team whose role is to set and monitor standards of facilitator selection; provide high-quality training, learning and support; quality assure all processes and data; provide strategic direction to the development of the conferencing program; and liaise at a force level with our partner agencies and voluntary community groups.

In the Thames Valley Police, the generic term 'conferencing' covers three classes of restorative intervention: restorative cautions, restorative conferences and community conferences. When a trained facilitator/officer delivers a police caution to the offender(s) in a restorative manner using selected features of the full conferencing process, the process is known as a restorative caution; family/supporters are present in this case, but not the victim or community representative(s). This shift to emphasising the consequences of crime for the offender's family, social network and wider community, also means the restorative caution will often last for 40–60 minutes, compared to the traditional police caution which was a ten-minute 'telling off'. Whether a community representative is present or not distinguishes the restorative conference from the community conference: in the restorative conference, there is no community representative present; in the full-blown 'community conference', there is.

By October 1999, Thames Valley had conducted over 5000 restorative cautions and restorative and community conferences. Two other police forces in the United Kingdom, Nottinghamshire and Surrey, have joined us in a strategic partnership for the continued development of police conferencing and other forces are also considering joining this consortium. The legislation on youth crime contained in the *Crime and Disorder Act 1998* may prove an additional spur to the adoption of police conferencing across the whole of England and Wales. This may be complemented by similar programs (run by joint-agency Youth Offending Teams) at the higher level of the new-style Youth Courts.

Evaluation of our conferencing program is being undertaken over three years by the Oxford University Centre for Criminological Research, on substantial independent funding provided by the Roundtree Foundation. The early evidence on reoffending rates points to significant reductions when compared to the traditional police caution. Quite apart from the sizeable reductions in reoffending at Milton Keynes, a small study of 175 cases at Aylesbury between January 1996 and March 1997 found that 17 percent had reoffended within a year of the conference/caution, as compared with the figure of around 30 percent attributed by the Audit Commission to 'normal' cautioning practices.

But even if conferencing does not provide dramatic reductions in reoffending, it will still be immensely valuable in view of the other qualitative benefits it brings to the criminal justice process. The chief beneficiaries may be those most affected by the crime – victims, offenders and their families (Sherman et al, 1998; Strang et al, 1999). As well, there is the potential for high impact on the policing of nuisance and disorder, on policing culture and on inter-agency cooperation.

Restorative justice could also bring far-reaching changes to the style and purpose of non-criminal interventions in civil society: to resolving neighbour and community disputes and dealing with school exclusion, bullying and truancy. One reason for this optimism is that the conference forum itself provides a much needed structure in which people can come together and identify a common threshold of standards regulating behaviour in public spaces, just as happened with the youths in the High Wycombe shopping mall. Restorative justice programs could be a starting point for the task of redefining the civic rights and responsibilities of individuals and their communities. From that may emerge a consensus that only where the police and public work *together* will communities start to feel safer from crime, disorder and fear.

Community Safety and the Limitations of the Formal Criminal Justice System

I now turn to the formal criminal justice system. Its failings, at least in Western-style jurisdictions, are well documented as are the differences between the values of formal justice and those of restorative justice. Central to the debate about the failings of the formal justice system is the criminal trial itself. At the beginning of the 1990s, a number of miscarriages of justice, dating mostly from the 1970s, returned to haunt the system in England and Wales. Damaging though these were to public confidence, the greatest harm came from the system's ineffectiveness in the face of the 1980s crime wave. One of the most disturbing findings of successive British Crime Surveys has been the way crime has embedded itself in the social fabric of some neighbourhoods; so much so that by 1991 residents in the highest crime areas in the UK experienced twice as much property crime and four times as much personal crime as people living in areas rated 'next worse' (Hope, 1996).

Seen in this light, the criminal justice system has clearly failed to give a lead in promoting public safety and crime prevention, nor has it responded to the corrosive effects of crime on communities already affected. I argue that this is partly the fault of the adversarial trial system itself, the result of its pivotal role in determining guilt or innocence and disposing of the convicted. Its position at the pinnacle of the criminal processing system gives it a disproportionate influence over the work of the criminal justice agencies. The need to feed this system with suspects (and victims) engenders a 'processing' mentality, where the needs of people – of victims, offenders and their communities – are subordinated to the all consuming demands of an unwieldy and bureaucratic system.

One telling difference between the British situation and that in Continental Europe is that the adversarial nature of the proceedings in Britain and the requirement that the judge play the role of neutral referee absolves many of those involved day-to-day in the higher courts of ownership or accountability for what happens outside the courtroom. However, in France for example, judges are expected as part of their job to focus and develop the work of *all* the statutory agencies: the formal criminal justice system there actively stimulates the search for a viable response to problems likely to have a social as a criminal dimension (Pitts, 1997).

Two issues in particular point up the difference between formal justice and restorative justice: first the adversarial process itself – that part of the trial up until conviction which I shall refer to as 'the game' – and second, that part of the process following conviction or a guilty plea, known as 'the disposal'. I should emphasise that in using these terms, which some might find inappropriate, I am not implying criticism of the many individuals who work conscientiously within our court processes. Any implied criticisms that I make are aimed purely at the system itself, a system which in culture and ethos is diametrically opposed to restorative justice, and particularly at a trial system I believe to be largely responsible for the criminal justice system's failure to develop an effective partnership with communities in tackling crime.

'The Game'

The combative atmosphere of an adversarial trial lends itself to the notion of the trial as a 'game'. The police service in England and Wales – and I myself – have been accused of belittling the trial system by describing it in this way (see Zander, 1994 and Pollard, 1994), but my own experience has been that if you speak with lawyers in the privacy of their own home or chambers, they will as likely as not introduce the sporting analogy themselves. An old man who, in his prime, used to play cricket with W.G. Grace was asked whether the rumours that his hero cheated were true. He replied without so much as a hint of irony: 'Cheat? No sir. Don't you ever believe it – he were too clever for that' (see Pepper, 1985) – and this same ambiguity hangs over the gamesmanship of the criminal trial.

This is not simply something that we should accept because 'it has always been that way', or because it will be difficult to change owing to the vested interests which support it. The point is that many offenders appearing in court see themselves as excluded from mainstream society, without a stake in citizenship (see Pavlich, this volume): they see things in the context of 'us' (they and their like-minded friends) and 'them' (everyone else, particularly those in authority). How they are treated in court – the way in which they are engaged by those present and con- fronted by reality – may be a critical factor in whether their offending behaviour can be stopped or reduced.

When offenders come to court (particularly in the higher courts) we see all the rituals that heighten the trial's sense of drama, the very oppo- site of the dispassionate, rational analysis of the facts which the trial is supposed to engage in. To many, the legal games and culture of the courtroom simply mirror and reinforce their own perception that crime itself is only a game; offenders who do feel remorse have little chance to say sorry or make amends.

Surely if you were designing a criminal justice system from scratch, is not the idea of engaging the conscience of the offender one of the very first principles that you would adopt? Yet that is one of the very things that our Western adversarial trial goes out of its way to eliminate from the start of the process. Contrast that with the ethos of restorative justice, which is about people: how they felt about crime and its effect on their lives; about what happened and why; about putting crime in its social context and then searching for solutions.

The criminal justice system shows the same level of ineptitude in its treatment of victims whose consent legitimises the system and whose co- operation is its lifeblood. It is not just that victims have no formal status in the adversarial trial – an important point regularly made by advocates of restorative justice – but that, as mere givers of evidence, they are frequently subjected to oppressive treatment and questioning by the trial process itself (see Strang, this volume). The effects of this are well documented: one of Britain's leading libel lawyers, George Carman QC, was being unusually revealing when he admitted in a newspaper interview to relishing the 'blood and sand of the arena' (de Bertodano, 1998). The cut and thrust of cross-examination might give the professional lawyer the satisfied glow of a job well done; but for many victims the verbal mauling is as bad as the initial victimisation – and this an ordeal that is legitimised by the state.

'The Disposal'

Another important difference between the formal and restorative systems arises when we examine the processes for dealing with defendants after they have pleaded guilty or been convicted. Once a verdict has been given, the formal criminal trial has no in-built process to test the truth of mitigation, something that stands in stark contrast to the intellectual rigour imposed by the rules of evidence during the trial. As things currently stand, mitigation given in court is not based on sworn evidence and, because there are insufficient checks on the content, there is no redress after the event even if the information is wrong. Much of the information given to the court about the personal circumstances of the defendant, certainly in the United Kingdom, comes from the defendant himself with only limited verification. We have seen in Thames Valley defence counsel put in mitigation that the defendant's girlfriend, sitting forlornly at the back of the court, was expecting a baby and that he would need to be in a position to support her – with the result that the sentence was appropriately light. Police officers have seen this same mitigation given in successive cases by the same offender, yet no baby has ever materialised. In a conference it is less likely that such errors of fact could go uncontested by the police or by some other participant from the family or neighbourhood. Courts may be superior to conferences in fact-finding in some respects, but not in others.

   Such practical examples vividly illustrate the failings of a 'disposal' system lacking precision and basic professionalism. This is a system which may show society's formal disapproval of what the offender has done, and the sentence may serve to provide some protection of the public for the immediate future, but the process actually encourages offenders to think they can shed their *personal* accountability for what they have done. They need say nothing themselves; they have a mouthpiece who will try to minimise their responsibility in a manner often full of exaggeration and untruths; and the system singularly avoids confronting offenders with the impact of their actions on others (Braithwaite, 1989).

Contrast this 'disposal' process to that of the conference, where the offender has had to account personally for what he has done and all parties are encouraged to contribute to the outcome so that it has the ownership of *everyone* affected by the crime. Particularly revealing is the overall comparison between offenders' and victims' perceptions of the court *vis-à-vis* conference, being carried out in Canberra as part of the Reintegrative Shaming Experiments (RISE) (Sherman et al, 1998; Strang et al, 1999). Most measures indicate that both victims and offenders were more satisfied with conferencing, and that despite the fact that the researchers felt the Canberra courts do a good job in treating offenders with respect and courtesy and no doubt epitomise all that is best in the formal justice system.

If the trial resembles a game, then it must be acknowledged that the conference is also a performance of sorts; not one where outcomes are manufactured by rules, bureaucracy and lawyers but rather as the result of spontaneous and involved emotions, actions and reactions. The crucial difference between the adversarial court and the restorative conference is that the structure of the conference allows the participants to see themselves in *social* terms, identifying themselves by their social relationships and the opinions that others have of them. This process makes the law come alive and invokes the bonds that cement individuals into a community.

The historical development of our trial system renders any wholesale change to the rules of the trial *process* unlikely to happen; but there is little reason why the courtroom should also be immune from the cultural values of restorative justice, which could have a profound influence on the atmosphere within which the trial operates. There is no reason why restorative processes should not rapidly be introduced into the 'disposal' end of the trial in the UK, something that is already happening in other Western jurisdictions, for example through sentencing circles in Canada (LaPrairie, 1995a). The challenge for the restorative justice movement is to provide the research and hard evidence that will create this new paradigm for the criminal trial and disposal process – a 'Third Way' for the future, that moves from demanding blind faith from the public to trusting them with a voice in the dialogue of justice; that does not just impose top-down judgements, but mobilises communities to generate solutions tailored to their own needs and circumstances; in short, a system of justice structured to respond to their aspirations for safe and secure communities. If restorative justice can deliver what it promises, it will be the bridge that surmounts the divide between the state criminal justice system and civil society.

Community Safety and Restorative Justice

It is one thing to talk about a 'Third Way', whether for the trial itself or for criminal justice in general, but another to consider how that might be accomplished. David Garland (1996) has described the idea of the sovereign state capable of providing security, law and order and crime control within its territorial boundaries as one of the 'foundational myths' of modern societies. However, this myth of state omnipotence has been steadily eroded since the 1960s, at least in Britain, and today the state, having taken over functions and responsibilities which once belonged to the institutions of civil society, is exposed as unable to deliver the expected levels of crime control.

The state's response has been to activate non-state agencies and organisations through partnership, multi-agency cooperation, and self-help (Crawford, 1997). At its simplest level, this takes the form of a publicity campaign or a Neighbourhood Watch scheme. Initiatives such as this further erode the notion of the state's monopoly as the citizen's protector against crime, and may mark the beginning of an important reconfiguration of the criminal justice system and its relation to the citizen (see Shearing this volume, Bayley this volume).

In England and Wales, another important driver for change has been the 1998 *Crime and Disorder Act*. This legislation moves from a narrow conception of crime prevention based on policing and security to a multi-agency approach of 'community safety'. It dovetails neatly with restorative justice initiatives promoting a problem-solving approach to community safety, and should give a boost to social crime prevention measures which have for too long been neglected in favour of situational prevention. Another ingredient is the newly articulated 'Overarching Aims' of the criminal justice system, namely: *to reduce crime and the fear of crime, and their social and economic costs*; and *to dispense justice fairly and efficiently and to promote confidence in the rule of law.*

In particular, this clarity of purpose about *reducing crime* and preventing offending – as opposed to processing offenders after the event – will have profound consequences for how the agencies relate to local communities. Merely processing crime is an admission of defeat for both agencies and the communities who bear the brunt; but actually reducing crime demands that the agencies work with and among the victims, offenders and communities most personally affected by crime. And the more influence that restorative justice has over police strategy and tactics, then the greater will be its impact on relations between the police and other statutory agencies. We have seen in Thames Valley that once everyone is working towards common goals of social cohesion and reintegration, there is greater agreement as to what constitutes legitimate intervention. It will be seen as politically acceptable for the agencies to pool resources and share information. This can only be to the advantage of the public they serve.

All these changes may turn out to be contributory factors to the growth and expansion of restorative justice. But other factors must also be considered for restorative justice to play the major role it deserves. For this to happen, it is vital that it is 'marketed' effectively, so that the man and woman in the street understand the idea and are comfortable with it. It is that to which I finally turn.

'Marketing' Restorative Justice

What we are in effect proposing with restorative interventions is that communities absorb, own and take responsibility for their own offenders, certainly in the case of minor offenders. The issue then is how best to market this to the public. What happened in Britain shortly after the ending of transportation to Australia sheds some unwelcome light on what could happen: some isolated murders became, in the hands of the press, a crime wave; the public, still getting used to the idea of absorbing what was seen as its own 'moral sewage', proved receptive to the panic generated by the papers and the effect of all this was to blow the Victorian penal reformers off course (Davis, 1970). The lesson for us may be that mobilising communities to get used to the idea of reintegrating offenders, even those who are remorseful and willing to change, will not be so easy, particularly when that public is routinely exposed to ideas of prison (where offenders are 'out of sight, out of mind') or other tough solutions to crime. While prison can remain the ultimate deterrent for the persistent and serious offender, we must point out that the restorative option offers sounder, more practical benefits for victims – as well as consolidating that most nebulous of concepts, a sense of community.

This makes it all the more important that we explain *why* restorative conferencing is such an effective option: to highlight (for example) the large percentage of offenders fulfilling the terms set by restorative conferences; the high levels of victim involvement and participant satisfaction with procedural justice and fairness; and the low cost (Hayes et al, 1998 Fercello & Umbreit, 1998). These need to be explained at both local and national level; otherwise advocates of restorative justice, at least in Britain, could find themselves in the same boat as the judiciary, frequently pilloried in the press for what is seen as an overly liberal sentencing policy when it may actually be more accurate to say the public do not understand, and cannot relate to, the underlying principles of current sentencing practice (Ashworth & Hough, 1996).

As restorative justice grows in influence, it is perhaps inevitable that it will develop its own core of 'professionals', just as the formal justice system has done. In New Zealand, some advocates of restorative justice have already voiced concerns that decision-making at a tactical level has been taken over by 'experts', including lawyers contracted to watch over the rights of young people (New Zealand Ministry of Justice, 1996). Just as the formal criminal justice system has judges and rules providing necessary quality assurance, restorative justice too will need some sort of umbrella offering an oversight process at the highest level.

I have the highest regard for the work of Real Justice (see Wachtel & McCold, this volume), Transformative Justice Australia (see McDonald & Moore, this volume) and other organisations working across national boundaries, but most tend to focus their work at the *tactical* level. Such work is essential, but so too are the development and promotion of restorative justice at the *strategic* level, on the national and international stages. My final thought then concerns the feasibility of an International Institute which could do just that.

Any such organisation would first be expected to promote awareness of restorative justice among the general public, the media and policymakers. Second, it will need to campaign, certainly in Western-style jurisdictions, for changes to the criminal trial that will make it less of a game, by highlighting how and where restorative conferencing could supplement the work of the formal system. Third, any such Institute would need to set standards and monitoring arrangements at a national level in each country, to coordinate the work of statutory agencies and voluntary community groups experimenting with restorative justice, by promoting good practice and weaving their diverse experiences into a coherent strategy.

Conclusion

The police occupy a unique position in Western democracies: they are meant to police with the consent of their communities, while at the same time exercising a monopoly on legitimate force. Janus-like, the police must face in two directions: the friend and potentially the foe of the public. Resolving these competing demands is never going to be easy so the key, indeed a cornerstone of the British approach, has always been to give officers the discretion to intervene where a response is required, but without resorting to force. The shift to a problem-solving style of policing underscores this commitment to operational flexibility, and restorative justice offers tools honed to precisely the sort of offences that are the staple of police work.

But the police also find themselves sharing in the public crisis of confidence currently affecting the whole of the criminal justice system. Fear of crime grows (Hough & Roberts, 1998), while public confidence in the legal system declines (Gallup Report, 1995, see also Sherman, this volume). One of the causes of this may be the sheer distance between the social reality of crime and the criminal courts' response to crime. This has generated a bureaucratic, processing attitude to criminal justice where legal rules and administrative efficiency count for everything and the dignity, confidence and hope of victims, offenders and their communities for very little. There is finally light dawning on the horizon. The new emphasis on partnership and problem-solving has already prompted a great deal of discussion between the agencies and within society at large about how to revitalise civic institutions. What restorative justice can do is to offer a compass that police, statutory agencies and community groups all need before they can realign their response to the *social* causes and consequences of crime.

CHAPTER 12

Restorative Justice and School Discipline: Mutually Exclusive?

Lisa Cameron and Margaret Thorsborne

In April 1994, the first school-based community conference in Queensland, Australia, was conducted at Maroochydore State High School in an attempt to repair the harm of a serious assault after a school dance. The demand for conference facilitator training which emerged as word spread in the education community clearly indicated that this process answered some urgent need within schools for an entirely different approach for dealing with such harmful incidents.

This chapter will outline briefly the results of two separate studies conducted by Education Queensland involving the introduction of restorative justice in the form of community conferencing into schools to deal with incidents of serious harm, as an additional tool in a broad spectrum of strategies which also included suspension and exclusion. Experiences during the two years in which these studies were conducted have highlighted a range of implementation issues which have exposed tensions between existing philosophies and practices in managing behaviour and restorative interventions such as conferencing. The incorporation of the restorative justice approach, while in itself a very useful addition, had limited potential because of these tensions.

The theory, philosophy and practice of conferencing has demonstrated to practitioners the value of and necessity for a restorative philosophy in all aspects of school discipline by: (a) providing opportunities for insight and learning when behaviour is deemed unacceptable; (b) providing opportunities for dialogue and reflection when behaviour threatens the social cohesion of the school community; and (c) identifying issues of harm to relationships and how to 'make things right' through strengthening relationships. Education theory clearly articulates the importance of healthy relationships between all members of the school community to discipline and pedagogy. Restorative justice has much to offer in this respect.

This chapter argues that the language and discourse relating to discipline need to change and begin to embrace a behavioural framework in which wholesome behaviours are actively promoted and that compliance is an outcome of understanding and sense of community, and is not an end in itself. Finally, it explores ways in which a restorative philosophy can be implemented and, perhaps more importantly, sustained in our schools, by shifting mindsets of those delivering our educational services both at policy level and in practice, away from punishment to an approach clearly focused on building and sustaining positive relationships in our school communities.

Community Conferencing in Queensland Schools

The introduction of community conferencing into Queensland schools was the first significant variation in Australia of the police-based justice conferencing program in NSW, which in turn had been adapted from the New Zealand model of family group conferencing. The early history of conferencing in Australia is well documented (Moore, 1995). The search for a non-punitive intervention for serious misconduct in schools had been underway for some time (Hyndman and Thorsborne, 1993, 1994). In particular, the target of such a search was an intervention for serious cases of bullying which did not put the victim at further risk and also involved parents of both the offender and victim. Research had already established (Olweus, 1993; Tattum, 1993) that bullies typically have low levels of empathy, tended to be highly impulsive, and often retaliated if they were punished. It is understandable that conferencing seemed to fit the bill as the ultimate intervention which increased empathy and lowered impulsivity on the part of the bully. The first evaluation study of conferencing in Queensland schools was completed in 1996 and recommendations for expansion of this reform to five other regions were adopted; the second was completed in 1997 (Education Queensland, 1998).

Results of the Queensland Studies

In the course of the two Queensland studies, 119 schools were involved across a range of regions, districts and settings (Department of Education, 1996, Education Queensland, 1998). A total of 379 school and district personnel were trained as conference facilitators, although a significant number of those trained never conducted a conference, nor became 'accredited' according to departmental guidelines. A total of 89 conferences were conducted during the two studies, and schools continue to use conferencing to deal with serious cases of harmful behaviour. The majority of conferences took place in response to assaults and serious victimisation, followed by property damage and theft. Conferences were also used to address incidents involving drugs, damaging the reputation of the school, truanting, verbal abuse, persistent disruption in class, and in one case, a bomb threat.

The first study concluded (Department of Education, 1996):

- participants were highly satisfied with the process and its outcomes, for example:
  - 96 percent of participants agreed they had a chance to have their say;
  - 87 percent reported satisfaction with the way agreements were reached;
  - 95 percent agreed they were treated with respect;
  - 99 percent reported feeling understood by others;
  - 91 percent agreed the terms of the agreement were fair; and
  - 89 percent of victims reported that they got what they needed out of the conference.
- 84 percent compliance with most or all of the terms of the agreement by offenders;
- 83 percent of offenders did not reoffend;
- the majority of offenders reported high levels of reintegration, for example:
  - 98 percent felt cared about during the conference;
  - 95 percent felt that those closest to them loved them afterwards;
  - 80 percent felt they were able to make a fresh start;
  - 70 percent felt forgiven.
- 94 percent of victims felt safer;
- 87 percent of offenders had closer relationships with other conference participants after conferencing;
- 100 percent of school administrators felt that conferencing reinforced school values;
- 94 percent of all family members expressed positive perceptions of the school and comfort in approaching the school on other matters; and
- 92 percent of all schools in the trial reported they had changed their thinking about managing behaviour from a punitive to a more restorative approach.

The second study by the Queensland Education Department in 1997 (Education Queensland, 1998) confirmed that conferencing was a highly effective strategy for dealing with incidents of serious harm in schools. A significant number of incidents (similar to those outlined above) were not conferenced by these same schools, being dealt with by traditional approaches which included suspensions, parent interviews, counselling and detentions. Reasons given by schools for choosing not to conference, in order, were:

- incidents not considered appropriate;
- perception of poor attitude on the part of the offender and/or offender supporters;
- too time-consuming;
- not considered as an option (reasons for this view were not offered); and
- positive outcomes were not guaranteed.

We suspect that the underlying reason for these results was that while schools generally became more positive towards a restorative approach, they still favour a traditional approach for students with a 'bad attitude'.

Restorative Philosophy in the School Setting

The introduction of community conferencing into schools, with the associated training of conference facilitators and awareness-raising exercises, provides schools with an opportunity for reflection on philosophies and practices of behaviour management. It allows school personnel, possibly for the first time, an opportunity to discuss notions of compliance and justice – a broader view of justice than that determined by school communities and codified in behaviour management plans. School behaviour management plans have focused largely on what should happen (penalties and tariffs) to offenders when (school) rules are broken, with only limited understanding of the impact on those in the school community of the offending behaviour. Restorative justice in the school setting views misconduct not as school-rule-breaking, and therefore a violation of the institution, but as a violation against people and relationships in the school and wider school community. Restorative justice means that the harm done to people and relationships needs to be explored and that harm needs to be repaired. Restorative justice provides an opportunity for schools to practise participatory, deliberative democracy in their attempts to problem-solve around those serious incidents of misconduct that they find so challenging. It also provides an opportunity to explore how the life chances of students (both offenders and victims) and their families might be improved, and how the system might be transformed in ways likely to minimise the chance of further harm.

Furlong (1991), in his sociological analysis of disruption and the disaffected student, calls for 'a reconstruction of a sociological perspective on deviance [which] must be at a psychological and particularly at an emotional level' (p 295). In describing his work, Slee (1995) advances a concept of 'hidden injuries' experienced by students:

> As students experience three sets of educational structures – the production of ability; the production of values; and the production of occupational

identity – these 'hidden injuries' are inflicted via pedagogy, curriculum, school culture and practices, and the calibration of students on an occupational scale. (p 114)

By practising a restorative approach to problem-solving, schools are also made accountable for those aspects of structure, policy, organisation, curriculum and pedagogy which have contributed to the harm and injury. Restorative approaches, as such, are generally discouraged by an authoritarian, control-oriented style of school management from the principal to the classroom teacher, and rewarded and modelled by departmental management. On a practical, 'consumer' level, restorative justice processes such as community conferencing generate greater levels of participant satisfaction (procedural, emotional and substantive) including a sense of justice, greater levels of social support for those affected and reduced levels of reoffending, borne out by the evaluations in both studies (Department of Education, 1996; Education Queensland, 1998). While some schools have adopted humane philosophies closely aligned with what we now understand to be a restorative justice philosophy, it would be rare that misconduct is generally viewed from a harm-to-relationships perspective, with decisions about what to do about the incident centring around how to repair the harm. It is more likely that responses to (even low-level) wrong-doing are still driven by a belief that punishment works, and compliance is all about maintenance of control.

In Morrison's analysis (see this volume) of conferencing studies in Queensland and New South Wales schools, she suggests that:

> ... while educators' thinking is not antagonistic towards principles of restorative justice, the practice as a whole is not upheld. A number of tensions remain in the system that draw schools into the maintenance of traditional approaches. Beyond the issue that teachers perceive parents to favour punitive over restorative practice, other issues include lack of a shared rationale for the adoption of a restorative justice approach within the school community, as well as issues of time in systems where professionals are already under stress.

In his extensive study of reintegrative shaming in Japanese elementary and secondary schools Masters (1998) describes the heavy emphasis that schools, in particular teachers, place on the obligations and accountabilities that members of the school community have towards each other. The following summary is adapted from his analysis of how misconduct is dealt with in Japanese schools in a rather restorative way:

- there is a great deal of contact and dialogue with all those affected (including parents) by an incident in the school with emphasis placed on the impact of the behaviour on others.
- when suspensions are invoked as punishment for serious offences, multiple visits by the student's teachers at his/her home seek to re-establish

positive relationships between them, to continue a dialogue which encourages reflection about the offending behaviour and the student's obligations to the school community, and to discover the factors in the life of the student that may be influencing their behaviour.

- there is emphasis on apology and making amends as an important part of the expected response from students in the event of offending behaviour.
- there is a mindset among teachers to 'never give up' on a student, with troublemakers consistently and repeatedly labelled as 'having the potential to achieve anything' and given many chances to learn from their mistakes.

Masters concludes that teachers, with their emphasis on reflection and understanding the consequences of their actions, are doing their best to educate students rather than control them. They believe that punishment makes one think only of oneself rather than the consequences of one's behaviour for another (corresponding with Braithwaite's view (1989) that rapid escalation to punishment makes young people more angry than thoughtful); that if the goal of any intervention is to instil a sense of community and relational thinking, then isolating someone (as in suspension and exclusion) is exactly the worst way to achieve it.

These observations of behaviour management in Japanese schools would appear to support Braithwaite's theory of reintegrative shaming (1989) which suggests that where there is an emphasis on reintegrating offenders back into their communities by attempts to disapprove of their behaviour within a continuum of respect and support, there will be lower rates of reoffending, and in the case of Japan, low rates of delinquency.

According to Masters (1998), it would appear that the Japanese education system, with its emphasis on relationships and sense of community as a reflection of Japanese identity, effectively operates as 'one grand, institutionalised and effective crime prevention project'. The same cannot be said of education systems in the West, although rhetoric abounds in political circles which espouse efforts at crime prevention as needing to involve education.

It is clear that the seeds for criminal behaviour are planted early in the development of young people and that early intervention is critical to reverse this trend. The comprehensive National Crime Prevention (1999) report on early intervention approaches to crime lists a number of factors associated with anti-social and criminal behaviour (p 136). Factors are categorised into groups: child, family factors, school context, life events and community and cultural factors. 'School context' factors list school failure, normative beliefs about aggression, deviant peer group, bullying, peer rejection, poor attachment to school and inadequate behaviour management. In contrast, the report also lists a range of protective factors which mitigate against anti-social and criminal behaviour. The protective 'school context' factors (p. 138) include positive school climate, pro-social peer group, responsibility and required helpfulness, sense of belonging/bonding, opportunities for some success at school and recognition of achievement and school norms re violence.

The lesson for our education system then is to introduce restorative measures as early as preschool, and build on creating a climate where relational values are translated into pro-social behaviour by all members of the school community. The teaching and modelling of emotional intelligence and relationship skills becomes part of the daily business in classrooms. In describing their experience in working with staff at Lewisham, an inner-city primary school in Sydney, Ritchie and O'Connell (this volume) have this to say:

> The primary lesson from Lewisham to date is how improved relational techniques promote consonance between the stated values of an institution and the actual behaviours of key institutional actors. A decent group of teachers who knew what wholesome behaviour looked like did not recognise that their own behavioural signals often contradicted the values to which they all subscribed. The needed change was accomplished by shifting their operating style from imposed compliance to voluntary compliance.

Children *can be* taught to understand what they are feeling and how to deal with difficult situations. Situations and their consequent emotions, which, when unacknowledged, feed the need for interpersonal violence, are dealt with openly. In such a classroom and school culture, the connections between people are valued and nurtured, creating wholesome, healthy individuals and school communities (Thorsborne, 1999).

Other commentators on school effectiveness have made the link between student outcomes and positive school relationships. Rutter et al (1979), Mortimore et al (1988), Pink (1988) and Reynolds and Cuttance (1992) have recognised that relationships between all members of the school community are a critical factor in school effectiveness (as measured by student behaviour and achievement). This appears to support the priority that Japanese schools place on relational thinking which is valued, taught, reflected on and modelled as a way of life.

Sergiovanni (1994) echoes these sentiments in emphasising the importance of shifting the focus from schools as organisations based on contracts and rewards to schools as communities bound by moral commitment, trust and a sense of purpose:

> values, beliefs, norms and other dimensions of community may be more important than the relationships themselves. But it is the web of relationships that stands out and it is through the quality and character of relationships that values, beliefs and norms are felt. (p 18)

In coming to understand why restorative processes such as conferencing produce such positive outcomes, an exploration of such theories as reintegrative shaming (Braithwaite, 1989) and affect theory (Tomkins, 1962, 1963, 1987, 1991 & 1992; Nathanson, 1992 and Kelly, 1996) has revealed a basis for understanding the sociological, psychological and biological bonds which exist between individuals. Furthermore, these authors have revealed what is required for the development and maintenance of healthy relationships.

While it is beyond the scope of this chapter to explore how this happens, perhaps the greatest gift restorative philosophy has given schools is this knowledge. Imagine if teachers and school administrators had a working knowledge of these 'relationship' theories. Imagine if they were able to translate this body of knowledge by modelling and teaching. What impact might this have on school governance, on decisions regarding policy and practice across curriculum, pedagogy, school organisation and behaviour management? One might even dream that this knowledge could be put to good use to uncover and minimise the chance of Furlong's 'hidden injuries'.

It is of little wonder then, that schools which had some vision of a better future and an instinct for the fresh opportunities the restorative philosophy represented, embraced conferencing with such enthusiasm. So, why the tensions? Why have the education bureaucracy and schools been so slow to take up this process when it is clear from the available research that positive relationships are fundamental to the health of the school community?

Exploring the Tensions

Slee (1995) in his wide ranging review of theories, policies and practices of managing behaviour in Australian schools suggests that the abolition of corporal punishment did not lead to a re-evaluation of the nature and exercise of power and authority in schools. Suspensions and exclusions simply became the substitute for the more extreme tool of punishment, the cane, and so began the search for new forms of control in the wake of the cane's demise. Slee explores the subsequent expansion of a 'behaviour industry' – the professionals who became allies in this search for new forms of control and concludes that policy-makers:

> ... who moved beyond traditional technologies of control such as corporal punishment, suspension and exclusion, found allies in the processes of reclassification of students according to pathologies of emotional behavioural disturbance and the mobilisation of counselling and special education support as surveillance and containment instrumentalities. (p 150)

Hence, Slee concludes:

> Policy has predominantly been framed within a control paradigm which lim-
> its the potential for addressing the culture, curriculum, organisation and ped-
> agogies of schooling which contribute to indiscipline. Education authorities'
> concern tends to revolve around questions of after-the-fact responses to dis-
> ruption and is beholden to political dynamics of competing professional cul-
> tures within the education organisation and to electoral politics which shape
> governments and, in turn bureaucratic agendas. (p 167)

This control paradigm has become embedded in Queensland's state
policy on behaviour management, despite its official emphasis on securing a supportive school environment (Queensland Department of Education, 1993). Our efforts to graft restorative practices on to a system
which is basically punitive have proved frustrating, to say the least. But
commendation is due here to those schools which, despite these overwhelming pressures to suspend and exclude difficult students, have
grasped the nettle and recognised the contributions that restorative
practices can make in the pursuit of a supportive school environment.

The apparent slowness of 'approval' of the conference process for
statewide adoption may have been a result of the bottleneck created by
such central 'approving' bodies as the Board of Management which
reviews all major proposals likely to have an impact across the department. Two changes of government occurred in the period spanning the
studies, putting conferencing further down the agenda while other political imperatives in education (such as the Anti-Bullying/Anti-Violence
Initiative and the Child Protection Strategy) took precedence.

To prove the point that this control paradigm is still vigorously pursued, in the period July 1997 to June 1998, the number of School Disciplinary Absences (SDAs) in Queensland government schools reached
25,692 for a student population of just over 300,000 (*Sunday Mail*, 18
October 1998). These included both short suspensions (1–5 days), longer
suspensions (6–20 days), exclusions and enrolment cancellation for students aged over 15. While the reduction in school exclusions by a factor
of five percent became a performance indicator for 1999 set by Education Queensland, schools and districts are yet to be made accountable by
the system for reducing the numbers and length of SDAs. SDAs, as Slee
(1995) suggests, are being used as tools of organisational efficiency, out-
weighing considerations of student learning and social improvement.

The increase in SDAs is a matter of some concern, given the identified
links between school suspension and exclusion and the drift to juvenile
crime, homelessness and long-term dependency on welfare agencies
(Human Rights and Equal Opportunity Commission, 1989). Policy and
practice which focus largely on rules and responses to rule infraction, fail
to take into account those complex factors which impact on the life of a
school student, namely: 'The labour market, familial change, cultural
diversity, gender relations, socio-economic status, changing patterns of

authority and the impact of new technologies on the way students receive and process information' (Slee, 1995: 172). Policy and practice which seek to exclude those very students who are in greatest need of social support and an education simply relocate the problem in time and place and may exacerbate it (McElrea, 1996).

> I am sure there are some schools where these criticisms have little or no application – where the student, the family, the school community and the wider community work together to find a way to solve the problem constructively and not destructively, inclusively and not by making outcasts. But my point is that such happy places are not the product of the [New Zealand] Education Act; they occur in spite of it, haphazardly and only because some individuals resolve to do it differently. (McElrea, 1996: 4)

Elsewhere, McElrea (1998) advocates the use of conferencing as a conflict resolution mechanism in schools, and to reverse the rising incidence of suspensions and expulsions in dealing with serious misbehaviour.

Implementation for Sustainability

Much needs to be taken into account if restorative justice practices such as conferencing are to be implemented successfully and, more importantly, sustained across a school system. The following guidelines are suggestions which are cognisant of some of the factors which have worked against the process of reform in Queensland and those we know already have produced a paradigm shift towards the restorative justice philosophy. Guidelines 1–3 represent the possibility for grassroots reform and will probably require some visionary leadership from a principal or energetic other who has influence in the school community. Guidelines 4–6 represent a greater challenge for reform because they require intellectual and organisational leadership and political will at state level. Our hope is that, over time, a critical mass of knowledge and skills firmly grounded in an understanding of what is required to develop healthy relationships and healthy communities will engender a top-down, bottom-up reform process which will produce the kinds of outcomes that improve the life chances of our young people.

Guidelines

1. Professional development in restorative justice philosophy and practices for all staff including those with a non-teaching role

The responsibility for managing student behaviour is not the sole turf of classroom teachers or administrators. As well, teacher aides, tuckshop convenors, office administrators and janitor-groundsmen all have contact with students, and attempt, whether or not they are aware of it, to influence behaviour. It is critical that all adult members of the school community, including school councils and parent bodies, are introduced to the philosophy and practice of restorative justice with its emphasis on building a sense of community through enhancing and restoring relationships; that they are given a structured opportunity to reflect on current practices, on notions of compliance, of justice, of democratic approaches to problem-solving, and what is important to them in relationships. Staff also need opportunities to broaden their discourse around the nature of disruption and conflict in the school, to be able to take into account those factors which impact on a young person's life and life chances. It is essential that this discourse places issues of behaviour management in an educational context rather than one of behaviourism or welfarism. It is important to share the knowledge and understanding of what does and does not work (Braithwaite, 1989 & 1996; Tomkins, 1962, 1963 & 1987, 1991 & 1992; Nathanson, 1992 & 1996; and Kelly, 1996) in the development and maintenance of healthy relationships. Skill acquisition in a planned program of professional development needs to be supported by adequate allocation of school funds, and a supportive learning environment.

This would form a sound basis for a critical review of policy and practice in the school including classroom management and whole-of-school packages, and offer staff insights into their own behaviour. It has already been established that modelling of appropriate wholesome behaviours and relationship-centred approaches to problem-solving which are not grounded in punishment, are important factors in delivering improved outcomes for students (see O'Connell & Ritchie in this volume).

2. Development and maintenance of a cohort of highly skilled conference facilitators

Schools preparing to adopt conferencing need to make careful decisions about who should be trained. In our experience, staff who have good process skills, who have already demonstrated some experience in problem-solving, and who are party to decisions about how an incident should be dealt with make good candidates. This group includes, in particular, principals, deputy principals, year coordinators, guidance officers, community education counsellors and heads of department. These people, with appropriate high-quality training, are more likely to be able to translate the microskills of conference facilitation to deal with other matters. It is helpful if the entire administration team is trained, and joint decision-making about what should happen in serious cases is encouraged to minimise the chance of knee-jerk, punitive responses.

While a critical mass of facilitators in a cluster or district is still developing, networking becomes an essential process for the sharing of stories, reflection on practice, peer support and supervision. Technical aspects of the conference process, while addressed during training workshops, need constant attention, and could form the basis of ongoing dialogue within these networks. These aspects include:

- how the decision is reached to convene a conference;
- inviting the 'right' combination of people to a conference;
- making sure participants understand the purpose of the conference;
- comprehensive preparation by the facilitator;
- writing the agreement in a way that quantifies and qualifies behaviour change in specific, realistic and measurable ways;
- planning for comprehensive agreement monitoring and follow-up; and
- ensuring conference facilitators can handle the sometimes high levels of emotion which arise in conferences.

Stories can also be shared about the creative ways schools are using the conference microskills and philosophy to resolve both smaller and larger scale situations. Someone with energy and commitment might assemble a collection of these restorative practices which can be published and distributed to schools.

3. Use of restorative processes for dealing with incidents of inappropriate behaviour and high-level conflict for staff

Not surprisingly, the practices for dealing with difficult staff situations are no less punitive than those used for students. While it is rare for staff to be 'suspended' or 'excluded' (except for criminal matters), experience in a wide range of school settings has led to our conclusions that current formal procedures for resolving diminished work-performance issues, and grievance processes, for example, if not wholly punitive, are extremely punishing emotionally, with the system paying the price through absenteeism, sick leave and resignations.

While no research findings are yet available, we believe on the basis of our direct experience of facilitating conferences dealing with a range of extremely challenging staff situations (diminished work performance, harassment, staff assaults on students, difficult workplace behaviours, conflicts around roles and responsibilities), that the practice and philosophy of restorative justice are equally applicable to adults in schools. Indeed, why should it not be so, given the need to 'practise what we preach', and that relationships 'work' in the same way, independent of age?

4. Provision of restorative justice philosophy and practice within pre-service teacher education

Beginning teachers and those in training need to experience the same opportunities for discussion around notions of compliance, justice and democracy. The curriculum of teacher education can focus on the range of factors which influence student outcomes, so that they may develop a broader view of behaviour management. They need to be equipped to analyse the agendas underlying the development of state and school policy and how it impacts on schools, particularly students. They need, at the very beginning of their professional lives (and before they acquire bad habits), to develop an understanding of how important relationships are to pedagogy, and to look for mentors among teaching staff in schools who can model appropriate behaviours and guide them supportively. They should be exposed to restorative practices, and have the acquisition of these skills built into their courses.

5. State policy development

Slee (1995) suggests that the first priority of discipline policy-making should be to focus on the overall goal of providing successful learning programs for all students, and must take into account the articulation between secondary schooling and higher education, training and the labour market. Advantages could be derived from a consideration of issues across teacher–student relationships, school governance and decision-making, uniforms, curriculum matters, treatment of youth concerns and teaching and evaluation methods; in short, curriculum, pedagogy and school organisation.

Slee (1995) also recommends the '... alignment of our conception of discipline with educational principles distinguishable from the control oriented paradigms of behaviourism and welfarism. Policy making at state level needs to be participatory and democratic, with emphasis on the inclusion of those (teachers in particular) who must implement the policy' (p 170). We also suggest that those recruited for policy-making undergo the same sort of professional development as suggested in Guideline 1, so that old paradigms of control and punishment are not embedded in new policy.

Education departments can set targets for schools that allow them to move beyond the traditional approach of developing codes of behaviour, and reflect on matters of curriculum, pedagogy and school organisation. Performance indicators at school level, for example, could be linked to reducing the number and length of school disciplinary absences, and the encouragement of restorative practices in achieving those outcomes.

6. School policy development

With appropriate broadening of views about school discipline which acknowledge the political economy, the cultural dimensions of schooling and the range of factors which impinge on students' lives, schools will be better able to generate disciplinary processes which reflect a more democratic, restorative approach. Healthy relationships must be considered a high priority in the achievement of the educational goals of the school. This approach will place an analysis of any 'pathology' firmly within the school itself rather than within the student body.

Attention also must be paid to the processes of policy development in the school community. Participatory democracy needs to be authentic. Dialogue and debate by all stakeholders (students especially) in the translation of state policy at the school site must include issues of philosophy, implementation and evaluation, and have a focus beyond how to handle episodes of disruption. School policy should also be tied to measurable outcomes (e.g., reducing the number of SDAs). These democratic processes should also provide a mechanism for communicating with state policy-makers.

Conclusion

It is clear that there is both an identified need and a desire for restorative processes such as conferencing in schools. The philosophy underpinning this offers schools a new perspective on the way they address behaviour issues. Restorative justice views indiscipline as harm to relationships and by doing so allows problem-solving to be focused on the present (repairing the harm), and the future (transforming the system in some way to prevent further harm). It focuses our attention on relationships between all members of the school community and teaches us the value of relationships in achieving quality outcomes for students. It might be useful to reframe 'behaviour' management as 'relationship' management. The theories which explain the success of restorative processes can inform professional development efforts aimed at building healthy relationships. These in turn underpin issues of pedagogy, curriculum and school organisation, all critical components determining school culture. Restorative justice represents an opportunity to address the complex issues which influence student outcomes and insists that schools become accountable for creating an authentic, supportive school environment.

The challenge of sustaining such a paradigm shift in the way schools 'do business' lies in addressing, in a most fundamental way, beliefs and practices which have a central theme of control, and use punishment and other disguised practices to achieve compliance. This paradigm shift requires intellectual and organisational leadership, commitment and energy, and must be focused at all levels within education, from policy-making at departmental level, to district offices which provide support to schools, and in classrooms, administrators' offices and school playgrounds.

CHAPTER 13

The School System: Developing its Capacity in the Regulation of a Civil Society

Brenda Morrison[1]

Developmental Institutions

Can our school system, through the adoption of restorative justice practices, play a role in the maintenance of a civil society? This chapter argues that it does hold an important role as a developmental institution in this capacity. An understanding of a civil society is advanced that highlights the reciprocal interplay between social capital and responsible citizenship. These arguments are substantiated through sociological and psychological theories that uphold the importance of social relationships to the regulation of social justice. Restorative justice is introduced as a participatory learning framework through which social bonds can be re-constituted and strengthened, thus building our capacity to sustain a civil society. Principles of restorative justice, in the context of addressing school bullying, are presented, as well as a preliminary survey of educators' attitudes towards these principles. Obstacles to the implementation of restorative justice are then examined. The chapter concludes with a final examination of the role of restorative justice in the maintenance of a civil society.

Civil Society

A current theme of social theory is that the development of social capital is essential to our capacity to build and sustain a civil society (Australian commentators: Cox, 1995; Krygier, 1997; Malouf, 1998). This thrust is also developing internationally, in countries as different as America and Russia (see Putnam, 1995; Kawachi et al, 1999; Kennedy et al, 1998). Further to this, the United Nations is now turning to social, as well as economic, indicators of national development and social health. Social capital has been conceived as '... the social glue, the weft and warp of the

195

social fabric which comprises the myriad of interactions that make up our public and private lives – our *vita activa*' (Cox, 1995: 18). This conception of social capital captures the regulatory power of a web of positive social relationships to the maintenance of a civil society. Selznick (1996) takes this point further; he argues that the development of communal bonds through a participatory regulatory framework is central to the development of personal responsibility:

> Personal responsibility is most likely to flourish when there is genuine opportunity to participate in communal life. These conditions require substantial investment by the community and its institutions. At the same time, how much the community invests, and what kind of investment it makes, will depend on the prevalence of a sense of personal responsibility for the common good. (p 14)

Strong institutions that develop genuine positive relationships within the nexus that sustains individual and collective life seem essential to our capacity to build a civil society (see also Ritchie & O'Connell, this volume). Within this web of regulatory frameworks, the school system provides a solid foundation on which to build, as it is a central institution in the development and education of all citizens. Given Selznick's (1996) emphasis on the reciprocal process of individual and collective life in building responsible citizenship, if we fail to make the investment of developing social capital in our schools we may miss a significant opportunity to nurture the development of a responsive civil society.

Social capital, then, is built and regulated through strong and effective developmental institutions, such as schools, that not only acknowledge and enforce the development of individual responsibility, but also the reciprocal processes of upholding the responsibilities of institutions that represent us as collectives and the claims they have on us. In other words, given that macrosocial processes of institutions inform and nurture the micropsychological processes of individuals and vice versa, what we know about the underpinnings of social life at the micro level should reflect practice at the macro level. Over the last century, our regulatory institutions have mostly assumed that individuals are solely motivated by individual self-interest. In line with this thinking, rewards and punishment have been the dominant mode of regulation. However, if we think that individuals are also motivated by the need for affirming social relationships (or to simply find meaning for themselves as group members), our institutions should acknowledge and carry the responsibility of building positive relationships. Institutions, in regard to the latter, would then need to develop the social glue that Eva Cox speaks of; the stuff that binds us and defines us in terms of the collective identities we share and nurture.

When social institutions give us the message that we don't belong, our pro-social attitudes and behaviours can quickly become anti-social. Thus, institutional frameworks can bring us together in terms of shared social identities (and collective goals) or they can disenfranchise us to the extent that individuals come to define themselves in terms of anti-institutional identities. For example, within the institutional framework of the school, students can take on the responsibilities of a good citizen and identify as one; but if students are not given the opportunity to find a respected place within the school community, they can also take on delinquent social identities. To this end, the school system plays a significant role in developing the capacity for good citizenship.

Whether it be the school system, or any other regulatory system, an interesting misfortune is that our most well developed theories of social regulation, and cooperation within these systems, are based on the assumption of individualism. In much of our theory and policy development we have failed to recognise the importance of the social groups to which we belong in regulating our social behaviour. More specifically, we have failed to acknowledge the psychological reality and importance of the social group to the individual (see Tajfel & Turner, 1979; Turner et al, 1987). In other words, the importance of collective identities that individuals hold and share, as responsive members of society, must be recognised and become an important aspect of the regulatory frameworks that are constituted within our institutions.

Restorative Justice: Practice into Theory

Restorative justice is a productive regulatory framework whose aim it is to maximise our capacity to reintegrate those disenfranchised from their communities, foster responsible citizenship and build social capital. One could argue that a central tenet of restorative justice is the assumption that the nature of our social relationships sustains our capacity to live as responsible citizens. For example, Braithwaite's (1989) reintegrative shaming theory maintains that caring relationships hold a central role in the process of family group conferencing:

> ... the support of those who enjoy the strongest love or respect with the offender structures reintegration into the ritual. It is not the shame of police or judges or newspapers that is most able to get through to us; it is shame in the eyes of those we respect and trust. (p 45)

Nathanson's (1992) use of affect theory (see also Moore & Forsythe, 1995; Retzinger & Scheff, 1996; Scheff, 1990; Tomkins, 1962) has argued that shame is 'the central social regulator that governs our social interactions with others' (p 99). The assumption is that because social relationships are psychologically important to an individual, the affect state

of shame regulates individual behaviour by bringing social awareness to
a wrong-doing. Psychologically, an individual is motivated to deal with
this state of shame. Bringing the importance of shame and social relations together, Nathanson (1992, 1997) has argued that positive reactions to shame evoke a change in our self-image; however, if social
relations break down, shame can have a negative effect. This can lead a
disenfranchised individual, be it victim or offender, to attack others,
attack self, avoid or withdraw.

Social identity theory (Tajfel & Turner, 1979) and self-categorisation
theory (Turner et al, 1987) also uphold the importance of group life,
through identity formation and maintenance, to self-regulation. These
theories argue that our self-concept is moulded through the functional
antagonism that exists between individual and group-level processes. We
self-stereotype in terms of social identities that create meaningful relationships for us. These social identities emerge within a framework that
gives meaning to our place within society. Specifically, self-stereotyping
has been defined as 'those aspects of an individual's self-image that
derive from the social categories to which he [sic] perceives himself [sic]
as belonging' (Tajfel & Turner, 1979: 40). Self-categorisation theory
developed this understanding further, conceptualising a social identity
as the psychological link between the self and the collective that emerges
through the psychological process of categorisation. The process of acting out by the offender and the victim can thus be conceived as manifestations of subjectively relevant social identities that create meaning for
the individual through the process of self-categorisation.

While these theories uphold the practice of restorative justice, an interesting aspect to the development of the field of restorative justice is that
practice has foreshadowed theory. Of significant influence in this development has been the family group conferencing model of restorative justice
used to address juvenile crime. This model provided a timely opportunity
for practice to inform theory. Within a context of genuine collaboration
between practitioners and academics, the theoretical emphasis turned
from debates about the pros and cons of different regulatory models (of
policing in this case) to the compelling question of: 'why does it work?' As
Braithwaite (1999a) states: 'Indeed, for all of us practice was ahead of theory, and it was well into the 90s before the North American label restorative justice subsumed what had been developing elsewhere for a long time'
(p 22). The steady momentum of the restorative justice movement is a
poignant example of the productivity that can emerge within a collaborative dynamic of theory and practice (see also Lewin, 1951).

Reintegrative shaming theory (Braithwaite, 1989) argues for a restorative process of crime prevention that: (1) makes it clear to the offender
that their behaviour is not condoned within the community; and (2) is

respectful of the individual while not condoning the behaviour. It is this process that allows for a change in attitude and behaviour to take place. In other words, in the context of important and meaningful social relationships, attitude change towards a community can occur through an individual taking on responsibility for a wrongful act. This process allows reintegration to occur and (hopefully) subsequent acts of wrong-doing to be reduced. It has been labelled reintegrative shaming in that the shaming process is reintegrative rather than stigmatising. The theory predicts that shaming processes of a stigmatising nature result in further wrongful acts. Applying this analysis to the school community: school suspensions handed down in a punitive (stigmatising) manner increase the likelihood of further wrongful actions while processes such as family group conferencing decrease the likelihood of further wrongful acts. A number of school districts have used this theoretical framework to develop a range of interventions within the school system (see Cameron & Thorsborne, this volume; Hyndman & Thorsborne, 1994; Moore, 1998; O'Connell, 1999; Ritchie & O'Connell, this volume; Wachtel & McCold, this volume).

Ahmed's (1999) analysis of bullying behaviour in schools further substantiates the importance of shame in the maintenance of social relations. Her analysis shows that bullies, victims, bully/victims and non-bullies/non-victims each used different strategies in the management of shame in relation to the acceptance of wrongful acts and feelings of acceptance in the school community: bullies by-pass shame; victims are caught in a cycle of persistent shame; bully/victims are swept up by denied by-passed shame; while non-bullies/non-victims discharge shame. Each of these shame-management styles relates to wrong-doing and social relations in the following way: bullies deny wrong-doing while not feeling rejected by others; victims are more likely to chronically accept wrong-doing and feelings of rejection by others; bully/victims do not accept wrong-doing but feel rejected by others; while non-bullies/non-victims accept wrong-doing without feeling rejected by others. Examining these categories in relation to an identity analysis: bullies are generally alienated from the school community, which would not be a positive reference group for bullies (and may even be a negative reference group); victims would feel insecure about their relationship with others in the school environment; bully/victims are chronically ambivalent about their relationship with the school community; while non-bullies/non-victims would feel secure in terms of their relationship with others at school.

Koh (1997) uses a social identity and self-categorisation analysis in her studies of social delinquency in schools. She argues that the current practice of exclusion, like other strategies for dealing with delinquent behaviour such as time out, behavioural counselling and community work, have one feature in common: they are individualistic, rather than social, in nature. These interventions typically pathologise the individual's behaviour. Contrary to this individualistic analysis, Koh argues that the role of acting out by the victim and the bully can be better understood as manifestations of subjectively relevant social identities that create meaning for the individual. She argues that delinquent behaviour can be more effectively understood as intergroup behaviour rather than interpersonal behaviour. Emler and Reicher (1995) have made similar claims:

> ... to address both the social contours and the individual variability of delinquent conduct. On the one hand, one must be able to explain the social determination of delinquency without being socially deterministic. On the other, one must be able to account for individual variability without succumbing to individualistic reductionism. What is required then, is an account of which factors feed into the proximal process by which individual actions are produced. (p 5)

In other words, an effective analysis of social delinquency must closely examine the proximal relationship between individuals, collectives and the social institutions that regulate them.

The social dilemma literature has examined the relationship between institutional structure and individual behaviour from a paradigm of social exchange and control (see Kormorita & Parks, 1994). Until very recently, this body of literature has been largely individualistic in nature. This line of thinking grew from the finding in the 1960s that in mixed-motive situations of interdependence, individuals fail to cooperate; that is, individuals fail to perceive themselves as members of a collective. Within the social dilemma paradigm, the assumption is that interdependence is a necessary condition for group formation; however, this assumption has been questioned by self-categorisation theory (see Morrison, 1998; Turner et al, 1987). Morrison's (1999) social identity analysis has shown that under certain conditions institutional frameworks which aim to foster positive social interdependence can be undermined and transformed into situations of negative interdependence. This process can be understood through an analysis of the conditions under which social identities become salient. Social cooperation is argued to be a product of a salient social identity. If the salient identification does not mirror the interdependence structure, cooperation will not ensue. In other words, group interaction in terms of the interdependence structure can be unproductive (if not antagonistic) in fostering positive social relations if the self-category (and associated meaning) that is salient for the individual does not foster positive social bonds.

School bullies, for example, may be objectively interdependent with others in the schools community, and rely on their dominance of others within this institution to achieve their sense of self-worth, but they are not psychologically interdependent with this community. There is no mutual positive regard between the school community and the individual. The school community would not be a shared social category with others in the school, and thus not a positive reference group. The reference group that would more likely be salient would be a delinquent subgroup of the school community. This is the group that would be psychologically relevant, and provide the motivational basis for bullying behaviour.

This social identity critique of interdependence theory brings new insights to reintegrative shaming theory as Braithwaite (1999a) acknowledges: '[The theory] is sloppily theorised on this question, slipping back and forth between interaction-based and identity-based accounts of how criminal subcultures influence action' (p 52). An important point should be made here. This identity analysis should not be confused with an identity analysis that emphasises uni-dimensional identities, such as with labelling theory. As Braithwaite and Mugford (1994) have argued:

> Labelling theorists did useful work, but their work was myopic, exclusively focused on 'front-end' processes that certify deviance. Above all, they envisage individuals to have 'total identities'. We suggest that by employing instead the notion of multiple identities one can recast the interest in transformation ceremonies, asking questions as much about ceremonies to decertify deviance as to certify it. ... In a reintegration ceremony, disapproval of a bad act is communicated while sustaining the identity of the actor as good. (p 142)

In contrast to the work of labelling theorists, social identities are conceived as context-specific self-categorisations that emerge as a property of group processes. For each individual many different social identities can emerge. As such, the theories emphasise multiple-dimensional identities over uni-dimensional identities.

Kawachi and Kennedy (1997; see also Kawachi, Kennedy, Lochner & Prothow-Stith, 1997) have made a similar point. They build on the fields of sociology and political science, where the concept of social capital is used to explain the means by which communities come together, that is cooperate, to overcome the dilemmas of collective action. What these researchers have added is how this framework can explain heterogeneity, as well as homogeneity. In other words, they have used social capital to capture the multi-dimensionality of social life.

Restorative Justice – What Message Does it Carry for Social Justice in Civil Society?

In line with the practice of restorative justice, this chapter has argued that social capital is built through strengthening dominion (freedom as non-domination; Pettit, 1997) in the lives of individuals. This can be achieved through thoughtful development of institutional design that aims to construct a web of productive social relationships (see also Ritchie & O'Connell, this volume). It is this web of relationships that maximises the dominion of individual lives. Too often our institutional designs have failed to recognise the importance of collective processes to individual lives, and when individuals don't fit into our social institutions, typically we find ways to exclude them rather than create opportunities to build mutual understanding through the enhancement of social relationships (see also Pavlich, this volume). At best, we hope that offenders will be rehabilitated (often in isolation from society as a whole) and subsequently conform to the institutional demands. How is restorative justice different?

Restorative justice seeks not to exclude the individual but to create mutual understanding. The participatory nature of restorative practices develops both individual and collective welfare. Between the extremes of individual and collective life reside a myriad of dominions that make up our individual lives. These dominions are sustained by both individualistic and collective needs. Normatively, our thinking is still caught up in the end points that define the dichotomy; that is, between liberals, who generally support a welfare model of social justice, and conservatives, who generally support a punitive justice model. Zehr (1990) has argued that 'Restorative justice is touted as a long-overdue third model or a new "lens", a way of hopping off the see-saw' (p 8). Instead of arguing in terms of these extremes of the legal system, restorative justice, in practice, recognises that citizens have both individualistic and collectivist needs and motivations. While, for the most part, the existing behavioural correction system rests on premises upheld by individualism, restorative justice practices recognise the importance of a theory of social relationships – the dominions of self-awareness that we share in terms of social identities – in the regulation of social justice.

As Wachtel, O'Connell and Ritchie, as well as Cameron and Thorsborne (this volume) have all argued, restorative justice practices fit nicely within the context of a school environment in that they are opportunities for the individual to learn from their experiences in a meaningful and supported environment. Two basic tenets of the practice are: (1) acknowledgement of and taking responsibility for harm resulting from inappropriate behaviour; and (2) acknowledgement of and restitution to those affected by the inappropriate behaviour. An effective restorative justice practice will take participants through a process that connects the inappropriate behaviour with the harm done to the victim, the offender and other collateral parties, while at the same time connecting the individual to a community of care and respect. The process aims to enable the offender to accept responsibility for the wrongful act and then create opportunities to strengthen the relationships that sustain individual responsibility. Through the development of mutual understanding between those affected, it is hoped that the offender will then carry through the process of 'making things right'.

'Making things right' could include a range of actions/behaviours taken on by the offender that constitute restitution to the individuals within the community affected. School suspensions (as opposed to permanent exclusion), for example, could constitute a restorative justice practice if it is seen as legitimate opportunity, by all involved in the process, to 'make things right'. If the offender shows a positive learning outcome and a renewed sense of belonging from the process of being suspended and reintegrated then the practice has been restorative. It is the social meaning that is given to the act of suspension that is important. If the offender gives meaning to the suspension through self-examination which engrains anti-institutional identity patterns (e.g., I don't belong at school; I'm just not cut out for school; I never can do the right thing at school), the intervention will only prove to further stigmatise the offender and encourage participation in other (often deviant) subcultures. If, on the other hand, the offender understands the intervention as an opportunity to 'make things right' then an effective learning outcome can be achieved and responsible citizenship fostered. While there are many ways to practise restorative justice, the common aim is to re-constitute the capacity of the offender, victim and community to sustain positive and productive relationships.

Schools, Social Justice and Civil Society

The importance of positive school relationships to developing a productive school environment, in terms of achievement and citizenship for students, has been well documented (Mortimore et al, 1988; Reynolds & Cuttance, 1992; Rigby & Slee, 1998). As Cameron and Thorsborne note in their chapter (this volume), Sergiovanni (1994) captures the essence of restorative justice when he emphasises the importance of shifting the focus in schools from contractual institutions based on rewards and punishment to communities bound by moral commitment, trust and a sense of purpose:

> Values, beliefs, norms and other dimensions of community may be more important than the relationships themselves. But it is the web of relationships that stands out and it is through the quality and character of relationships that values, beliefs and norms are felt. (p 18)

Schools are one of our most important institutions. They harbour a microcosm of society and they teach us many things through both an overt and a hidden curriculum. Explicitly they teach us about numeracy, literacy and other core business; implicitly they teach us about our place in the world. If we alienate a child from the school community, we essentially have created the potential to alienate a child from society as a whole. Repetitive bullies and other offenders within the school system, as well as their victims, are at a high risk of proceeding down the route of social alienation and subsequent anti-social behaviour. For bullies, this cycle can lead to lives of crime and violence; for victims, the cycle can be one of social isolation and suicidal tendencies (see Callaghan & Joseph, 1995; Dietz, 1994; Farrington, 1993; Olweus, 1991; 1992a). There is a significant link between students who are most likely to be involved in school bullying and later incidents of juvenile delinquency at school, as well as beyond this community (Gottfredson, Gottfredson & Hybl, 1993; Huesmann et al, 1984). In particular, it is those students who suffer suspensions, exclusions and truancy who are most at risk. Given the unsupervised nature of suspension and exclusion from the school community, there is a good chance that these young people will become involved with subcultures that participate in a wide range of anti-social behaviours. If the subculture then begins to define the individual's life, the rate of suspension is likely to increase as they become disenfranchised from the school community.

While violence in schools is often viewed as part of a much larger 'culture of violence' in society, schools, more than any other social institution, have the potential to curb behavioural problems and front-end the process of social regulation. To this end, school curriculums should include programs that explicitly teach children how to deal with conflict in social relationships. Not only will this develop an important skill that underlies personal and social growth, it will also provide an early intervention process in social regulation. Too often our institutions try to mask social conflict. Given that social conflict is a necessary and important aspect of human development, would it not be more productive to teach children how to work through conflict? Often it is not conflict, *per se*, that is the problem but how well the conflict is approached and handled. Do we choose channels that impose punitive sanctions? Do we do nothing or permit it to happen? Or do we try to create mutual understanding through a learning process for all involved? Schools, as educational systems, are an appropriate institution in which to provide a learning process for not only core business but also the business of building responsible citizens.

Justice Einfeld (1998), in his keynote address to a national conference on safe schools, recognises the important role that schools play in imparting a sense of justice in the community. As he states:

> If it is the obligation of society as a whole to address the social injustices that confront the disadvantaged and the victims of discrimination, it is the responsibility of schools to impart to children the equal worth of all peoples. ...

Knowledge is the key to overcoming prejudices and ignorance, and school is the environment to which society has entrusted the responsibility of providing the foundations of a lifetime of learning.

The lesson a child learns when he or she is cast out from the school community becomes one of their stronger lessons in life.

What Principles could Constitute a Process of Restorative Justice in Schools?

Given the diversity of practices that could constitute restorative justice, is it possible to develop a set of principles that underpin restorative justice? A few will be suggested as a starting point. These principles will be examined in the context of restorative justice as applied to school bullying. School bullying has been chosen as it presents itself as one of the most effective early intervention targets for a number of reasons. First, the school environment is the one institutional framework that we all participate in from an early age into our young adult life, and as such it is an important institution to target. Second, bullying is one of the first signs of social behaviour that signals the breakdown of social relationships. Thus, bullying at school is an important target to front-end the regulation of social justice.

Drawing on current literature, the following six principles have been put forward in targeting, designing and evaluating the effectiveness of restorative justice intervention programs: (1) bullying and being bullied are ways of behaving that can be changed (Rigby & Slee, 1998; Olweus, 1991, 1992b); (2) wrong-doing, such as bullying, concerns actions and should not involve the denigration of the whole person (Moore & O'Connell, 1994); (3) the harm done by bullying to self and others must be acknowledged (Retzinger, 1991; Scheff, 1990, 1994); (4) reparation for the harm done is essential (Retzinger & Scheff, 1996); (5) both bullies and victims are valued members of the school community whose supportive ties with others should be strengthened through participation in communities of care (Bazemore & Umbreit, 1994); and (6) forgiveness is necessary for social reintegration (Tavuchis, 1991). Together, these six principles should constitute an effective restorative justice intervention program. The question now turns to how one implements an effective and sustainable program.

How Ready is the School Community to Work With the Principles of Restorative Justice?

A number of commentators have noted the importance of acknowledging where the school community is at when implementing a behavioural change program (see O'Connell, 1999; Slee, 1992). With this in mind, a survey of ten primary schools (96 staff members) in Canberra was carried out at the end of 1998 asking educators about behavioural management at their school (see Morrison, forthcoming, a). Within this survey, a number of questions were asked about agreement with these principles. Responses were given on a five-point scale ranging from 'strongly disagree' (1) to 'strongly agree' (5).

In terms of the first principle of behaviour change for bullies and victims, teachers agreed that both bullying (M = 4.30) and victimisation (M = 4.32) were ways of behaving that could be changed. They also agreed that both bullies (M = 3.29) and victims (M = 3.34) are basically good kids who, respectively, have done some bad things or couldn't stand up for themselves. There was further agreement that bullies (M = 3.43) and victims (M = 4.13) are valued members of the community who deserve support. In terms of actions taken to effectively deal with an act of bullying, it was agreed that the harm done to those affected must be acknowledged by the bully (M = 4.46) and the victim (M = 4.05). It was also agreed that some form of reparation by the bully is essential (M = 4.19) and that the form of reparation should focus on the victim and his/her family (M = 3.75). Finally, there was general agreement that it is important that the bully (M = 3.53) and the victim (M = 3.63) be forgiven for his/her actions.

Given this general agreement in terms of principles that underlie restorative justice, why is it that suspension rates and incidents of bullying are increasing in our school communities? For example, in Canberra suspensions rose significantly in the years 1993 to 1997. In 1993, 592 students generated 770 suspensions (some students having multiple suspensions), and in 1997, 1138 students generated 1963 suspensions (ACT [Australian Capital Territory] Council of P&C Associations). Thus, in a five-year period the number of students suspended almost doubled and the number of suspensions generated almost tripled. This indicates that not only are suspension rates increasing but the rate of multiple suspensions is growing at an even faster rate. It seems for a growing group of students suspension is the option most often adopted. One may think that the process of implementing restorative justice would be a practical option to trial to address this worrying trend; however, in practice this has not been the case. The evidence suggests that there are a number of obstacles to the implementation of restorative justice practices.

Restorative Justice in Schools: What are the Obstacles?

One obstacle to implementing restorative justice practices that was highlighted by this survey is the perception by teachers that parents want more punitive interventions. Teachers were asked how they think problems of bullying should be brought under control and how they thought most parents wanted the problem of bullying to be brought under control. Responding on the same five-point scale, ranging from 'strongly disagree' (1) to 'strongly agree' (5), three questions were posed. 'Do you think the problem of bullying should be brought under control: (1) through a dialogue involving teachers/students/parents; (2) through enforcing stricter rules and discipline; (3) through a participatory dialogue backed up by stricter enforcement.' The frequency data revealed that 67 percent of the teachers strongly agreed with the participatory dialogue approach, followed by 56 percent of teachers strongly agreeing with the combined approach, and with only 30 percent of the teachers strongly agreeing with the enforcement approach.

These results are interesting when compared with what they thought parents wanted. The pattern is reversed. The dialogic and combined approaches drop significantly, to 32 percent and 33 percent respectively, while the enforcement approach rises to 60 percent. These trends indicate that teachers perceive parents not to be 'on side' with restorative principles. However, data from Ahmed's (1999) survey indicate that 53 percent of parents strongly agree with the combined approach, followed by the dialogic approach (33.5 percent) and the enforcement approach (34 percent). That is, the teachers' view of what parents want is not what parents actually report wanting.

These results were mirrored in the data collected from teachers on how much they trusted various groups in contributing in a constructive way to controlling the problem of school bullying. Teachers responded on a scale ranging from 'not at all' (1) to 'a great deal' (4). School teachers (M = 3.69) and principals (M = 3.66) rated highest, followed by students (M = 3.23). This was followed by parents in general (M = 3.07), with parents of bullies (M = 2.43) and parents of victims (M = 2.51) rating significantly lower. These data highlight the importance of implementing a dialogic intervention that includes teachers and parents. One reason is that this can help teachers understand that parents are not as opposed to restorative principles as the teachers assume. Assumptions about the punitiveness of the other party's attitude have in themselves been an obstacle to restorative justice. We see it in the resistance of some restorative justice advocates to engage the victims' movement with restorative justice (see Strang, this volume). We also see it in politicians' and judges' assumptions that people are more punitive and less restorative than they really are (Roberts & Stalins, 1997; Braithwaite, 1999a).

New Models of Practice

A number of obstacles to implementing behavioural change in school programs have also been highlighted by O'Connell (1999) in his review of different attempts to introduce restorative justice practices into schools. Three of these programs will be briefly summarised.

Community Accountability Conferencing (CAC) was introduced into Queensland schools beginning in 1994. This was one of the first attempts in Australia to introduce restorative justice practices into schools with the aim of addressing incidents of serious harm in the school community. The promising results of the initial trial led to the development of a pilot program throughout Queensland (see Thorsborne and Cameron, this volume). Nearly all schools in the trial reported that they had changed their thinking about managing behaviour from a punitive to a more restorative approach. Participant satisfaction with the fairness of outcomes was very high. However, these same schools failed to practise CAC on a number of incidents, opting for more traditional approaches.

School Community Forums were introduced in New South Wales schools in 1997 as part of the Alternatives to Suspension pilot project (McKenzie, 1999). Based on the successes of the CAC process in Queensland, the forum process was established on a similar model. The results of this program suggested that these forums worked best in the context of school bullying and harassment, in that the forums had a great capacity to build empathy among participants. The process worked effectively at exposing the complexity of the bullying–victimisation cycle at many levels, such as the grey boundaries of bullying and victimisation and the extent of collateral damage. While many teachers reported that they developed insights into behavioural management, this pilot was inconclusive in the context of the wider project, which aimed to reduce and find alternatives to suspension. This was due to the fact that so few forums were run, only 20 in an 18-month period. Concerns were also raised in respect to the heavy investment of time and resources that the forum process draws. Again the insights gained did not lead to a system-wide change in behavioural management practice.

The Lewisham Primary School Community Project was implemented at the beginning of 1998. The program involved the NSW Police Restorative Justice Group and the Port Jackson Behavioural Management Team working with the school (see Ritchie & O'Connell, this volume). The aim of the program was to achieve a reduction in suspension rates and the need for police involvement at this culturally diverse inner-city school. At the beginning of 1998 the school teachers received 24 hours (over eight weeks) of training in the theory and practice of restorative justice. Teachers made the commitment to incorporate restorative justice principles within their classrooms on a day-to-day basis. This involved their interaction with all members of the school community – students, teachers, and parents. They also developed and standardised a continuum of practices such that each student had the opportunity to learn from his/her experiences. At the end of 1998 the results were encouraging. The number of playground incidents that resulted in formal disciplinary entries dropped from an average of 20 per week to around two or three. The number of suspensions was also reduced. Further, where a suspension did result, this was in the context of a conferencing process to allow for learning and reintegration into the school community to occur. Police involvement was reduced and teachers felt increasingly confident about handling serious incidents within the school. Despite this apparent success, the school continued to struggle with the ideals of restorative justice and its place within the school.

The evidence suggests that while the thinking about managing behaviour can change, this often does not lead to systematic changes in practice. And while educators' thinking is not antagonistic towards principles of restorative justice, the practice as a whole is not upheld. A number of tensions remain in the system that draw schools into the maintenance of traditional approaches. Beyond the issue that teachers perceive parents to favour punitive over restorative practice, other issues include lack of a shared rationale for the adoption of a restorative justice approach within the school community, as well as issues of time in systems where professionals are already under stress. This begs the question: what constitutes effective levers in moving from 'thinking about' restorative justice practices to 'participating' in restorative justice practices? Discovering these levers defines a central part of our future research agenda.

Conclusion: Pessimism and Hope

It has been argued that the school does have an important role to play in the development and maintenance of a civil society. Building skills in conflict resolution is an important aspect in the development of responsible citizenship (Morrison, forthcoming, b). The effectiveness of these skills is developed further when nurtured in the context of both family and school, and even more so in mutual collaboration.

Selznick's (1996) argument remains valid: strong institutional investment that enables the capacity for individuals to participate in communal life is the cornerstone of building responsible citizenship. We have found the evidence to show that schools are an important institution in the maintenance of a civil society. The question is how to best achieve this end. Restorative justice could play a central role in this regard. As Braithwaite (1999a) has argued, restorative justice seems to have the leverage to capture the hearts and minds of both libertarians and conservatives. Our attitudinal data, while indicating teacher support for restorative justice principles, also reveal teacher pessimism about parental support for those same principles. It may be, however, that restorative justice institutionalises a solution to this central obstacle to its own realisation. It is the simple solution of institutionalising a dialogue between parents and teachers that will reveal, contrary to the pessimistic beliefs of each about the other, that both sides evince strong support of the six core restorative justice principles we have identified.

O'Connell (forthcoming) states that: 'Hope is what makes everything worthwhile. .... [Yet] our existing [institutional] practices do not engender hope and optimism.' O'Connell's years of experience as a practitioner of restorative justice tell him that hope is the common outcome sought by participants, victim and offender alike (see also Sherman & Strang, 1997). Hope is the emotional stimulant of responsible citizenship. Krygier (1997) made this a theme of his Boyer lectures: 'Our institutions ... will have to be looked at not just from the perspective of reducing our fears but also from that of securing our hopes' (p 110). Restorative justice programs in schools offer one practical institutional mechanism for Krygier's aspiration to cultivate hope as we allay fears.

Note

1   My thanks to Valerie Braithwaite and Helen Berry for their reading of and comments on this chapter.

CHAPTER 14

Security and Justice for All

David H. Bayley

In most countries the state has for many years been the chief custodian of criminal justice. Its institutions bear the primary responsibility for providing protection from enemies both foreign and domestic and for adjudicating criminal offences and civil disputes. In the last few years, however, state-based criminal justice has been challenged with respect to its monopoly on security and to the character of its justice.

The provenance of security has been multilateralised through privatisation and volunteerism (Bayley & Shearing, 1996). Security is being provided increasingly by commercial firms through the market, by businesses to their own employees and customers, and by private residential communities. Volunteers – people working without pay – have also been encouraged to share responsibility for public safety with the public police, as in Neighbourhood Watch, citizens' patrols, and community crime prevention councils.

The character of justice provided by the state is being challenged by the restorative justice movement. One of its tenets is that crime prevention is more likely to be achieved through social reintegration and shaming rather than ostracism and punishment (Braithwaite, 1989). This outcome is achieved through meetings ('conferences') between offenders and victims, usually accompanied by their respective families and friends, where guilt is admitted, hurt revealed, restitution explored, commitments about future behaviour made, and responsibility for carrying out obligations shared.

These two challenges to state-based criminal justice – multilateralisation of security and restorative justice – are closely related to one another in practice. Philip Stenning and Clifford Shearing noted some time ago that the crime prevention activities of private security were very different from those of the state because they stressed restoration rather than

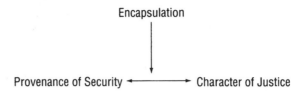

Figure 14.1 Level of Social Organisation

punishment, prevention rather than reaction, and regulation rather than punishment (Stenning & Shearing, 1979). In other words, 'commodified' security relies less on deterrence and more on restoration. Conversely, restorative justice involves more than a sharing of responsibility between perpetrator and victim. It insists on undertakings that reduce the likelihood that the same person will offend again. In short, privatisation of security tends to work in restorative ways; restorative justice tends to encourage particularistic crime prevention.

There is a strong theoretical reason why these challenges to the state with respect to the provenance of security and to the character of justice should be related. Both involve the relocation of authority, either to non-state auspices altogether or to lower levels of government. Multilateralisation as well as devolution involve the reconstruction of criminal justice in decentralised ways so that it responds to local needs, reflects local morality, and takes advantage of local knowledge. As Shearing has noted, both developments involve the 'responsibilising' of communities (see Shearing, 1994 and this volume).

The theoretical proposition that explains the connection between these twin challenges to the state is that the auspices under which both security and justice are organised affect their character as well as their effectiveness (Bayley, 1985). More precisely, when social sanctioning is located at a single level in large-scale societies encapsulating all others, it is likely to be reactive and to depend on deterrence; when social sanctioning is located at less aggregated levels of authority, especially primary social groups and peers, it is more likely to act in premonitory and restorative ways (see Figure 14.1). In layman's language, states organise security and justice differently from families and colleagues. When both security and justice are multilateralised and decentralised, they rely more on shame, anticipatory regulation, and restoration.

Because the multilateralisation of security and restorative justice challenge so directly the authority of the central state, there is a giddy sense at the moment among many intellectuals that the state is passé. For reasons of both circumstance and morality, the governance of security is being transformed (Shearing, 1994).

But is the state passé with respect to criminal justice? And should it be? Curiously, both Clifford Shearing and John Braithwaite, respectively the most influential students of security multilateralisation and restorative justice, depend upon the state to achieve the benefits implicit in both. Shearing, with Michael Brogden, wants the state to ensure equality in the distribution of public safety, especially so as to avoid disadvantaging the poor (Brogden & Shearing, 1993). The state, they propose, should give localities 'security budgets' which allow them to bid for the police services, public or private, that best fit their needs. In order for institutions of restorative justice to be created, John Braithwaite wants the state to share some of its adjudicating authority and to provide money for evaluating success of the new programs.

So a dilemma arises. Is it reasonable to expect that the state will assist in minimising the adverse effects of the multilateralising movement that is undermining its own authority? Is it reasonable to expect the state to undertake experiments in restorative justice that are designed to show that its own approach is less effective? Moreover, if the state does provide the assistance suggested by advocates of both multilateralisation and restorative justice, will their integrity be affected? Can the state assist without changing these movements fundamentally? In sum, in the face of these twin challenges to its authority, what should we expect as well as require the state to do? I shall try to answer these questions, examining first the security dimension and second the justice dimension.

The Provenance of Security

The multilateralisation of security has not occurred through the planned activities of states. Indeed, until recently, most governments viewed private security as well as volunteerism in policing as dangerous (Shearing & Stenning, 1992). The role that is being proposed for the state with respect to multilateralisation is not its encouragement, but rather the mitigation of its adverse effects. Two of these have attracted particular concern: the inequitable distribution of security in society in favour of the rich and the abuse of policing power in private hands (Bayley & Shearing, 1996). I shall devote most of my attention to the former, although some of the regulatory considerations that arise in the former also could be used to alleviate the latter.

One important qualification needs to be made to the statement that the state has not actively encouraged multilateralisation. Volunteerism in policing is very largely the result of state action, specifically, the community policing movement. The philosophy of community policing calls for police to share responsibility for crime control and prevention with local communities. Police do so through consulting with communities about security problems and priorities, allowing commanders to adapt their strategies to local conditions, mobilising civilian resources in supportive ways, and devising strategies for resolving conditions that generate crime, disorder, and insecurity (Bayley, 1994). If the enthusiasm of governments for community policing were to decline, it is unclear what would happen to volunteerism as a source of multilateralisation. In places where it is well established, it might endure, but in many others it would almost certainly die.

It would be unfortunate if volunteerism were to die from governmental neglect because it is a partial antidote to the inequitable distribution that results from the 'marketising' of security. Patrick Murphy, the former Commissioner of the New York City Police Department, has observed that community policing is private security for the poor. Community policing allows them to become 'customers' shaping the kind of security services they receive without having to participate in commercial markets. It follows, therefore, that unless private security can be expanded to poor, socially disorganised communities, state action in the form of community policing will continue to be required. For those communities, community policing may be their best hope for providing more effective security founded on preventive, restorative principles.

Community policing may, however, be very costly in precisely the areas where it is needed most. Research has shown that community policing is most difficult to implement in communities that have high rates of crime, unemployment, and transience, and low levels of income and education (Rosenbaum, 1994). Perversely, then, the volunteerism that community policing engenders may magnify rather than mitigate the inequitable distribution of non-state security unless it is actively supported by government in disadvantaged communities.

Besides the effective maintenance and expansion of community policing in disadvantaged communities, what else might the state do to ensure the equitable distribution of multilateralisation's security benefits? One idea, proposed by Clifford Shearing, is that governments should provide 'security budgets' to poor communities in the form of cash or vouchers that could be used to purchase security.[1]

Is it reasonable to expect that governments will provide money for the purchase of security directly by communities? I am very doubtful, for several reasons:

Economic: Equalisation of security by the state among its constituent communities in order to compensate for commercialisation requires either the reallocation of existing state revenue or the raising of new revenue. The police, as well as other criminal justice agencies, are unlikely to accept security subsidies to communities if the money comes out of their own budgets. So far, multilateralisation through both markets and volunteerism has not reduced government investments in police. Public and private policing have grown together, although the private sector has grown much faster (Bayley, 1994; Bayley & Shearing, 1996). However, if security budgets require supplemental government investment in policing, then either existing public security agencies or the general tax-paying public must pay. I think it unlikely that public agencies would selflessly submit to a reduction in their operating budgets in favour of community-based commodification. Given their political power, security budgets on the backs of existing criminal justice institutions seem unlikely.

I am also doubtful about the willingness of the tax-paying public to spend more on security enhancement that will be allocated primarily to the poor. Affluent tax-payers might reasonably conclude that they are paying three times for security – taxes to support the public police, the expense of hiring private security, and now more taxes to subsidise the entry of the poor into the commercial security market. In the field of education, there is mounting evidence that tax-payers resent paying for public education when their own children go to private schools. Might the same thing happen with respect to security? The effect of educational 'voucher' programs in the United States on tax-payer support for public schools could be a bell-wether for the effect that security budgets might have on public support for the public police.

On the other hand, there are some reasons for thinking that providing security budgets to poor communities might be attractive to governments and the public. If the costs of effective policing are less when provided by private security, then governments could get more security for poor communities at the same cost by allowing competition between the private and public sectors. This is the logic of privatisation throughout criminal justice, whether in prisons or policing. Through the competition that security budgets generate, government gets a 'bigger bang for the buck'. The assumption behind this expectation is, of course, that private security purchased with state funds replaces, rather than supplements, public policing. This is not a prospect that will be regarded favourably by the public police establishment.

But the privatisation of security in this way, even if accepted by the public sector police, poses a serious danger to the very groups whose security is of concern. The budgetary gains from privatisation might come at the expense of the safety of the poor if security budgets become an excuse for governments to wash their hands of responsibility for protecting the poor. Safety is a right and cost alone cannot be allowed to become the criterion of success. 'Responsibilising' communities is a good idea, but 'de-responsibilising' states is not. The implication is clear:

even if states provide security budgets to local communities so that they may purchase whatever policing they see fit, governments must retain the capacity to assess their success.

It seems to me, therefore, that in order for the corrective of security budgets to achieve genuine equalisation of security across class boundaries in the face of increasing privatisation, a fairly restrictive set of conditions must be present. Countries must be relatively well developed economically so that they can afford public policing at existing levels plus subsidised security budgets for communities. Furthermore, the tax-paying public must be prosperous enough to afford both private policing for itself and public policing for others. This condition diminishes in importance where there is hard evidence that communities can use state money more effectively for security than public agencies. In this case, an enlightened and courageous government might prevail in reallocating resources from existing agencies to local communities. Even if it does so, however, it must continue to monitor the quality of public safety throughout its communities and be ready to take corrective action under public auspices if necessary.

Furthermore, tax-payers must be willing out of self-interest or humanity to pay for the equalisation of security across social classes. While I believe a strong case can be made that governments protect the rich by protecting the poor, convincing the general public will be difficult. Moreover, I suspect, but cannot demonstrate, that countries with more egalitarian distributions of income are more likely to respond to humanitarian arguments that security should be equalised.

In addition to these rather restrictive economic conditions, there may be political and social constraints as well.

Political: States are unlikely to provide security budgets to communities if they fear decentralised political competition. When states are founded by voluntary unification, as in the United States, decentralisation is not threatening to a regime; when states are founded by enforced submission, as in France or China, decentralisation is to be feared. The traditions established early in state-building persist, severely restricting the likelihood that states will delegate authority (Bayley, 1985). It follows that security budgets are unlikely in countries with weak, unstable, or authoritarian governments.

Social: It follows as well that security budgets are less likely to find favour in countries with heterogeneous populations, especially where residency is structured by race, ethnicity, or religion. It is worth remembering that 'neighbourhood policing' was rejected in the United States in the late 1960s when it was associated with the 'black power' movement, but was accepted in the 1980s in the form of community policing when it was developed by the public police.

Community capacity: Security budgets presuppose that local communities have the capacity to use money wisely. As is well known, however, poor communities lack the 'social capital' to create effective institutions of local government. In such circumstances, the state must not only provide money for security, it must develop the community's capacity to use it (Rosenbaum, 1994). This raises the cost appreciably.

In conclusion, I am not optimistic that many states will choose to provide money directly to poor communities in order to offset the inequality in security that multilateralisation is bringing. The enabling conditions are too limiting. Security budgets are feasible in countries that are affluent, democratic, relatively egalitarian in income, not politically destabilised by ascriptive social divisions, and possessing a strong market economy.

Providing security subsidies and community police are not the only actions, however, that states might take to ensure that multilateralisation through commodification does not cruelly disadvantage the poor. One alternative is to regulate the growth of private security so that it includes the poor. Shearing and I may have underestimated the extent to which the privatisation of security, especially in public spaces, leads to the neglect of the poor (1996). Private security organised by location creates 'bubbles of security' that cover everyone within them. Thus, the poor as well as the rich may be protected by privatisation where they work, bank, shop, travel, recreate, or learn. To the extent that the poor are employed and can consume, commodified security may cover them. What commodification leaves out, of course, is protection of the poor where they live.

The solution to this problem might be to regulate private security so that it includes the residential communities of the poor. Governments might, for example, offer tax-incentives to private employers who extend their security 'bubbles' to adjacent residential communities. On the assumption that crime is often opportunistic, businesses might protect themselves by enhancing security nearby, transforming adjacent neighbourhoods from crime sanctuaries to safety zones. The costs of extending security perimeters might be offset in part by lower insurance rates. The additional security provided by 'business improvement districts' in the United States has this effect in mixed-zoned neighbourhoods. More ambitiously, companies might be given tax-incentives for providing residential security to their workers, either in company housing or in enclaves where large numbers of them live. Companies in many countries are already providing vans and buses to transport their workers safely and efficiently to work; why not expand the umbrella of corporate security to their residential neighbourhoods?

Whether governments subsidise private security for the poor directly or encourage it through regulation, there are three policing functions they cannot give up.

First: states must maintain the capacity to be the police of last resort. If 'responsibilising' neighbourhoods does not work or 'bubbles of security' cannot be sufficiently extended, then governments must be prepared to step into the breach. Security is a right that should not be distributed according to class. Failure to ensure this right can have serious political consequences by undercutting the rationale for government.

Second: providing effective security throughout modern countries requires creation and maintenance of an infrastructure beyond the capacity of multilateralised agents, such as coordinating and standardising communication and information systems, creating national databases, and maintaining forensic laboratories and research facilities. Furthermore, certain crime and disorder problems, such as terrorism, political subversion, illegal immigration, computer crime and illegal drugs, can only be addressed across jurisdictions and agencies. Something as commonplace but essential as traffic regulation also requires coordination across security perimeters.

Third: governments must retain the ability to monitor and evaluate public safety throughout their territories. This is required whether they subsidise communities in the market-place, regulate private security, fill security gaps, or provide essential infrastructure. In other words, even if the instrumental security activities of the public police diminish, their intelligence and analytic activities must not. They must also be prepared to act on the analyses they make. For this reason, Ian Blair, former Chief Constable of Essex England, has argued that all security agents – private, volunteer, or devolved – should be 'police compliant', meaning that their actions should be subject to continual oversight and correction by the public police (Blair, 1998).

The Character of Justice

The second challenge to state-based criminal justice is to its character. This challenge has required more collaboration by the state in order to make it meaningful than is the case with security. Of course, privatisation, as Shearing has pointed out, does rely less on deterrence and more on restoration and premonitory prevention than public security. And restorative principles of justice persist among Indigenous communities that have been left alone. Their practices have often been the intellectual inspiration for the restorative challenge to state-based justice (Braithwaite, 1989). But proponents of restorative justice are not proposing the creation of a justice system under new auspices. They are proposing the transformation of the state's existing justice system. They want the state to collaborate with them in changing the way justice is administered. Default by the state, then, is not an option as it is with respect to the growth of private security. The state must sponsor and evaluate restorative justice experiments and later remould state practices according to the lessons learned.

Is it reasonable to expect that the state will assist in transforming the character of its own justice as the proponents of restorative justice want? The answer to this question depends in part on the extent to which restorative principles are already accepted in the culture of a country. Countries with cultures stressing individualism will be less inclined to do so than countries with communitarian cultures (Bayley, 1991). They may also be affected by structural elements in their histories that inhibited the rise of rehabilitative and reintegrative criminal justice practices. John Braithwaite has recently argued that slavery in the United States has contributed to its attachment to deterrence, especially with respect to offending by African-Americans, while settlement by convicts in Australia encouraged practices of reintegration (Braithwaite, 1999b). Paradoxically, then, countries that might profit most from restorative reforms are those that will have the greatest difficulty implementing them. If Braithwaite is right, it also follows that governments in countries where politics is sharply contested along ascriptive lines, even if the culture is relatively communitarian, will be less likely to assist in moving from a deterrent to a restorative justice paradigm.

In terms of cost, rich countries have an advantage because they can afford the existing justice system and restorative alternatives at the same time. Restorative transformations are a boot-strapping operation in the sense that states must explore the cost-benefits of the new paradigm out of additional expenditures. Whether governments invest meaningfully depends initially on the marginal costs and in the long run on the proven benefits in crime prevention, recidivism, and community response. However, even where governments are willing to support pilot ventures that demonstrate cost-effective results, governments may for political reasons baulk at the cost of extensive institutional change.

Even when rigorous evaluation shows that restorative justice is cost-effective, governments may be inhibited from investing because of public opinion or ideology. There are fashions in justice. Restorative justice may seem to be 'soft', too solicitous of criminals, and not sufficiently retributive. I suggest, therefore, that governments are more likely to sponsor restorative justice in countries that are communitarian in culture, inclusive politically, economically developed, and not unduly fearful of crime.

Even when governments are committed to a restorative transformation, there are formidable problems of implementation. The most fundamental is that justice, like security, is a right. Communities can be allowed to 'responsibilise' justice only within limits. States in western Europe and North America during the nineteenth century created rights for women, children, religious and ethnic minorities, and workers in the face of institutionalised oppression in local communities. Social pressure in local communities cannot be allowed to restrict this hard-won expansion of human rights. Furthermore, citizens have the right to expect that laws will be applied equally throughout their country. For this reason, the New Zealand Court of Appeal recently overruled a restorative justice conference for being too lenient in the punishment it awarded, arguing that the state had an abiding interest in equalising punishment across offences (Mason, 2000).

Moreover, the state's justice system protects procedural as well as substantive rights. Restorative justice is being proposed as an alternative that nests within the overarching system of a state's courts. But can states do this successfully? Can they maintain and coordinate systems of justice that operate on different principles?

This issue has been studied by a variety of scholars (Bayley, 1985; Galanter, 1979; Moore, 1972; Nader, 1969; Starr, 1974). Two observations from this literature are especially worth noting. First, affluent, powerful parties to a dispute are more likely to appeal to the larger, encapsulating, often state-based, institutions of justice when they do not get their way in subordinate venues. This follows Donald Black's proposition that there is 'more law' the greater the social distance between disputants, and that the 'more law' is produced in response to actions by the party with higher status (Black, 1976). Second, although grievances may rise from micro- to macro-systems of justice, the procedures of macro-systems have a tendency to percolate downward, influencing the way in which micro-systems conduct business (Galanter, 1979). As Galanter observed, principles of 'legal centralism' contaminate the practice of 'Indigenous law'. Consider, for example, the way in which very small-scale meetings are regulated by appeals to Robert's Rules of Order when decisions might more easily be made by agreement. In just this way, participants in restorative justice conferences may feel that in order to ensure fairness, lawyers must be present, rules codified, and punishments made subject to appeal.

The point is that in order for restorative justice to grow, governments must not only encourage it but manage the boundary between it and their own dominating systems. The principles and procedures of state-based criminal justice percolate down and penetrate micro-practices. In order to become real, the restorative justice challenge requires states to sponsor without inhibiting. This is very tricky intellectually and daunting bureaucratically.

Conclusion

There is great humane potential in the multilateralisation of security and in the transformation of justice from retributive to restorative practices. However, the ability to overcome the shortcomings of the first – unequal distribution in the character and efficacy of policing – and to successfully accomplish the second under state auspices will be uneven across the world. Success will be affected by powerful social and political forces. Most important will be the level of economic development, the character of government, the incidence of both collective violence and crime, the stability as well as the capacity of central governments, the relative importance of the individual versus the community, and the capacity of local institutions.

In neither case is the conclusion warranted that the state, in the sense of strong central governments, should wither away. It has two essential and enduring roles with respect to security and justice: (1) it must create agencies of both when natural auspices are inadequate, and (2) it must guarantee equal measures of both throughout society. As Peter Grabosky (1996) has said, 'The design and guidance of hybrid law enforcement systems is an essential task of government in the next century' (p 6).[2] However much we are committed to the 'communification' of security and justice, we will not be able to escape the gritty politics of the nation-state. Both multilateralisation and restorative justice will require high-minded action by national governments.

Indeed, the fundamental lesson from my analysis is that in order for both movements to be fair and just, strong rather than weak central governments are required, what Gunnar Myrdal referred to as 'hard' rather than 'soft' states (Myrdal, 1968). Clifford Shearing believes that the multilateralisation of security and restorative justice constitute changes in the 'governance of security'. I believe that neither will occur in satisfactory ways unless attention is paid to the 'security of governance'. As the French might say, *L'état est mort. Vive l'état.*

Notes

1 Clifford Shearing has proposed this when writing with Michael Brogden and myself as well as on his own. Since I know him to be the prime mover in these proposals, it is not unfair to write as if he was solely responsible. I should also add that some of the views I attribute to him come from long conversations over many years. These have been some of the most stimulating moments of my intellectual life and, although I disagree with him at points, I am deeply in his debt.

2 Peter Grabosky (1996) has described an array of mechanisms which states can use to devolve or shift the responsibility for security to private auspices. He has organised them according to their directiveness (coerciveness).

Bibliography

Abel, Richard L (1982) *The Politics of Informal Justice*, New York, Academic Press.

ACT Council of P&C Associations (March/April 1998) *Feedback*, Canberra, ACT P&C Association.

Ahmed, Eliza (1999) 'Shame management and bullying', unpublished PhD dissertation, Research School of Social Sciences, Australian National University.

Anderson, Benedict R (1983/1991) *Imagined Communities: Reflections on the Origin and Spread of Nationalism*, London & New York, Verso.

Anderson, Elijah (1999) *Code of the Street: Decency, Violence, and the Moral Life*, New York, Norton.

Ashworth, A (2000) 'Victims' rights, defendants' rights and criminal procedure', in A Crawford and J Goodey (eds) *Integrating a Victim Perspective within Criminal Justice*, Aldershot, Ashgate.

Ashworth, A & Hough, M (1996) 'Sentencing and the climate of opinion', *Criminal Law Review*, 776–787.

Ashworth, A & Von Hirsch, A (1993) 'Deserts and the three Rs', *Current Issues in Criminal Justice*, 5 (1): 9–12.

Association of Chief Police Officers of England and Wales (1993) *Statement of Common Purpose and Values*, London, Association of Chief Police Officers of England and Wales.

Ayto, John (1990) *Bloomsbury Dictionary of Word Origins*, London, Bloomsbury.

Balint, J (1994) 'Towards the anti-genocide community: the role of law', *Australian Journal of Human Rights*, 1 (1): 12–42.

—— (forthcoming) 'Genocide and the law: a holistic approach to state crime', unpublished PhD thesis.

Baltzell, E Digby (1979) *Puritan Boston and Quaker Philadelphia: Two Protestant Ethics and the Spirit of Class Authority and Leadership*, New York, Free Press.

Barber, B R (1992) *An Aristocracy of Everyone: The Politics of Education and Future of America*, New York, Oxford University Press.

Barkan, E (2000) *The Guilt of Nations*, New York, W W Norton.

Barr, Gladys H (1961) *Master of Geneva*, New York, Holt, Rinehart and Winston.

Bauman, Zygmunt (1989) *Modernity and the Holocaust*, Cambridge, Polity Press.

—— (1997) *Postmodernity and its Discontents*, Cambridge, Polity Press.

Baumrind, D (1971) 'Current patterns of parental authority', *Developmental Psychology Monograph*, 4 (1).

—— (1978) 'Parental disciplinary patterns and social competence in children', *Youth and Society*, 9: 239–276.

Bayley, David (1985) *Patterns of Policing*, New Brunswick, NJ, Rutgers University Press.

—— (1991) *Forces of Order*, Berkeley, CA, University of California Press (revised edition).

—— (1994) *Police for the Future*, New York, Oxford University Press.

Bayley, David and Shearing, Clifford (1996) 'The future of policing', *Law and Society Review*, 30 (3): 585–606.

Bazemore, G & Umbreit, M (1994) *Balanced and Restorative Justice: Program Summary, Balanced and Restorative Justice Project*, Washington DC, US Department of Justice, Office of Juvenile Justice and Delinquency Prevention.

Bean, Clive (1995) 'Citizen beliefs and attitudes about Australian institutions', an overview paper presented to the Reshaping Australian Institutions Conference, Research School of Social Sciences, Australian National University, 2–3 November.

Beck, Ulrich (1992) *Risk Society: Towards a New Modernity*, London, Sage.

Bernard, T J (1992) *The Cycle of Juvenile Justice*, New York and Oxford, Oxford University Press.

Berndt, R M (1962) *Excess and Restraint*, Chicago, Chicago University Press.

Biderman, A, Johnson, L, McIntyre, J & Weir, A (1967) 'Report on a pilot study in the District of Columbia on victimization and attitudes towards law enforcement', *President's Commission on Law Enforcement and Administration of Justice, Field Surveys 1*, Washington DC, US Government Printing Office.

Black, Donald (1976) *The Behavior of Law*, New York, Academic Press.

—— (1983) 'Crime as social control', *American Sociological Review*, 48: 34–45.

Black, H (1990) *Black's Law Dictionary*, 6th edition, St Paul, MN, West Publishing.

Blagg, H (1998) 'Restorative visions and restorative justice practices, conferencing, ceremony and reconciliation in Australia', *Current Issues in Criminal Justice*, 10 (1).

Blair, Ian (1998) 'The governance of security: where do the police fit into policing?', speech to the Conference of Assistant Chief Police Officers, Great Britain, 16 July.

Blake, R R & McCanse, A A (1991) *Leadership Dilemmas: Grid Solutions*, Houston, Gulf Publishing.

Blake, R R & Mouton, J S (1964) *The Managerial Grid*, Houston, Gulf Publishing.

Boraine, A (1999) 'Alternatives and adjuncts to criminal prosecutions', in R I. Brooks (ed) *When Sorry Isn't Enough*, New York, New York University Press.

Bowers, D G & Seashore, S E (1966) 'Predicting effectiveness with a four-factor theory of leadership', *Administrative Science Quarterly*, 2: 238–263.

Box, S (1981) *Deviance, Reality and Society*, London, Holt, Rinehart and Winston.

Braithwaite, John (1989) *Crime, Shame and Reintegration*, Cambridge, Cambridge University Press.

—— (1996) 'Restorative justice and a better future', Dorothy J Killam Memorial Lecture, Australian National University.

—— (1998a) 'Linking crime prevention to restorative justice', North American Conference on Conferencing Papers, Minneapolis, Minnesota, 23–29.

—— (1998b) 'Institutionalizing distrust, enculturating trust', in V Braithwaite and M Levi (eds) *Trust and Governance*, New York, Russell Sage.

—— (1999a) 'Restorative justice: assessing optimistic and pessimistic accounts', In M Tonry (ed) *Crime and Justice, A Review of Research*, 25, Chicago, University of Chicago Press, 1–127.

—— (1999b) 'Crime in a convict republic', unpublished paper presented to the conference on Restorative Justice and Civil Society, Australian National University, 16–18 February.

—— (forthcoming) *Restorative Justice and Responsive Regulation*, New York, Oxford University Press.

Braithwaite, John & Grabosky, Peter (1993) (eds) *Business Regulation and Australia's Future*, Canberra, Australian Institute of Criminology.

Braithwaite, John & Mugford, S (1994) 'Conditions of successful reintegration ceremonies: dealing with juvenile offenders', *British Journal of Criminology*, 34 (2): 139–171.

Brogden, M & Shearing, Clifford (1993) *Policing for a New South Africa*, London, Routledge.

Brooks, R L (1999) (ed) *When Sorry Isn't Enough*, New York, New York University Press.

Brown S & Yantzi, M (1980) *Needs Assessment for Victims and Witnesses of Crime*, Ontario Mennonite Central Committee.

Brownlie, I (1998) *Principles of Public International Law*, 5th edition, Oxford, Clarendon Press.

Bull, R, Bustin, B, Evans, P & Gahagan, D (eds) (c 1983) *Psychology for Police Officers*, Chichester, Sussex; New York, Wiley.

Burchell, Graham (1993) 'Liberal government and techniques of the self', in Andrew Barry, Thomas Osborne & Nikolas Rose (eds) *Foucault and Political Reason, Liberalism, Neo-Liberalism and Rationalities of Government*, Chicago, University of Chicago Press.

Burford, G and Pennell, J (1998) 'Family group decision making project, outcome report, volume I', Newfoundland, St John's, Memorial University.

Burns, James MacGregor (1978) *Leadership*, New York, Harper & Row.

Callaghan, S & Joseph, S (1995) 'Self concept and peer victimization among school children', *Personality and Individual Differences*, 18 (1): 161–163.

Canada, Indian and Northern Affairs (1998) *Gathering Strength*, Ottawa, available online at www.inac.go.ca.

Carrier, Ryan (forthcoming) 'The dissolving boundaries between private and public, private security and policing in South Africa', *African Security Review*.

Carrington F (1975) *The Victims*, New Rochelle, NY, Arlington House.

—— (1977) 'Victims' rights legislation', *University of Richmond Law Review*, 11 (3): 447–470.

Chan, Wai Yin (1996) 'Family Conferences in the juvenile justice process: survey on the impact of Family Conferencing on juvenile offenders and their families', Subordinate Courts Statistics and Planning Unit Research Bulletin, February 1996, Singapore.

Charles, C M (1985) *Building Classroom Discipline: From Models to Practice*, 2nd edition, New York, Longman.

Chesney, S & Schneider, C (1981) 'Crime victims crisis centers: the Minnesota experience', in B Galaway & J Hudson (eds) *Perspectives on Crime Victims*, St Louis, Mosby.

Chowning, A (1973) *An Introduction to the Peoples and Cultures of Melanesia*, Massachusetts, Addison-Wesley Publishing Company.

Christie, Nils (1977) 'Conflicts as property', *British Journal of Criminology*, 17 (1): 1–15.

—— (1986) 'The ideal victim', in E Fattah (ed) *From Crime Policy to Victim Policy*, London, Macmillan.

Clifford, W (1976) 'Crime prevention in Papua New Guinea', in David Biles (ed) *Crime in Papua New Guinea*, Canberra, Australian Institute of Criminology, 79–90.

Cohen, Stanley (1985) *Visions of Social Control, Crime, Punishment and Classification*, Oxford & New York, Polity Press.

Collins, Deborah (1998) 'Evaluation of the behavioural change program of the NSW Police Service' (internal Police Service document).

Consedine, Jim (1995) *Restorative Justice, Healing the Effects of Crime*, Lyttelton, NZ, Ploughshares Publications.

Corlett, William (1989) *Community Without Unity , A Politics Of Derridian Extravagance*, Durham, NC, Duke University Press.

Cox, E (1995) *A Truly Civil Society*, ABC Boyer Lectures, Sydney, ABC Books.

Crawford, Adam (1997) *The Local Governance of Crime: Appeals to Community and Partnerships*, Oxford, Clarendon Press.

—— (1998) 'Community safety and the quest for security: holding back the dynamics of social exclusion', *Policy Studies*, 19: 237–253.

—— (2000) 'Salient themes towards a victim perspective and the limitations of restorative justice: some concluding comments', in A Crawford and J Goodey (eds) *Integrating a Victim Perspective within Criminal Justice*, Aldershot, Ashgate.

Crawford, T, Strong, K, Sargeant, K, Souryal, C & Van Ness, D (1990) *Restorative Justice: Principles*, Washington DC, Justice Fellowship.

Critchley, Simon (1992) *The Ethics Of Deconstruction: Derrida And Levinas*, Oxford & Cambridge, Mass, Blackwell.

Cruikshank, Barbara (1999) *The Will to Empower, Democratic Citizens and Other Subjects*, Ithaca, NY, Cornell University Press.

Cunneen, C (1997) 'Community conferencing and the fiction of Indigenous control', *Australian and New Zealand Journal of Criminology*, 30 (3): 292–311.

—— (1998) 'Restorative justice and the recognition of Indigenous rights', paper presented to the Second Annual International Conference on Restorative Justice for Juveniles, Florida, Atlantic University, Fort Lauderdale, 7–9 November 1998.

Cunneen, C & Libesman, T (2000a) *A Review of the Federal Government's Response to the National Inquiry into the Separation of Aboriginal and Torres Strait Islander Children from their Families*, AIATSIS Research Discussion Paper No 10, AIATSIS, Canberra.

—— (2000b) 'Postcolonial trauma: the contemporary removal of Indigenous children and young people from families in Australia', *Australian Journal of Social Issues*, 35 (2): 99–116.

Dahl, Robert (1998) *On Democracy*, New Haven, Yale University Press.

Daly, K, and Immarigeon, R (1998) 'The past, present, and future of restorative justice: some critical reflections', *Contemporary Justice Review*, 1: 21–45.

Damasio, A R (1994) *Descartes' Error: Emotion, Reason, and the Human Brain*, New York, Avon Books.

Damaska, M R (1986) *The Faces of Justice and State Authority: A Comparative Approach to the Legal Process*, New Haven, Yale University Press.

Davis, J (1970) 'The London garrotting panic of 1862: a moral panic and the creation of a criminal class in mid-Victorian England', in V Gattrell, B Lenman & G Parker (eds) *Crime and the Law: A Social History of Crime in Western Europe Since 1500*, London, Europa.

Davis, R (1987) *Providing Help to Victims: A Study of Psychological and Material Outcomes*, New York, Victim Services Agency.

Davis, R, Kummenther, R & Connick, E (1984) 'Expanding the victim's role in the criminal court dispositional process', *Journal of Criminal Law and Criminology*, 12.

de Bertodano, H (1998) 'Lawyer of the jungle', *Sunday Telegraph* Features Section, 8 February, p 3.

de Tocqueville, Alexis (1848; 1969) *Democracy In America*, translated by George Lawrence and edited by J P Mayer, New York, Anchor Books.

Demos, E V (ed) (1994) *Exploring Affect: The Selected Writings of Silvan S Tomkins*, Cambridge, Cambridge University Press.

Derrida, Jacques (1976) *Of Grammatology*, Baltimore, Johns Hopkins University Press.

—— (1992) 'The force of law, the "mystical foundation of authority"', in D Cornell, M Rosenfeld, D Carlson & N Benjamin (eds) *Deconstruction And The Possibility Of Justice*, New York, Routledge.

—— (1994) *Specters Of Marx: The State of The Debt, The Work of Mourning, and The New International*, New York, Routledge.

—— (1995) *Points, Interviews, 1974–1994*, Stanford, CA, Stanford University Press.

Derrida, Jacques (1997) *Deconstruction in a Nutshell: A Conversation with Jacques Derrida* (edited by J D Caputo), New York, Fordham University Press.

Dietz, B (1994) 'Effects on subsequent heterosexual shyness and depression of peer victimisation at school', paper presented at the International Conference on Children's Peer Relations, Institute of Social Research, University of South Australia, Adelaide.

DiIulio Jr, John J (1998) 'Inner-city crime, what the Federal Government should do', in Amitai Etzioni (ed) *The Essential Communitarian Reader*, Lanham, MD, Rowman & Littlefield.

Dinnen, S (1994) 'Public order in Papua New Guinea – problems and prospects', in Alan Thompson (ed) *Papua New Guinea – Issues for Australian Security Planners*, Canberra, Australian Defence Studies Centre, 99–115.

—— (1995a) 'Custom, community and criminal justice in Papua New Guinea', in Jonathan Aleck & Jackson Rannells (eds) *Custom at the Crossroads*, Port Moresby, Faculty of Law, University of Papua New Guinea, 148–170.

—— (1995b) 'Praise the Lord and pass the ammunition – criminal group surrender in Papua New Guinea', *Oceania*, 66 (2): 103–118.

Doob, A N (1999) 'Understanding public views of what should be accomplished at sentencing', paper presented to Canadian Institute for the Administration of Justice Conference, Saskatoon.

Dorney, S (1990) *Papua New Guinea – People, Politics and History Since 1975*, Sydney, Random House.

Drucker, Peter (1994) 'The age of social transformation', *The Atlantic Monthly*, 274: 53–80.

Duffee, D, Hussey, F & Kramer, J (1978) *Criminal Justice: Organization, Structure, and Analysis*, Englewood Cliffs, NJ, Prentice-Hall.

Education Queensland (1998) *1997 Pilot of Community Accountability Conferencing Report*, unpublished paper, Brisbane, Education Queensland.

Eggers, William D & O'Leary, John (1995) *Revolution at the Roots: Making Government Smaller, Better, and Closer to Home*, New York, Free Press.

Einfeld, M (1998) 'Schools as a microcosm of society', paper presented at Australian Council of State School Organisations, May 8, Canberra, ACT.

Elias, N [1939] (1978/1982) *The Civilising Process: I The History of Manners; II State Formation and Civilisation*, Oxford, Blackwell.

Elias, R (1986) *The Politics of Victimisation, Victims, Victimology and Human Rights*, New York, Oxford University Press.

—— (1990) 'Which victim movement? The politics of victim policy', in A Lurigio, W Skogan & R Davis (eds) *Victims of Crime, Problems, Policies and Programs*, New York, Sage.

Emler, N & Reicher, S (1995) *Adolescence and Delinquency: The Collective Management of Reputation*, Oxford, Blackwell.

Erez, E (2000) 'Integrating a victim perspective in criminal justice through victim impact statements', in A Crawford and J Goodey (eds) *Integrating a Victim Perspective within Criminal Justice*, Aldershot, Ashgate.

Ericson, Richard & Haggerty, Kevin (1997) *Policing the Risk Society*, Toronto, University of Toronto Press.

Etzioni, Amitai (ed) (1998) *The Essential Communitarian Reader*, Lanham, MD, Rowman & Littlefield.

Farrington, D (1993) 'Understanding and preventing bullying', In M Tonry and N Morris (eds), *Crime and Justice*, 17, Chicago, University of Chicago Press.

Fattah, E (1986) 'Prologue: On some visible and hidden dangers of victims movements', in E Fattah (ed) *From Crime Policy to Victim Policy*, London, Macmillan.

—— (1993) 'The rational choice/opportunity perspectives as a vehicle for integrating criminological and victimological theories', in R Clarke & M Felson (eds) *Advances in Criminological Theory*, vol 5, New Brunswick, NJ, Transaction.

Federal Bureau of Investigation, United States Department of Justice (1993), *Crime in the United States: Uniform Crime Reports*, Washington DC, Government Printing Office.

—— (1999) *Crime in the United States: Uniform Crime Reports*, Washington DC, Government Printing Office.

Fercello, C & Umbreit, M (1998) *Client Evaluation of Family Group Conferencing in Twelve Sites: First Judicial District of Minnesota*, Minneapolis, Center for Restorative Justice and Mediation, University of Minnesota.

Fisher, R & Ury, W (1991) *Getting to Yes: Negotiating an Agreement without Giving In*, 2nd edition, London, Arrow Books.

Fisher, Robert Hartley (1972a) 'Agricola, Johann', *Encyclopedia Britannica*, vol 1.

—— (1972b) 'Antinomianism', *Encyclopedia Britannica*, vol 2.

Fishkin, J (1995) *The Voice of the People: Public Opinion and Democracy*, New Haven, Yale University Press.

Fonseka, Leo (1999) 'Good urban governance: a toolkit of indicators and positive references' (draft document, 1 August), mimeo.

Forsythe, Lubica (1995) 'An analysis of juvenile apprehension characteristics and reapprehension rates', in David Moore, with Lubica Forsythe and Terry O'Connell (eds) *A New Approach to Juvenile Justice: An Evaluation of Family Conferencing in Wagga Wagga*, A Report to the Criminology Research Council, Wagga Wagga, Charles Sturt University.

Foucault, Michel & Gordon, Colin (1980) *Power/Knowledge, Selected Interviews And Other Writings, 1972–1977*, Brighton, Sussex, Harvester Press.

Frank, A & Fuentes, M (1990) 'Social movements', in *New Directions in the Study of Justice, Law and Social Control*, prepared by the School of Justice Studies, Arizona State University, Temple, Arizona; Plenum Press, New York.

Friedman, L, Bischoff, L, Davis, R & Person, A (1982) *Victims and Helpers: Reactions to Crime*, Washington DC, US Government Printing Office.

Fukuyama, Francis (1992) *The End of History and the Last Man*, New York, Free Press.

Furlong, V J (1991) 'Disaffected pupils: reconstructing the sociological perspective', *British Journal of Sociology of Education*, 2 (3): 293–307.

Gabor, T (1994) *Everybody Does It! Crime by the Public*, Toronto, University of Toronto.

Galanter, M (1979) 'Justice in many rooms', Working Paper No 4, Madison, WI, University of Wisconsin Law School, Dispute Resolution Program.

Galaway, B & Hudson, J (eds) (1996) *Restorative Justice: International Perspectives*, Monsey, NY, Criminal Justice Press.

Gallup Report on Social Trends (1995) Report 419 (July).

Garap, S (2000) 'Struggles of women and girls – Simbu Province, Papua New Guinea', in Sinclair Dinnen & Alison Ley (eds) *Reflections on Violence in Melanesia*, Sydney & Canberra, Hawkins Press & Asia Pacific Press.

Garland, David (1996) 'The limits of the sovereign state: strategies of crime control in contemporary society', *British Journal of Criminology*, 36 (4): 445–471.

Gay, M, Holtom, C & Thomas, S (1975) 'Helping the victims', *International Journal of Offender Therapy and Comparative Criminology*, 19 (3): 263–269.

Geis, G (1990) 'Crime victims: practices and prospects', in A Lurigio, W Skogan & R Davis (eds) *Victims of Crime: Problems, Policies and Programs*, New York, Sage Publications.

Gendreau, P, and Ross, R R (1983) 'Correctional treatment: some recommendations for effective intervention', *Juvenile and Family Court Journal*, 34 (4): 31–39.

Giddens, Anthony (1991) *Modernity and Self-Identity in the Late Modern Age*, Oxford, Polity Press.

—— (1998) *The Third Way: The Renewal Of Social Democracy*, Cambridge, UK & Malden, Mass, Polity Press.

Giddings, L (1986) 'Some alternatives to states of emergency', in Louise Morauta (ed) *Law and Order in a Changing Society*, Canberra, Australian National University, Political and Social Change, Monograph No 6, 86–109.

Glaser, D (1969) *The Effectiveness of a Prison and Parole System*, Indianapolis, Indiana, Bobbs-Merrill.

Goddard, M (1992) 'Big-man, thief: the social organization of gangs in Port Moresby', *Canberra Anthropology*, 15 (1): 20–34.

—— (1995) 'The rascal road: crime, prestige and development in Papua New Guinea', *The Contemporary Pacific*, 7 (1): 55–80.

—— (2000) 'Three urban village courts in Papua New Guinea: some comparative observations on dispute settlement', in Sinclair Dinnen and Alison Ley (eds) *Reflections on Violence in Melanesia*, Sydney & Canberra, Hawkins Press & Asia Pacific Press.

Goodin, E (1998) 'Communities of Enlightenment' (review article), *British Journal of Political Science*, 28: 531–559.

Gordon, R J (1983) 'The decline of the kiapdom and the resurgence of "tribal fighting" in Enga', *Oceania*, 53: 205–223.

Gottfredson, D C (1998) 'School-based crime prevention', in L W Sherman, D Gottfredson, D MacKenzie, J Eck, P Reuter & S Bushway (eds) *Preventing Crime, What Works, What Doesn't, and What's Promising: A Report to the United States Congress* prepared for the National Institute of Justice Department of Criminology and Criminal Justice, University of Maryland.

Gottfredson, D, Gottfredson, G & Hybl, L (1993) 'Managing adolescent behavior: a multiyear, multischool study', *American Educational Research Journal*, 30 (1): 179–215.

Grabosky, P (1996) 'The future of crime control', *Trends & Issues in Crime and Criminal Justice*, No 63, Canberra, Australian Institute of Criminology.

Hahn, P H (1998) *Emerging Criminal Justice – Three Pillars for a Proactive Justice System*, California, Sage Publications.

Harrington, Christine B (1985) *Shadow Justice: the Ideology and Institutionalization of Alternatives to Court*, Westport, Conn, Greenwood Press.

Harris, B M (1988) *The Rise of Rascalism: action and reaction in the evolution of rascal gangs*, Port Moresby, Institute of Applied Social and Economic Research Discussion Paper No 54.

Hawthorne, Nathaniel (1900) *The Scarlet Letter*, Boston, Houghton Mifflin.

Hayes, H, Prenzler, T & Wortley, R (1998) *Making Amends: Final Evaluation of the Queensland Community Conferencing Pilot*, paper prepared for Queensland Department of Justice, Juvenile Justice Branch, Brisbane.

Haynes, J (1996) *Third World Politics: A Concise Introduction*, Oxford, Blackwell.

Hepworth, M & Turner, B (1982) *Confession: Studies in Deviance and Religion*, London, Routledge and Kegan Paul..

Herzberg, F (1968) 'One more time: How do you motivate employees?', *Harvard Business Review*, January–February, 27–35.

Hindelang, M (1976) *Criminal Victimization in Eight American Cities: A Descriptive Analysis of Common Theft and Assault*, Cambridge, Mass, Ballinger Publishing Company.

Hirschi, T, and Gottfredson, M (1983) 'Age and the explanation of crime', *American Journal of Sociology*, 89 (3): 522–584.

Hofrichter, Richard (1987) *Neighborhood Justice In Capitalist Society: The Expansion of the Informal State*, New York, Greenwood Press.

Hofstadter, Richard (1963) *Anti-Intellectualism In American Life*, New York, Albert A Knopf.

Holtom, C & Raynor, P (1988) 'Origins of victims support policy and practice', in M Maguire & J Pointing (eds) *Victims of Crime: A New Deal?*, Milton Keynes, Open University Press.

Home Office (1993) *White Paper on Police Reform*, London, Her Majesty's Stationery Office.

—— (1998) *Statistics on Race and the Criminal Justice System, a Home Office Publication under Section 95 of the Criminal Justice Act 1991*, London, Her Majesty's Stationery Office.

Hope, T (1996) 'Communities, crime and inequality in England and Wales', in T Bennett (ed) *Preventing Crime and Disorder*, Cambridge, Institute of Criminology, University of Cambridge, pp 165–194

Hough, M & Roberts, J (1998) *Attitudes to Punishment: Findings from the British Crime Survey*, Home Office Research and Statistics Directorate Report, pp 7–10.

Hudson, J, Morris, A, Maxwell, G & Galaway, B (eds) (1996) *Family Group Conferences: Perspectives on Policy and Practice*, Sydney, The Federation Press.

Huesmann, L R, Eron, L D, Lefkowitz, M M & Walder, L O (1984) 'Stability of aggression over time and generations', *Developmental Psychology*, 20: 1120–1134.

Human Rights and Equal Opportunity Commission (1989) *Our Homeless Children, Report of the National Inquiry into Homeless Children* (Burdekin Report), Canberra, Human Rights and Equal Opportunity Commission, Australian Government Publishing Service.

—— (2000) Submission to the Senate Legal and Constitutional References Committee's Inquiry into the Stolen Generations, HREOC, Sydney.

Hyndman, M & Thorsborne, M (1993) 'Bullying: a school focus', in D Evans, M Myhill & J Izard (eds), *Proceedings of the 1993 National Conference on Student Behaviour Problems*, University of South Australia.

—— (1994) 'Taking action on bullying: whole school and multi-stage approach to intervention and prevention', *In Proceedings of First International Conference on Peer Relations, Conflict and Cooperation*, Institute of Social Research, University of South Australia.

Independent Commission (1999) *A New Beginning, Policing in Northern Ireland* (The Report of the Independent Commission on Policing for Northern Ireland).

Inglehart, Ronald (1997) 'Postmaterialist values and the erosion of institutional authority', in Joseph S Nye Jnr, Philip D Zelikow and David C King (eds) *Why People Don't Trust Government*, Cambridge, Mass, Harvard University Press, pp 217–236.

Jacobs, J (1993) *Systems of Survival: A Dialogue on the Moral Foundations of Commerce and Politics*, London, Hodder and Stoughton.

Johnston, Les (1992) *The Rebirth of Private Policing*, London, Routledge.

Johnstone, G (1996) *Medical Concepts and Penal Policy*, London, Cavendish Publishing.

Katz, Jack (1988) *Seductions Of Crime: Moral and Sensual Attractions in Doing Evil*, New York, Basic Books.

Kawachi, I & Kennedy, B P (1997) 'Health and social cohesion: why care about income inequality?', *British Medical Journal*, 314: 1037–1040.

Kawachi, I, Kennedy, B P & Wilkinson, R G (1999) 'Crime, social disorganisation and relative deprivation', *Social Science and Medicine*, 48: 719.

Kawachi, I, Kennedy, B P, Lochner, K & Prothow-Stith, D (1997) 'Social capital, income inequality, and mortality', *American Journal of Public Health*, 87: 1491–1498.

Kelling, G L & Coles, C M (1996) *Fixing Broken Windows: Restoring Order and Reducing Crime in Our Communities*, New York, Martin Kessler.

Kelly, V C, Jr (1996) 'Affect and the redefinition of intimacy', in D L Nathanson (ed) *Knowing Feeling*, New York, W W Norton.

Kennedy, B P, Kawachi, I & Brainerd, E (1998) 'The role of social capital in the Russian mortality crisis', *World Development*, 26: 2029.

King, D (1992) 'The demise of the small towns and outstations of Papua New Guinea: trends in urban census populations and growth from 1966 to 1990', *Yagl-Ambu*, 16 (3): 17–33.

Koh, A C E (1997) 'The delinquent peer group: social identity and self-categorization perspectives', unpublished PhD dissertation, Australian National University.

Kormorita, S S & Parks, C D (1994) *Social Dilemmas*, Wisconsin, Brown and Benchmark's.

Krygier, M (1997) *Between Fear and Hope: Hybrid Thoughts on Public Values*, ABC Boyer Lectures, Sydney, ABC Books.

Kuper L (1981) *Genocide: Its Political Use in the Twentieth Century*, New Haven and London, Yale University Press.

LaFree, Gary (1998) *Losing Legitimacy, Street Crime and the Decline of Social Institutions in the United States*, Boulder, CO, Westview Press.

LaFree, Gary & Drass, Kriss A (1996) 'The effect of changes in intraracial income inequality and educational attainment on changes in arrest rates for African Americans and whites, 1957–1990', *American Sociological Review*, 61: 614–634.

LaPrairie Carol (1995a) 'Altering course, new directions in criminal justice', *Australian and New Zealand Journal of Criminology*, Special Supplementary Issue.

—— (1995b) 'Community justice or just community? Aboriginal communities in search of justice', *Canadian Journal of Criminology*, 37: 521–545.

—— (1999) 'Some reflections on new criminal justice policies in Canada, restorative justice, alternative measures and conditional sentences', *Australian and New Zealand Journal of Criminology*, 32 (2): 139–152.

Law Commission of Canada (1999) *From Restorative Justice to Transformative Justice, A Discussion Paper*, Canada.

—— (2000) *Restoring Dignity: Responding to Child Abuse in Canadian Institutions*, available on-line at www.lcc.gc.ca.

Law Enforcement News, John Jay College of Criminal Justice, City University of New York.

Lawrence, P (1969) 'The state versus stateless societies in Papua New Guinea', in Bernard J Brown (ed) *Fashion of Law in New Guinea*, Sydney, Butterworths, 15–37.

Levantis, T (1997) 'The labour market of Papua New Guinea: a study of its structure and policy implications', unpublished PhD thesis, Australian National University.

Levantis, T & Gani, A (1998) 'Labour market deregulation, crime and Papua New Guinea's severe drought', *Pacific Economic Bulletin*, 13 (1): 89–97.

Lewin, K (1943) *Forces Behind Food Habits and Methods of Change*, Bulletin 108, Washington DC, National Research Council.

—— (1948) *Resolving Social Conflicts: Selected Papers on Group Dynamics*, New York, Harper.

—— (1951) *Field Theory in Social Science*, New York, Harper.

Lewin, K, Lippit, R & White, R (1939) 'Patterns of aggressive behavior in experimentally created social climates', *Journal of Psychology*, 271–299.

Likert, R (1961) *New Patterns of Management*, New York, McGraw-Hill.

—— (1967) *The Human Organization*, New York, McGraw-Hill.

Lindblom, C (1990) *Inquiry and Change: The Troubled Attempt to Understand and Shape Society*, New Haven, Yale University Press.

Luthans, F (1985) *Organizational Behavior: Modification and Beyond*, Glenview, IL, Scott Foresman.

Lyster, R (2000) 'The South African experience of truth and reconciliation: some comments on the South African model and possible lessons for Australia', *Current Issues in Criminal Justice*, 12 (1).

MacKenzie, D L (1998) 'Criminal justice and crime prevention', in L W Sherman, D Gottfredson, D MacKenzie, J Eck, P Reuter & S Bushway (eds) *Preventing Crime, What Works, What Doesn't, and What's Promising: A Report to the United States Congress*, prepared for the National Institute of Justice, Department of Criminology and Criminal Justice, University of Maryland.

Maguire, M (1991) 'The needs and rights of victims of crime', in M Tonry (ed) *Crime and Justice, A Review of Research*, vol 14, Chicago and London, The University of Chicago Press.

Maguire M & Corbett, C (1987) *The Effects of Crime and the Work of Victims Support Schemes*, Aldershot, Gower.

Maguire, M & Shapland, J (1990) 'The "victims movement" in Europe', in A Lurigio, W Skogan & R Davis (eds) *Victims of Crime, Problems, Policies and Programs*, Newbury Park, Sage Publications.

Malinowski, B, (1972) *Argonauts of the Western Pacific, An account of native enterprise and adventure in the archipelagoes of Melanesian New Guinea*, London, Routledge and Kegan Paul.

Malouf, D (1998) *A Spirit of Play: The Making of Australian Consciousness*, ABC Boyer Lectures, Sydney, ABC Books.

Markus, A (1990) *Governing Savages*, Sydney, Allen and Unwin.

Marongiu, P & Newman, G (1987) *Vengeance: The Fight Against Injustice*, Totowa, NJ, Rowman and Littlefield.

Marshall, T F (1992) 'Restorative justice on trial in Britain', in H Messmer & H-U Otto (eds) *Restorative Justice on Trial*, Netherlands, Kluwer Academic Publishers, pp 15–28.

Marshall, Tony (1985) *Alternatives to Criminal Courts* Aldershot, Gower.

Mason, Anthony (2000) 'Restorative justice, courts and civil society', in H Strang & J Braithwaite (eds) *Restorative Justice: From Theory to Practice*, Aldershot, Ashgate.

Masters, Guy (1997) 'Reintegrative shaming in theory and practice: thinking about feeling in criminology', unpublished PhD thesis, Department of Applied Social Science, Lancaster University.

Mawby, R (1988) 'Victims' needs or victims' rights: alternative approaches to policy making', in M Maguire & J Pointing (eds) *A New Deal for Crime Victims?*, Milton Keynes, Open University Press.

Mawby, R & Gill, M (1987) *Crime Victims, Needs, Services and the Voluntary Sector*, London, Tavistock.

May, R J (1982) *Micronationalist Movements in Papua New Guinea*, Canberra, Australian National University, Political and Social Change, Monograph No 1.

McBarnett, D (1988) 'Victim in the witness box – confronting victimology's stereotype', *Contemporary Crises*, vol 7, pp 279–303.

McCold, P (1996) 'Restorative justice, variations on a theme', in L Walgrave (ed) *Restorative Justice for Juveniles: Potentialities, Risks and Problems for Research*, Belgium.

—— (2000) 'Toward a mid-range theory of restorative criminal justice: a reply to the Maximalist Model', *Contemporary Justice Review*, 3 (4): 357–414.

McCulloch, H (1996) *Shop Theft: Improving the Police Response*, Home Office Police Research Group, Crime Detection and Prevention Series Paper No 76, London, Her Majesty's Stationery Office.

McDonald, J M & Moore, D B (1995) 'Achieving the good community: a local police initiative and its wider ramifications' in K Hazlehurst (ed) *Justice and*

Reform, vol 2, Regenerating Communities Through Crime Prevention, Aldershot, Avebury.

McElrea, F (1996) 'Discipline and restorative justice', unpublished paper for the Legal Research Foundation on Education.

—— (1998) 'The New Zealand model of Family Group Conferences', *Awhi Newsletter*, 5 (3).

McGregor, D (1960) *The Human Side of Enterprise*, New York: McGraw-Hill.

McKenzie, A (1999) 'An evaluation of school community forums in New South Wales Schools', paper presented at Restorative Justice and Civil Society Reshaping Australian Institutions Conference, Research School of Social Sciences, Australian National University, February 16–18, 1999.

McLaren, K (1992) *Reducing Reoffending: What Works Now*, Wellington, NZ, Penal Division, New Zealand Department of Justice.

Meggitt, M J (1977) *Blood is their Argument, Warfare among the Mae Enga Tribesmen of the New Guinea Highlands*, Palo Alto, CA, Mayfield.

Merry, Sally Engle, and Neal A Milner (1993) *The Possibility of Popular Justice: A Case Study of Community Mediation in the United States*, Ann Arbor, University of Michigan Press.

Miller, D & Swanson, G (1960) *Inner Conflict and Defense*, New York, W W Norton.

Moore, D B (1996a) 'Shame, forgiveness, and juvenile justice', in M Braswell, B McCarthy & B McCarthy (eds) *Justice, Crime and Ethics*, 2nd edition, Cincinnati, OH, Anderson Publishing. [Originally published in *Criminal Justice Ethics*, 12, 1993. Also available at www.lib.jjay.cuny.edu/cje/html/sample2.html.

—— (1996b) 'Shame: human universal or cultural construct?', in R Dalziell, D Parker & I Wright (eds) *Shame and the Modern Self*, Melbourne, Australian Scholarly Publishers.

—— (1996c) 'Criminal action – official reaction, affect theory, criminology and criminal justice', in D L Nathanson (ed) *Knowing Feeling*, New York, W W Norton.

—— (1998a) 'Justice in the workplace: the transformation of economic communities', *Humanity and Society*, 22 (3): 78–96.

—— (1998b) 'Pride, shame and empathy among peers: community conferencing as transformative justice in education', in K Rigby & P Slee (eds) *Children's Peer Relations*, London, Routledge.

Moore, D B, Forsythe, L and O'Connell, T (1995) *A New Approach to Juvenile Justice, An Evaluation of Family Conferencing in Wagga Wagga*, Wagga Wagga, Charles Sturt University.

Moore, D B and O'Connell, T (1994) 'Family conferencing in Wagga Wagga, A communitarian model of justice', in C Alder and J Wundersitz (eds) *Family Conferencing and Juvenile Justice*, Canberra, Australian Studies in Law, Crime, and Justice, Australian Institute of Criminology.

Moore, D B & McDonald, J (2000) *Transforming Conflict in Workplaces and Other Communities*, Sydney, TJA.

Moore, S (1972) 'Legal liability and evolutionary interpretation, some aspects of strict liability, self-help and collective responsibility', in Max Gluckman (ed) *The Allocation Of Responsibility*, Manchester, Manchester University Press.

Morgan, Edmund S (1964) *The Founding of Massachusetts: Historians and Sources*, Indianapolis, Bobbs-Merrill.

Morris, Allison & Young, Warren (1987) *Juvenile Justice In New Zealand: Policy and Practice*, Institute of Criminology Victoria University of Wellington, Wellington, NZ.

Morris, Edmund (1978) *The Rise of Theodore Roosevelt*, New York, Coward, McCann & Geoghegan.

Morris, Ruth (1995) 'Not Enough!', *Mediation Quarterly*, 12 (3): 285–291.

Morrison, B E (1998) 'Social cooperation, re-defining the self in self-interest', unpublished PhD dissertation, Australian National University.

—— (1999) 'Interdependence, the group and social cooperation: a new look at an old problem', in M Foddy, M Smithson, S Schneider and M Hogg (eds) *Resolving social dilemmas: dynamic, structural and intergroup aspects*, Psychology Press.

—— (forthcoming, a) *Behavioural management in ACT schools: Current issues and trends*.

—— (forthcoming, b) *Developing responsible citizenship in our schools: A restorative justice approach to school bullying*.

Mortimore, P, Sammons, P, Ecob, R & Stol, L (1988) *School Matters: The Junior Years*, Salisbury, Open Books.

Mosteller R (1998) 'Victims' rights and the United States Constitution: moving from guaranteeing participatory rights to benefiting the prosecution', *St Mary's Law Journal*, 29: 1053–65.

Myrdal, G (1968) *Asian Drama: An Inquiry Into The Poverty Of Nations*, New York, Random House, Pantheon Books.

Nader, L (ed) (1969) *Law In Culture And Society*, Chicago, IL, Aldine Publishing.

Nancy, Jean-Luc (1991) *The Inoperative Community*, Minneapolis, MN, University of Minnesota Press.

Nathanson, D L (1992) *Shame and Pride, Affect, Sex, and the Birth of Self*, New York, W W Norton.

—— (1996) (ed) *Knowing Feeling*, New York, W W Norton.

—— (1997) 'Affect theory and the compass of shame', in M Lansky & A Morrison (eds) *The Widening Scope of Shame*, London, Analytic Press.

—— (1998) 'From empathy to community', paper presented at 'Conferencing: A New Response To Wrongdoing', Minneapolis, MN, August 6–8. Available on-line at www.realjustice.org.

National Crime Prevention (1999) *Pathways to Prevention, Developmental and Early Intervention Approaches to Crime in Australia*, Canberra, Attorney-General's Department.

National Inquiry into the Separation of Aboriginal and Torres Strait Islander Children from Their Families (1997), *Bringing Them Home*, Report of the National Inquiry into the Separation of Aboriginal and Torres Strait Islander Children from Their Families, HREOC, Sydney.

National Police Research Unit (1998) *The Police Role Survey: A Tool for Comparing Public and Police Perceptions of the Police Role*, Adelaide, National Police Research Unit.

Nelsen, J (1996) *Positive Discipline*, 2nd edition, New York, Ballantine Books.

Neustadt, Richard & May, Ernest (1986) *Thinking in Time: The Uses of History For Decision Makers*, New York, Free Press.

Newman, G (1978) *The Punishment Response*, Philadelphia, J B Lippincott Co.

Newman, Otto & de Zoysa, Richard (1997) 'Communitarianism, the new panacea?', *Sociological Perspectives*, 40: 622–38.

New Zealand Ministry of Justice (1995) *Restorative Justice: A Discussion Paper*, Wellington, NZ, Ministry of Justice.

—— (1996) *Restorative Justice: A Discussion Paper* Wellington, NZ, Ministry of Justice.

Nisbett, Richard E & Cohen, Dov (1996) *Culture Of Honor: The Psychology of Violence in the South*, Boulder, CO, Westview Press.

Norquay, G & Weiler, R (1981) *Services to Victims and Witnesses of Crime in Canada*, Ottawa, Canadian Ministry of the Solicitor General.

NSW Parliamentary Hansard (1998), 28th October.

NSW Police Service (1998) *Cultural Survey, IBM Consulting*, March 1998.

Nye, Joseph S, Jr & Zelikow, Philip D (1997) 'Conclusion, reflections, conjectures and puzzles', in Joseph S Nye, Jr, Philip D Zelikow & David C King (eds) *Why People Don't Trust Government*, Cambridge, Mass, Harvard University Press.

O'Collins, Maeve (1999) 'Images of violence in Papua New Guinea: whose images, whose reality?', in Sinclair Dinnen & Alison Ley (eds) *Reflections on Violence in Melanesia*, Annandale, NSW & Canberra, Federation Press & Asia Pacific Press.

O'Connell, T (1999) 'In what way can the introduction of restorative justice practices into schools reduce or prevent youth crime?', a discussion paper initiated by Thames Valley Police Chief Constable Charles Pollard.

—— (forthcoming) 'Restorative justice and policing', unpublished Master's thesis, University of New South Wales.

Oliver, D L (1955) *A Solomon Island Society, Kinship and Leadership among the Siuai of Bougainville*, Cambridge, Mass, Harvard University Press.

Olweus, D (1991) 'Bully/victim problems among schoolchildren: basic facts and effects of a school-based intervention program', in D J Pepler and K H Rubin (eds) *The Development of Treatment of Childhood Aggression*, Hillsdale, NJ, Erlbaum.

—— (1992) 'Victimization by peers: antecedents and long-term outcomes', in K H Rubin and J B Asendorpf (eds) *School Withdrawal, Inhibition, and Shyness in Childhood*, Hillsdale, NJ, Erlbaum.

—— (1993) *Bullying at School: What We Know and What We Can Do*, Oxford, Blackwell.

O'Malley, Pat & Palmer, Darren (1996) 'Post-Keynesian policing', *Economy and Society*, 25 (2, May): 137–155.

Orentlichter, D (1994) 'Addressing gross human rights abuses: punishment and victim compensation', in L Henkin & L Hargrave (eds) *Human Rights: An Agenda for the Next Century*, Washington DC, American Society of International Law.

Orren, Gary (1997) 'Fall from grace: why people don't trust government', in Joseph S Nye, Jr, Philip D Zelikow & David C King (eds) *Why People Don't Trust Government*, Cambridge, Mass, Harvard University Press.

Osborne, David & Gaebler, Ted (1993) *Reinventing Government: How the Entrepreneurial Spirit is Transforming the Public Sector*, New York, Plume.

Packer, H (1968) *Limits of the Criminal Sanction*, Stanford, CA, Stanford University Press.

Pavlich, George (1996) *Justice Fragmented, Mediating Community Disputes Under Postmodern Conditions*, London, Routledge.

—— (1999) 'Preventing crime: "social" versus "community" governance in Aotearoa/New Zealand', in R Smandych (ed) *Governable Places: Readings on Governmentality and Crime Control*, Aldershot, Dartmouth-Ashgate, pp 103–132.

Peachey, D E (1992) 'Restitution, reconciliation, retribution: identifying the forms of justice people desire', in H Messmer and H-U Otto (eds) *Restorative Justice on Trial*, Netherlands, Kluwer Academic Publishers, pp 551–557.

Pepper, F S (1985) (ed) *Dictionary of Biographical Quotations*, London, Sphere Books.

Pettit, P (1997) *Republicanism*, Oxford, Clarendon Press.

Pettit, P & Braithwaite, John (1993) 'Not just deserts, even in sentencing', *Current Issues in Criminal Justice*, 4 (3).

Phillips, Kevin (1999) *The Cousins' Wars: Religion, Politics and the Triumph of Anglo-America*, New York, Basic Books.

Pink, W T (1988) 'School climate and effective school programmes in America', in R Slee (ed) *Discipline and Schools: A Curriculum Perspective*, Melbourne, Macmillan.

Pitts, J (1997) 'Youth crime, social change and crime control in Britain and France in the 1980s and 1990s', in H Jones (ed) *Towards a Classless Society?*, London, Routledge.

Pollard, Charles (1994) 'A law unto themselves', *Police Review*, 102, 11 February.

—— (1997) 'From problem solving policing to problem solving justice', paper presented at CIAJ National Conference, Montreal, April 1997.

Pranis, Kay (1998) 'Conferencing and the community', paper presented at 'Conferencing: A New Response To Wrongdoing', Minneapolis, MN, August 6–8. Available on-line at www.realjustice.org.

Pritchard, S (1997) 'The Stolen Generations and reparations', *UNSW Law Journal*, Forum on Stolen Children, From Removal to Reconciliation, 4 (5): 225–239.

Prunier, G (1995) *The Rwanda Crisis: History of a Genocide*, New York, Columbia University Press.

Putnam, Robert D (1993) *Making Democracy Work: Civic Traditions in Modern Italy*, Princeton, Princeton University Press.

—— (1995) 'Bowling alone: America's declining social capital', *Journal of Democracy*, 6: 65–78.

Queensland Department of Education (1993) *School and Discipline, Managing Student Behaviour in a Supportive School Environment*, Brisbane, Department of Education.

—— (1996) *Community Accountability Conferencing, Trial Report*, Brisbane, Department of Education.

Radzinowicz, Leon (1948) *A History Of English Criminal Law*, London, Macmillan.

Ramachandran, V S & Blakeslee, S (1998) *Phantoms in the Brain: Probing the Mysteries of the Mind*, New York, William Morrow.

Rasmussen, David M (1990) *Universalism Versus Communitarianism: Contemporary Debates in Ethics*, Cambridge, Mass, MIT Press.

Ratner, R S (1999) 'Tracking "crime": a professional odyssey', in J Hodgson (ed) *Social Control Versus Social Justice*, Toronto, Canadian Scholars Press.

Redeker, J (1989) *Employee Discipline: Policies and Practices*, Washington DC, The Bureau of National Affairs, Inc.

Reed, R S (1943) *The Making of Modern New Guinea, with special reference to culture contact in the mandated territory*, Philadelphia, American Philosophical Society.

Reeves, H & Mulley, K (2000) 'The new status of victims in the UK: opportunities and threats', in A Crawford & J Goodey (eds) *Integrating a Victim Perspective within Criminal Justice*, Aldershot, Ashgate.

Reiss, A (1981) 'Public safety, marshalling crime statistics', *The Annals of the American Academy of Political and Social Science*, 453: 222–236.

Retzinger, S (1991) *Violent Emotions*, Newbury Park, CA, Sage Publications.

Retzinger, S & Scheff, T J (1996) 'Strategy for community conferences: emotions and social bonds', in B Galaway & J Hudson (eds) *Restorative Justice: International Perspectives*, New York, Criminal Justice Press.

Reynolds D & Cuttance, P (eds) (1992) *School Effectiveness, Research, Policy and Practice*, London, Cassell.

Richardson, James (1970) *The New York Police: Colonial Times to 1901*, New York, Oxford University Press.

Riesman, David (1950) *The Lonely Crowd: A Study Of The Changing American Character*, New Haven, Yale University Press.

Rigby, K (1996) *Bullying in Schools and What to Do About It*, Melbourne, Australian Council for Educational Research.

Rigby, K & Slee, P (eds) (1998) *Children's Peer Relations*, London, Routledge.

Roach, K (1999) *Due Process and Victims' Rights: The New Law and Politics of Criminal Justice*, Toronto, University of Toronto Press.

Roberts, J V & Stalins, L J (1997) *Public Opinion, Crime, and Criminal Justice*, Boulder, CO, Westview.

Rose, Nikolas (1996) 'The death of the social: refiguring the territory of government', *Economy and Society*, 25 (3): 327–356.

—— (1999) *Powers of Freedom*, Cambridge, Cambridge University Press.

Rose, Nikolas & Miller, Peter (1992) 'Political power beyond the state: problematics of government', *British Journal of Sociology*, 43 (2): 173–205.

Rosenbaum, D (ed) (1994) *The Challenge Of Community Policing*, Thousand Oaks, CA, Sage Publishers.

Rothman, David (1971) *The Discovery of the Asylum*, Boston, Little, Brown.

Royal Commission on Aboriginal Peoples (Canada) (1996) *Report of the Royal Commission on Aboriginal Peoples*, Ottawa, Canada Communication Group.

Rumsey, Alan (1999) 'Women as peacemakers in the New Guinea Highlands: a case from the Nebilyer Valley, Western Highland Province', in Sinclair Dinnen & Alison Ley (eds) *Reflections on Violence in Melanesia*, Annandale, NSW & Canberra, Federation Press & Asia Pacific Press.

Rutter, M, Maughan, B, Mortimore, P & Ouston, J (1979) *Fifteen Thousand Hours: Secondary Schools and Their Effects on Children*, London, Open Books.

Santos, Boaventura de Sousa (1982) 'Law and community: the changing nature of state power in later capitalism', in R Abel (ed) *The Politics of Informal Justice*, New York, Academic Press.

Schaef, A W & Fassell, D (1997) *Addictive Organisations*, San Francisco, Harper & Row.

Scheff, T J (1990) *Microsociology: Discourse, Emotion and Social Structure*, Chicago, University of Chicago Press.

—— (1994) *Bloody Revenge: Emotions, Nationalism and War*, Boulder, CO, Westview Press.

Scheff, T & Retzinger, S (1991) *Emotions and Violence: Shame and Rage in Destructive Conflicts*, Lexington, MA, Lexington Books.

Scheingold S, Olson, T & Pershing, J (1994) 'Sexual violence, victim advocacy and republican criminology: Washington State's Community Protection Act', *Law and Society Review*, 28 (4): 729–763.

Schulman, Ronca & Bucuvalas, Inc (1999) *What Do We Want (and what are we getting) From the Criminal Justice System?*, study conducted for the Council of State Governments/Eastern Regional Conference, 5 World Trade Center 9241, New York.

Schur, E M (1973) *Radical Non-Intervention: Rethinking the Delinquency Problem*, Englewood Cliffs, NJ, Prentice-Hall.

Selznick, Philip (1995) 'Ten theses: thoughts on communitarianism', *Current*, 378: 11, 14.

—— (1996) 'Social justice: a communitarian perspective', *The Responsive Community*, 6 (4): 14–23.

Sergiovanni, T J (1994) *Building Community in Schools*, USA, Josey Bass.

Shapland, J (1988) 'Fiefs and peasants: accomplishing change for victims in the criminal justice system', in M Maguire & J Pointing (eds) *Victims of Crime: A New Deal?*, Milton Keynes, Open University Press.

—— (2000) 'Victims and criminal justice: creating responsible criminal justice agencies', in A Crawford & J Goodey (eds) *Integrating a Victim Perspective within Criminal Justice*, Aldershot, Ashgate.

Shapland, J, Willmore, J & Duff, P (1985) *Victims in the Criminal Justice System*, Cambridge Studies in Criminology, Aldershot, Gower.

Shapland, J, Hibbert, J, L'Anson, J, Sorsby, A & Wild, R (1995) *Milton Keynes Criminal Justice Audit*, The Institute for the Study of the Legal Profession, University of Sheffield.

Shearing, Clifford (1993) 'A constitutive conception of regulation', in John Braithwaite & Peter Grabosky (eds) *Business Regulation and Australia's Future*, Canberra, Australian Institute of Criminology.

—— (1994) 'Reinventing policing: policing as governance', unpublished paper for the Conference on Privatisation, Bielefeld, Germany, March 24–26.

—— (1997) 'The unrecognized origins of the new policing: linkages between public and private policing', in Marcus Felson and Ronald Clarke (eds) *Business and Crime Prevention*, Monsey, NY, Criminal Justice Press.

Shearing, Clifford & Stenning, Philip (1981) 'Modern private security: its growth and implications', in Michael Tonry & Norval Morris (eds), *Crime and Justice: An Annual Review of Research*, 3, Chicago, IL, University of Chicago Press, 193–246.

—— (1992) 'The relation between public and private policing', in Michael Tonry & Norval Morris (eds), *Modern Policing – Crime and Justice: An Annual Review of Research*, 15, Chicago, IL, University of Chicago Press, 399–434.

Shearing, Clifford & Wood, Jennifer (forthcoming) 'Reflections on the governance of security: a normative enquiry', *Police Research and Practice: An International Journal*.

Sherman, Lawrence W (1998) 'Thinking about crime prevention', in L W Sherman, D Gottfredson, D MacKenzie, J Eck, P Reuter & S Bushway (eds) *Preventing Crime, What Works, What Doesn't, and What's Promising: A Report to the United States Congress*, prepared for the National Institute of Justice and the University of Maryland.

Sherman, Lawrence W & Strang, H (1997) *The Right Kind of Shame for Crime*, RISE Working Paper No 1, Law Program, Research School of Social Sciences, Australian National University, Canberra.

Sherman, Lawrence W, Strang, H, Barnes, G, Braithwaite, J, Inkpen, N & The, M (1998) *Experiments in Restorative Policing: A Progress Report on the Canberra Reintegrative Shaming Experiments*, Law Program, Research School of Social Sciences, Australian National University, Canberra. Available on-line at www.aic.gov.au/rjustice/rise/index.html.

Sherman, Lawrence W, Strang, H & Woods D J (2000) Recidivism Patterns in the *Canberra Reintegrative Sharing Experiments (RISE)*, Centre for Restorative Justice; Research School of Social Sciences, Australian National University, Canberra. Available on-line at www.aic.gov.au/rjustice/rise/index.html.

Shonholtz, Raymond (1988/89) 'Community as peacemaker: making neighborhood justice work', *Current Municipal Problems*, 15: 291–330.

Skogan W, Davis, R & Lurigio, A (1990) 'Victims' needs and victims' services', Final Report to the National Institute of Justice, Washington DC.

Slee, P (ed) (1992) *Discipline in Australian Public Education: Changing Policy and Practice*, Melbourne, ACER.

Slee, R (1995) *Changing Theories and Practices of Discipline*, London, The Falmer Press.

Snyder, J & Patterson, G (1987) 'Family interaction and delinquent behavior', in H C Quay (ed) *Handbook of Juvenile Delinquency*, New York, John Wiley and Sons, pp 216–243.

Souryal, S (1995) *Police Organization and Administration*, 2nd edition, Cincinnati, Anderson Publishing.

Starr, J (1974) 'The impact of a legal revolution on rural Turkey', *Law And Society Review* (Summer): 533–560.

Stenning, P & Shearing, C (1979) 'Modern private security – its principal characteristics and role, some general legal implications', in Law Reform Commission of Canada, *Seizure: Power of Private Security Personnel*, Ottawa, Canada, Ministry of Supply and Service.

Stodgill, R M (1974) *Handbook of Leadership: A Survey of Theory and Research*, New York, Free Press.

Stodgill, R M & Coons, A (1957) *Leader Behavior: Its Description and Measurement*, Bureau of Business Research, University of Ohio.

Strang, H, Barnes, G, Braithwaite, J & Sherman, L (1999) *Experiments in Restorative Policing: A Progress Report on the Canberra Reintegrative Shaming Experiments (RISE)*, Law Program, Research School of Social Sciences, Australian National University, Canberra. Available on-line at www.aic.gov.au/rjustice/rise/index.html.

Strathern, A J (1971) *Rope of Moka: Big-Men and Ceremonial Exchange in Mount Hagen, New Guinea*, Cambridge, Cambridge University Press.

Strathern, A M (1972) *Official and Unofficial Courts: Legal Assumptions and Expectations in a Highlands Community*, Port Moresby, New Guinea Research Bulletin, No 47, 1–166.

—— (1985) 'Discovering social control', *Journal of Law and Society*, 12 (2): 111–134.

Suarez, Ray (1999) *The Old Neighborhood: What We Lost in the Great Suburban Migration, 1966–99*, New York, Free Press.

Sunday Mail, October 18 (1998) Article titled 'Classroom crimes', p 4.

Tajfel, H & Turner, J C (1979) 'An integrative theory of intergroup conflict', in S Worschel and W G Austin (eds) *The Social Psychology of Intergroup Relations*, Chicago, Nelson-Hall.

Tam, Henry Benedict (1998) *Communitarianism: A New Agenda For Politics And Citizenship*, Basingstoke, Macmillan.

Tattum, D (ed) (1993) *Understanding and Managing Bullying*, London, Heinemann Books.

Tatz, C (1999) *Genocide in Australia*, Australian Institute for Aboriginal and Torres Strait Islander Studies (AIATSIS), Research Discussion Paper No 8, AIATSIS, Canberra.

Tavuchis, N (1991) *Mea Culpa: A Sociology of Apology and Reconciliation*, Stanford, Stanford University Press.

Taylor, F W (1913) *The Principles of Scientific Management*, New York, Harper & Brothers.

Taylor, G (1985) *Pride, Shame and Guilt: Emotions of Self-Assessment*, Oxford, Clarendon Press.

Taylor, M (1982) *Community, Anarchy and Liberty*, Cambridge, Cambridge University Press.

Thames Valley Police (1998) *Annual Report of the Chief Constable of Thames Valley Police 1997–98*.

Thorsborne M (1999) Presentation to the 'Guidance Counsellors and the Law, A Conference for Best Practice' Conference, The Australia and New Zealand Education Law Association (Queensland Chapter) in conjunction with The School of Professional Studies (Queensland University of Technology), Brisbane.

Tomkins, S S (1962) *Affect/Imagery/Consciousness, Vol 1, The Positive Affects*, New York, Springer.

—— (1963) *Affect/Imagery/Consciousness, Vol 2, The Negative Affects*, New York, Springer.

—— (1987) 'Script theory', in J Aronoff, A I Rabin & R A Zucker (eds) *The Emergence of Personality*, New York, Springer.

—— (1991) *Affect/Imagery/Consciousness, Vol 3, The Negative Affects – Anger and Fear*, New York, Springer.

—— (1992) *Affect/Imagery/Consciousness, Vol 4, Cognition – Duplication and Transmission of Information*, New York, Springer.

Truth and Reconciliation Commission (South Africa) (1998) Final Report, available at www.truth.org.za

Turner, J C, Hogg, M A, Oakes, P J & Reicher, S D (1987) *Rediscovering the Social Group: A Self-Categorization Theory*, London, Basil Blackwell.

Turow, Scott (1999) 'Order in the court, the jurors were starved, jailed – and victorious', *New York Times Magazine*, April 18, p 109.

Tyler, Tom (1990) *Why People Obey The Law*, New Haven, Yale University Press.

—— (1998) 'Trust and democratic governance', in Valerie Braithwaite & Margaret Levi (eds) *Trust and Governance*, New York, Russell Sage Foundation.

UCLA Management Review (1989), University of California, Los Angeles, Summer.

US Department of Justice (1986) *Four Years Later: A Report on the President's Task Force on Victims of Crime*, Washington DC, US Government Printing Office.

van Dijk, J (1986) 'Victims' rights: a right to better service or a right to "active participation"?', in J van Dijk (ed) *Criminal Law in Action*, Arnhem, Gouda Quint.

—— (1988) 'Victims' needs or victims' rights: alternative approaches to policymaking', in M Maguire & J Pointing (eds) *Victims of Crime: A New Deal?*, Milton Keynes, Open University Press.

van Dijk J, Mayhew, P & and Killias, J (1990) *Experiences of Crime Across the World: Key Findings from the 1989 International Crime Survey*, Deventer, The Netherlands, Kluwer.

Van Ness, D (1996) 'Restorative justice and international human rights', in B. Galaway & J Hudson (eds) *Restorative Justice: International Perspectives*, Monsey, NY, Criminal Justice Press.

Viano, E (1983) 'Violence victimization and social change: a socio-cultural and public policy analysis', *Victimology, An International Journal*, 8 (3–4): 54–59.

—— (1987) 'Victims' rights and the Constitution', *Crime and Delinquency*, 33: 438–451.

—— (1990) *The Victimology Handbook: Research Findings, Treatment and Public Policy*, New York, Garland.

Vincent, Andrew (1997) 'Liberal nationalism and communitarianism: an ambiguous association', *The Australian Journal of Politics and History*, 43: 14–28.

Von Hirsch, A (1976) *Doing Justice: The Choice of Punishment*, New York, Hill and Wang.

Wachtel, T (1998) *Real Justice*, Pipersville, PA, Piper's Press.

Waller, I (1989) 'The needs of crime victims', in E Fattah (ed) *The Plight of Crime Victims in Modern Society*, Basingstoke, Macmillan.

Weber, Max (1922–23 [1948]) 'The Protestant sects and the spirit of capitalism', in *From Max Weber: Essays in Sociology*, translated, edited and with an introduction by H H Gerth and C Wright Mills, London, Routledge & Kegan Paul.

—— (1958) *The Protestant Ethic and the Spirit of Capitalism*, New York, Scribner's.

West, D J & Farrington, D P (1977) *The Delinquent Way of Life*, London, Heinemann.

Wilkins, Leslie T (1966) *Social Deviance*, Englewood Cliffs, NJ, Prentice-Hall.

Williams, George H (1972) 'Anabaptists', *Encyclopedia Britannica*, vol 1.

Williamson, D (1999) *Two Plays, 'Corporate Vibes' and 'Face to Face'*, Sydney, Currency Press.

Wood, James (1997) *Royal Commission into the New South Wales Police Service, Final Report*, Volume 11, Chapter 1, Sydney.

Wood, Jennifer & Shearing, Clifford (1998) 'Inclusions and exclusions in governance: an examination of campus security', *Canadian Journal of Criminology*, 40: 81–95.

Wright, M & Galaway, B (1989) *Mediation and Criminal Justice: Victims, Offenders and Community*, London, Sage.

Young, Iris Marion (1990) 'The ideal of community and the politics of difference', in Linda J Nicholson (ed) *Feminism/Postmodernism*, New York, Routledge.

Zaleznik, A (1989) *The Managerial Mystique*, New York, Harper & Row.

Zander, M (1994) 'Is the criminal justice system a game?', *Police Review*, 102, 28 January.

Zedner, L (1994) 'Victims', in M Maguire, R Morgan & R Reiner (eds) *The Oxford Handbook of Criminology*, Oxford, Clarendon Press.

Zehr, Howard (1990) *Changing Lenses: A New Focus for Criminal Justice*, Scottsdale, PA, Herald Press.

Index

Lightning Source UK Ltd.
Milton Keynes UK
UKOW05f2239260913

218035UK00001B/94/P